PART SWAN,
PART GOOSE

PART SWAN, PART GOOSE

An Uncommon Memoir of
Womanhood, Work and Family

SWOOSIE KURTZ

with JONI RODGERS

A PERIGEE BOOK

A PERIGEE BOOK
Published by the Penguin Group
Penguin Group (USA) LLC
375 Hudson Street, New York, New York 10014

USA • Canada • UK • Ireland • Australia • New Zealand • India • South Africa • China

penguin.com

A Penguin Random House Company

PART SWAN, PART GOOSE

ISBN: 978-0-399-16850-5

An application to register this book for cataloging
has been submitted to the Library of Congress.

First edition: May 2014

PRINTED IN THE UNITED STATES OF AMERICA

10   9   8   7   6   5   4   3   2   1

Text design by Tiffany Estreicher

Penguin is committed to publishing works of quality and integrity.
In that spirit, we are proud to offer this book to our readers;
however, the story, the experiences, and the words
are the author's alone.

While the author has made every effort to provide accurate telephone numbers,
Internet addresses, and other contact information at the time of publication, neither the
publisher nor the author assumes any responsibility for errors, or for changes that occur
after publication. Further, the publisher does not have any control over and does not
assume any responsibility for author or third-party websites or their content.

Most Perigee books are available at special quantity discounts for bulk purchases for sales
promotions, premiums, fund-raising, or educational use. Special books, or book excerpts, can
also be created to fit specific needs. For details, write: Special.Markets@us.penguingroup.com.

For Margo and Frankie,
who gave me the world

Contents

1. Enter Breathing   1

2. Descendants of Art and Grace   25

3. Imaginary Friends   45

4. My Last First Day   65

5. Why I Wasn't at Woodstock   85

6. Love and Squalor   109

7. Uncommon Women   127

8. Like a Beach House at the Winter Olympics   147

9. Singing, Dancing and Schizophrenia   177

10. Degrees of Separation   205

11. Heartbreak and Daisies   243

12. More Later   283

   Acknowledgments   309
   Credits and Permissions   313
   Work and Awards   315
   Index   319

Poolside at the Miami Beach Aquacade in 1948. "Lucky me."

CHAPTER ONE

Enter Breathing

There are two time-honored professions in which the first thing you do when you get to work is take off your clothes.

I'm in the other one.

Arriving backstage or on a back lot, ascending the winding staircase in a Broadway theater or climbing into my trailer at Warner Brothers, my first order of business is to shed my street clothes (my father would have called them "civvies") and be delivered into the skin of whomever it is I'm getting paid to be that day. I'm surrounded by nimble artists who appraise my appearance with unforgiving technical eyes and craft me from heel to eyelash, evaluating my rear end, propping up my meager décolletage, making sure my earlobes and knuckles don't clash, checking for knee wrinkles and hem threads.

Rarely does all this happen with any deference to my dignity. In my line of work, while humility is an asset, modesty is a bother.

I'm lucky enough to have been brought up by two people who knew the difference.

My father, Frank Kurtz, was an Olympic diver in his youth. There's not much room for modesty up there on the ten-meter platform and even less room in a pair of aerodynamically snug swim trunks. But to make that leap without humility—without respect for gravity, without remembering how applause disappears under water—that would be a terrible mistake.

My mother, Margo Rogers Kurtz, was Frankie's foil in witty dinner table repartee and his staunch ally in every other aspect of life. She was the "ever-fixed mark" Shakespeare noted in sonnet, a small, brilliant pin on his private map of the world. Margo was the model wartime bride in the 1940s: industrious, beautiful, capable, the perfect combination of stiff upper lip and fire-engine red lipstick. She could pilot a small airplane, feed a small army and fit nicely into those tailored peplum skirt suits that were all the rage.

Newspapers and newsreels couldn't help noticing her as my father flew higher and farther, collecting scars and medals. Every time he made it home in one piece, it was a stunning blow for the cause of hope, and during World War II—under the darkness and din of the air-raid sirens, as inhumanity sucked innocence into a genocidal oven—hope was highly prized. It was sought after.

Frankie and Margo were recruited along with Hollywood stars and other celebrities for war-bond tours. These junkets were utterly purpose driven: no frills, no egos, just as many recognizable names as the organizer could cram into a train car and parade to the autograph tables. In one town after another, starstruck fans lined up to buy bonds. Even the most pampered celebrities

"I look at that photograph on a bookshelf behind my desk and see nothing but hope, hope, hope." Margo and me, September 6, 1944.

were gung ho about these rustic excursions. I'm certain any attempts at modesty would have been laughed out of the tiny train car water closet, so Margo and Frankie fit right in. He was a hero, and she was the classy, garrulous sidekick who kept his clay feet warm.

My mother's book, *My Rival, the Sky*, came into the world the same year I did. We both grew inside her while my father flew bombing runs over Italy in 1944. G. P. Putnam (the publishing magnate who was also the husband of Amelia Earhart) had taken an interest in my parents after they collaborated with W. L. White on the book *Queens Die Proudly*, which told the story of the great Flying Fortress bombers, including my father's heroically cobbled together B-17D, the Swoose. A contract was proposed and accepted: Margo was to write a war memoir from the home-front perspective, title to be determined, $250 to be remitted on signing and $250 on delivery of the manuscript.

I was born in the fall of 1944, a few weeks after Nazi forces put a brutal end to Hungarian resistance, a few weeks before U.S. troops landed in the Philippines. My father was somewhere in the thick of that as my mother and day-old me were being photographed for the newspaper. People desperately needed to see this beautiful, young mother treasuring her fresh baby and believe in a God who would either bring that baby's daddy home or send straight to Hell the scurvy tail gunner who took him out.

I look at that photograph on a bookshelf behind my desk and see nothing but hope, hope, hope. My mother's face is filled with optimism and love. It's hard to turn away. But it's time.

"Margo, darling?" I call on my way to the car. "I'm off."

"No, you're not," she says. "You're just right."

A quick hug, and I'm out the door. I drive myself to work

(mechanically and metaphorically), and it doesn't take long. Every day I'm grateful for this five-minute commute to the studio. The kismet is unbelievable. After decades of bicoastal and intercontinental commutes, almost always working more than one job at any given time, just when I needed it most, I landed a steady gig on that rarest of beasts: a television show that is a critical *and* commercial success. That's something we hardly dare hope for in this business. Most people have no idea how many pilots disappear into the mosh pit, how many promising starts go the way of the pet rock before a show comes along with a genuine heart and exactly the right creative team, writers, cast and production crew. You're more likely to find narwhal steaks on special at Ralph's. Above and beyond that, this particular cast and crew—all souls counted—are smart, delightful, mellow, ego-light professionals who've become my dear friends.

When I saw the pilot script, I knew this show, *Mike & Molly*, had the potential to go the distance. In the back of my mind, I heard Frankie telling me the same thing he told me when I started *Sisters* on NBC in the early 1990s: "Five years," he said with certainty. When I puffed something about not counting chickens, he smiled a confident ready-for-takeoff smile and repeated, "Five years." The show lasted six more seasons. As did Frankie.

Ready to wrap our third season of *Mike & Molly*, I believe this one could last even longer, but every time I allow myself to speculate, I feel the urge to spit, throw salt over my shoulder and sacrifice a goat. Karma is a bitch, as they say; we all must have suffered tremendously in our previous lives to have this great job. I don't want to jinx it.

The main characters, Mike Biggs and Molly Flynn (Billy Gardell and Melissa McCarthy) are so easy to be with, on screen and off, our merry cast and crew quickly developed a healthy chemistry. I think people truly can feel that through the screen; the show immediately attracted a large audience of loyal fans, despite the fact (or perhaps because of the fact) that precious few successful sitcoms feature characters who look like real people instead of successful sitcom characters.

At first blush, the show is about a schoolteacher and a police officer who meet at Overeaters Anonymous. In their quest to lose weight, they find each other. That sweetly simple premise is injected with an impossible amalgam of highly evolved and low-brow. The moral scruples of this show are refreshingly intolerant of cynicism. A lot of the humor is below the belly button, and the zingy dialogue is boner blunt, but it doesn't feel crass because the relationships are so authentic, the atmosphere so unabashedly romantic and the storyline so much about love.

I've played broad, and I've played bawdy, but I've never inhabited a character quite like Joyce Flynn, Molly's mother. She's given me the opportunity to be more free-spirited and painfully candid than I could even dream of being when I'm being myself. If Holly Golightly and Groucho Marx got drunk and slept together, the unapologetic fruit of that union would be Joyce Flynn. She's a fiercely loving mother, but she sees herself as a contemporary of her beautiful young daughters, a sensual woman in her sexual prime. She has a good soul, but her moral compass is slightly bent. (And you could count on her to jump on the word "bent" with a double entendre that leaves the rest of the room blushing.)

When Joyce is asked by her daughters if she was lonely while their late father was in Vietnam, Joyce quips, "Lonely, no. Horny, yes." With a nostalgic sigh, she goes on to overshare that her remedy for that was sitting on the washing machine. Joyce not only

The M& M *family: Nyambi Nyambi, Chuck Lorre, Melissa McCarthy, me, Katy Mixon, Billy Gardell and Reno Wilson.*

UNDERWOOD/INVISION FOR THE ACADEMY OF TELEVISION

ARTS AND SCIENCES/AP IMAGES

inspires me to be more direct and less self-censoring, she provides me with a vehicle in which to do it with impunity on a weekly basis.

I learn something from every character I play. Each one of them bears a gift. The personal reward for doing the work of developing the character is the excavation of that gift and the sharing of it with an audience. To a large extent, that's what the craft of acting is about: the joy of that challenge, whether you're doing Molière or a Monday night sitcom. I noticed early in my career that almost every role I play is somewhat off-kilter—a bit dark, driven or crazy or driven crazy during the course of the show—and playing characters so utterly unlike myself is a job and a vacation at the same time; climbing into their lives, I get to leave my own reality behind for a little while. I don't hide behind the character—quite the opposite; I'm liberated in one way or another by every character I play, hitting my marks with sternum held high. "Lead with the breastbone," Michael Bennett used to say.

When I arrive on the set, Billy Gardell is sitting in the makeup chair where he and I take turns, since we share a makeup artist.

"I'm afraid we're starting to look alike," I tease him, and he laughs his big laugh.

Before we walk out in front of the cameras, he gathers us in a tight circle to pray. Usually it's something like, "Dear God, once again here we are. Help us do our best for the people who came to see us. We want to thank you for the gift of this amazing job. Please, help us remember it's a privilege, not an entitlement. Help us keep everyone in this building employed."

I always find myself profoundly affected, enormously grateful for each of these people and just plain happy to be here with them. Sometimes I'm so moved, I have to pay another visit to the makeup chair. And I'm not the only one. Particularly tonight.

"Lord, we have some troubled souls tonight," Billy says. "Give us strength to do what we need to do. Help us support and love each other."

I blink, trying to preserve my mascara. Around the tight circle, we grip each other's hands, clearing throats, swallowing hard. Reno Wilson's mother has died, and Reno, who plays Mike's partner, Officer Carl, has a lot of material to deliver in this episode.

The news took my breath away when I heard it. Our first week on the set, I mentioned to Reno how thrilled I was to be working a steady gig just a few minutes from the home Margo and I share. Since then, he and I have talked a lot about our moms, sharing memories, fears and funny stories. We talked about what home remedies and pharmaceuticals worked—or not—for various symptoms. *Oh, stay away from that one. Margo went psycho after the first two hundred milligrams. Organic black licorice root for constipation? I wouldn't have thought of that.* Eldercare is an odd conversation in a specific language that is by turns clinical, sentimental and cringe-inducing.

All week, Reno's sisters have kept him posted on his mother's rapid decline. *Oh, God*, I kept thinking, *don't let it be this week.* Having to get out there and be hilarious just a few hours after losing one's mother takes the body slam of losing one's mother to a whole new level. Reno is a multitalented pro who's been doing this work since he was one of the college kids on *The Cosby Show.* We're not worried about Reno's performance; we're just heartbroken for him. It's one of the moments theatre elitists forget about when they say that TV acting is for sissies.

We Broadway actors are legendary troupers, famous for our "show must go on" work ethic. We're tasked with nailing every scene, every time, eight shows a week—fractured ankles, broken hearts and vocal nodes be damned. On a TV show, you get do-overs. But you don't get understudies, and your missteps are not contained in the hallowed walls of one theater for one afternoon. On the day your mother dies, not only do you go to work, you go to work in front of millions of people, and whatever you do will be available for applause and/or ridicule until YouTube perishes from Earth.

At the end of the day, Reno is completely focused and funny, while the rest of us work our butts off, determined not to let him down. The audience leaves aching from laughter. Reno departs for his mother's funeral. Billy flies to Vegas where he burns the other end of the candle with a stand-up show. The rest of us go home emotionally exhausted. We'll all be back in less than fifty hours to start the whole process over again.

"How are you, my darling?" Margo asks when I walk in the door.

"Tired," I admit. "But it's a joyful tired."

I'm quoting her, but she opens her hands and collects the phrase from the air as if she's never heard it before.

"Frankie's coming home tonight, isn't he?" she asks.

"Yes, I think he is," I tell her.

Sometimes I say he's in Japan, at the Pentagon on a mission or at his office in Washington. The lies trip from my tongue without hesitation. (I'm a professional!) The truth is, Margo was resilient and dignified when Frankie died in 1996, but no one should have to be that resilient every damn day. Can you imagine what it would be like to roll out of bed every morning and be clobbered with that? No, darling, you're not twenty-seven, you're ninety-seven, and that ardent lover lying beside you a few minutes ago was a dream, and now even the dream is dead. *Good morning, sunshine!*

I think it's healthier—and more honest, ironically—to tell her the emotional truth: that she is loved, that she is young in spirit and enduringly beautiful and will see her great love soon. She won't remember what I said six minutes from now anyway.

"Why stand on ceremony?" Margo says. "Take a look at my breasts."

"Oh. Okay. Let's see."

Margo raises her soft jersey tunic, and we both look lovingly at her breasts. She nudges the one that hangs somewhat lower than the other.

"They're beautiful," I tell her, pulling her into my arms.

"I could tuck this one into my waistband if I wanted to," she says, and then, distracted by the waistband of her black yoga pants, she says, "Look at the color of this thread. What would make them use blue? My God, what a wonderful world we live in!"

This way of looking at the world can't be entirely put down to the dementia. The increasing seepage of non sequiturs and apparitions has made conversation a challenge, but Margo's personality is essentially intact. I have an early memory of my Aunt Mici striding into the kitchen stark naked and smoking a cigarette. Getting ready for a bath, she'd had a thought and didn't want to lose it. This made perfect sense to Margo. Logic over convention. Action over inhibition. This hierarchy of necessary values worked well for my mother throughout her unconventional and uninhibited life, and it's worked well for me in mine.

Nonetheless, thinking about that moment makes me laugh now, and as if she heard the story brush by the back of my mind, Margo laughs too, pressing her palms to my cheeks as she gives me a kiss.

I relish the feeling, a stingingly sweet element in my life that has remained unchanged through every tectonic shift of fortune, fame and circumstance: my mother loves me, and I love her. We are we. Always have been. Always will be.

"Joined at the heart," Margo says. "I love you, you precious child."

"I love you too, Mommie."

Oddly, I've started calling her "Mommie" lately, after sixty-*frshashm* years of calling her "Margo." Perhaps I'm cherishing my last remaining moments of being someone's precious child. Or maybe I'm occasionally taken into her world where time is no longer linear. A woman can be forty at breakfast and fifteen for dinner. At any moment, someone you loved and lost in your childhood might walk through the door. In Margo's world, a Japanese porcelain fisherman on the credenza winks and nods. A little girl in white hangs a left at the corner of your eye and vanishes down the hallway. Sometimes I feel her holding her breath, and I know Frankie is poised on the ten-meter platform, still as a tin soldier, hands flat at his sides.

He opens his arms wide, just before he dives.

Margo lives with me in a house I bought back in the 1990s when *Sisters* was going strong. Frankie searched long and hard and found this place for me while I was boomeranging back and forth between my New York apartment and various movie locations and my L.A. base of operations, my parents' home in Toluca

Lake—the home Frankie and Margo bought when I was about to start high school. Typical military transients, we'd moved around a lot prior to that, but Margo thought they should find a sticking place for my teen years, and they stuck with it for the next forty years, providing my hub throughout much of my bicoastal career. I'd spent so much of my life living with them, it was a natural turn to have Margo move in with me after Frankie died.

The great architect Harwell Hamilton Harris built this house in the early 1950s. It's a perfect exemplar of modernist sensibility, featuring the iconic angular light, open posture and floating staircase that branded postwar, pre–*Mad Men* martini temples and Ayn Rand–era movie sets. Margo and I have rebranded it as our own with memorabilia from our travels, books everywhere, overstuffed sofa—homey comforts Atlas could never fully shrug off.

For many years, I zealously protected the hermitage I thought I needed for my work, but I've come to love the quiet constancy of people in my space. I dread Margo's inevitable departure and all the existential impact of losing her, and part of that is the thought of losing the ad hoc family we've gathered, our small, fond staff of trusted caregivers. Angela, a pragmatic earth mother with endless patience and broad humor. Antonio, a devastatingly handsome Brazilian with a deeply sweet heart. Cielito, a lovely Filipino gentleman with Zen to spare. Meanwhile, Konrad, my unstoppable manager, periodically blows through (on the phone or in person) with the energy, aplomb and fervent tone of a swamp-cooler, which delights Margo. Perry, my indispensible right arm, does everything from hair color to correspondence, life coaching, soul feeding—actually, it's hard to quantify. Perry is the authentic force of nature who makes my life happen. His job title is assistant, which doesn't begin to cover the wonder that is Perry, proof that God exists and gallantry is not dead. Konrad gets me through the sprints; Perry gets me through the marathon.

There's an alchemy to Margo's care; it's taken a long time to achieve this delicate balance. Whenever she feels the need to migrate from one place to another, one of us is always walking behind her with our hands on her shoulders. At her age, tripping on a dog toy can be fatal. We refuse to let her fall. We may not be able to stop the seepage of memory or the progression of cell death, but we aim to make sure that she passes in her sleep, hips unbroken, knees unbruised. We intend to spend every day of her life being alive.

That's been my bond with these people over the years. We compare notes on small victories, commiserate over mounting defeats, lend comfort, share clinical information, tell each other our mother stories. My heart goes bone dry when I think of Reno alone on an airplane. I know how empty and vast the sky can be, and I wonder where I'll be when I'm orphaned. My preference, of course, would be that I'm here, holding Margo's hand. Barring that, I selfishly hope to be at work with strong hearts and strong arms around me. I don't dwell on the specifics of the inevitable, but I don't deny it. We're allowing it to lead us for the moment.

Why stand on ceremony?

These days, it's as if Margo and I are the ones who stand with our toes at the edge of the platform. Poised. She opens her arms wide.

"I wanted to tell you something," she says, "but it slipped under a chair."

Time and gravity are jealous gods. We all know where this is going.

Frankie and Margo pose with the Swoose in an Air Corps PR shot in 1943.
You couldn't find better spokesmodels for war or peace.

California, 1944

"Margo," says Frank, "there's a little item I wanted to talk to you about."

"Okay," I answer, floating, just us, so close and free, on a smooth drifting river. I should have known, though. We never drift for long.

A book, he is saying. He wants me to write a book.

There've been plenty of jobs I could do all right—diving coach, and learning to fly, and helping to produce aquacades. The war bond drives, I did those, and the radio programs. You've told me I'm a pretty good copilot, Frank, it's written here on the back of this little gold watch you gave me . . .

But a book—oh, Frank.

"All right. I'll write a book." And I smile because I know a little joke. I'll write it all about him.

We never say good-by, finally, but just goodnight. It's easier to get this word out, and when you think back and hear him saying it, it will sound better.

"I'll be so busy all day, and at night I'll say goodnight into the pillow. I'll talk to you when I first wake up, and a thousand times a day I'll look up at the sky and say, 'Hello, Frank.'"

Quiet and so calm. And Frank walks over to the army car. Just before he closes the door, he smiles, and I smile at him.

"Good night, Frank."

"Good night, Beloved."

Then the car drives away. I can see the car lights lead the

way. And I can see Frank hop out and walk into our plane. The men are all at attention, and now they follow him inside. The door of the plane closes. But I can't see any more because the army car has turned away, and it was the car's lights which gave me the picture. And with her four motors growling, our Fortress starts the turn which will take her down the runway.

But now I'm a little lost. I can't see our plane. She's lost out there in the dark. I can hear her engines, but I can't see anything. This has gotten to be such a big war. And it seems I wait so long and listen so hard . . .

I was a precocious child who loved books in general and was very curious about my mother's book in particular because grown-ups were always talking about Margo's *wonderful* book, Margo's *very important* book that told the story of how she and Frankie fell in love and survived the war. At age seven or eight, as soon as I was able to comprehend it (to the extent that any child is able to comprehend love and war), I inhaled *My Rival, the Sky* for the first time. It was a bit magical to meet Margo and Frankie as teenagers and be swept up in their adventures the same way I was swept up in the adventures of Nancy Drew and the Bobbsey Twins and Christopher Robin.

I read the book again when I was fresh out of college, a textbook twentysomething enjoying my early success in New York theatre, hanging out at Sardi's discussing Proust and Sartre, and test-driving a mild disdain for my parents. I knew my way around words well enough to know that my mother was a very good writer, but by this time, the rote recitation of our family lore had worn rather thin for me, and all those dusty war remembrances in the context of the 1960s were a total drag, man. Still, I thought it was adorable how she'd gotten her little book published and everything. I smiled and tucked it away with a few other quaint keepsakes.

It's interesting how a book evolves while we're away. I've heard it compared to a spiral staircase; you keep returning to the same place, but each time, you're a level higher. When I read *My Rival, the Sky* again in 2003, when the news was full of the war in Iraq, it took my breath away. The wrenching separations and joyful homecomings resonated as if the words had been written yesterday. I was taken back to what it means to be a military family in a time of war, and I felt a bond with all those who had a son, or daughter, or husband, or wife in harm's way on the other side of the world. For the first time, I saw how the arc of my parents' lives had been bowed by those years when they were each other's only safe haven.

Standing in the short hallway between the kitchen and Margo's room, I hear her talking quietly with my father. I can't make out what she's saying, but I recognize the very specific way she always says his name, as if she's catching it in a butterfly net. I strain forward a little, knowing I won't hear what she hears, but hoping I might feel a little of what she feels. The nearness of him.

That's what missing someone is, I suppose, and I do miss my father terribly, but the grammar of that phrase begs inspection: the person being missed is, in fact, the one who *is* missing. He is *missing* in exactly the sense that car keys go missing; you know they still exist somewhere, but you wish like hell they could be at hand when you need them.

"Hello, Frank!" she calls out to him again. "Frankie? *Hello . . .*"

My first performance with Frankie at the Miami Aquacade in 1947.

COURTESY OF THE AUTHOR

This time I hear a fragment of fear in her voice, shrapnel left over from her war injuries, all those days and nights in the wake of Pearl Harbor when she lay in the upstairs bedroom at her parents' home in Omaha. He was missing. There were places she could identify in both earth and sky where Frankie belonged, and he wasn't in any of them. In the fall of 1941, he'd been sent to Clark Air Base; rumors of an impending attack by Imperial Japan circled Luzon Island like shark shadows in the pristine blue ocean. Frankie was there, Margo knew, not in Hawaii on December 7, but it was as if the smoke billowing out of Pearl Harbor obscured everything in the Pacific Theater. The blackout curtains dropped; not a phone call, not a letter slipped through. The grainy news on the radio provided barely a keyhole. Margo studied maps and newspaper clippings on her bedroom floor, piecing together slivers of terrifying information. If Frankie was still alive, he was alone in a sea of inconceivable destruction.

"Mommie," I call down the hall, "are you getting hungry?"

This is to give her a little warning before I push through the door. When I enter the room, she's sitting on the edge of her bed, a pillow in her arms.

"Hello, darling," I say, stroking the soft nape of her neck.

She pushes her face into the fresh linen and says, "Hello, Frankie." But there's no confusion in her face when she looks up at me. "That's just something I always do," she says, preempting the obvious.

"Do you feel like eating some dinner, Margo? Angela went to the chicken place for some Greek food."

"*Greek* food," she marvels. "Human beings never know how well off they are."

We straighten the bedding from her nap, and I follow behind her, hands on her shoulders, as we turtle toward the kitchen table.

"I'm not one hundred percent today," she admits. "I've been a little low."

"You're doing fine, darling." I kiss the crown of her head.

At first it seems we're headed for the dining room, but then we're off like Israelites on a long wander, taking a forty-year scenic route to the Promised Land. By the time we arrive at the table, Angela has returned, and Margo's dinner is on a placemat with evening meds and a bottle of Vitaminwater.

"Oh, yes," she says with relish, "this is the good stuff."

Gratitude is the defining emotion in Margo's personality, and it feels good to be around that. She gratefully settles into her chair, gratefully inhales the steam over a cup of instant coffee, gratefully downs the pharmacopoeia with Vitaminwater. She experiences each beat as a gift, and I have to gratefully acknowledge how healthy that is for all of us.

I sit kitty-corner to her, facing the patio and the temple ruins that will someday be a swimming pool—or so the contractor keeps promising. I hope it'll happen sooner rather than later. It's lovely to imagine that Margo and I will get out there every afternoon, soak up some vitamin D–enriched sunlight, do some kind of nice workout and then let our muscles and bones float. But that will never happen. She's not remotely capable of being in the water, even if it were remotely possible to get the water warm enough. Still, it feels important to have it there.

Swimming pools were a big part of my life growing up. Frankie never really left his diving days behind. He maintained that same precision in everything he did. There was always an order, a fine line, a protocol to be followed. The discipline of platform diving dovetailed nicely with the discipline of military life, and Frankie saw no reason to live his personal life any differently. It had worked well for him, so he reasonably concluded that it would work well for anyone, including me. (Especially me, in fact.)

Constancy. Morning coffee. A good night's sleep. A person should be independent, neatly groomed and well prepared unless he or she had a very good reason not to be. Daily exercise "as the sun rises and sets" consisted of sit-ups, leg scissors, headstands and a brisk walk. (I inherited his "Where's the fire?" gait, so it's always been a challenge to go walking with Margo, the easily distracted Israelite who feels compelled to stop and smell every rose.)

Frankie could be the hard-edged commander, but he was never overbearing or *Great Santini* about it. He had a naturally soothing tenor voice and would gently touch the top of my head when conveying the high expectations that were unapologetic and never hazy. He wasn't stingy with praise or sparing with criticism, and on the receiving end of either, I always knew he was being completely honest. He was Frank without fail, and I derived a genuine security from that. Not just warm, fuzzy security-blanket security, but security as a stance that served me well in my professional and personal life.

When I was a little girl, a lot of people were digging holes in their backyards to install either a swimming pool or a bomb shelter. We were definitely the swimming pool types, and I think that speaks volumes about my father, who saw the absolute worst that war had to offer and came home to organize aquacades instead of "Duck and Cover" drills. He also emerged from a wretchedly abusive childhood to be an enormously loving husband and father. Everyone fell in love with Frankie. Central Casting couldn't have come up with a better spokesmodel for war or peace.

Anyway, at the early aquacades, I've been told, Esther Williams performed along with the Hopkins Twins of synchronized swimming fame. (My uncle Homer, who was quite a swimmer himself, accidentally saw Esther naked in the locker room, the highlight of his young life.) At later events, I entertained the crowd between the headliners, diving from the poolside or low boards and swimming gracefully around in trendy swim shorts and a ruffled bra I could probably still fit into. I might have danced too. I remember a striking pair of gold sandals, and knowing me at that age, I couldn't have done less than dance in them.

Honestly, Central Casting couldn't have improved much on me as a spokesmodel either. If Margo was Frankie's sidekick, I was like that precocious little dog in *The Artist*: a knowing and unrepentant scene-stealer. The plot never revolved around me, but I never lacked for attention.

Margo has a photograph of me as a four-year-old, sitting in full sun on a white bench near the bleachers from which the spectators had cheered my aquatic entr'acte a few minutes earlier. My damp hair is mosquito-fine and all over the place. I'm wearing a sporty T-shirt emblazoned "The SWOOSE," legs daintily crossed like an Elvgren pinup illustration, toes pointed, hands on my hips. Attitude to spare.

But the expression on my face doesn't say, "Look at me."

It says, "Lucky me."

Visiting my namesake, the Swoose, at the Smithsonian in the late 1970s.
COURTESY OF THE AUTHOR

CHAPTER TWO

Descendants of Art and Grace

Margo and I have been singing the same duet for years.

"My sweetheart's a mule in the mine. I drive her with only one line, And as upon her I sit, Tobacco I spit, All over my sweetheart's behind!"

She's lying in the stirrups at the urologist's office, and he is doing something unnamable to her urethra. She grips my hand, and I launch into verse two.

"My sweetheart's a mule in the mines, way down where the sun never shines. That's appropriate for the occasion, isn't it, Mommie?"

The urologist smiles at us from between Margo's knees but doesn't pause in his task. It's one of those "do whatcha gotta do" days all the way around. My part is to stay calm, provide entertainment and hold her hand against my cheek. The infrastructure from wrist to knuckles feels as fragile and weightless as the brittle armor left by the passing of a cicada.

"I have the skeleton of an autumn leaf," she recently told a friend.

In general, Margo's quite good-humored about the indignities that have come with her decline and always grateful to the caregivers who manage to do what needs to be done while making her feel respected and loved. There's a point at which private bodily functions become acceptable conversation again, just like they are when there's a baby in the house. Between toddlerhood and old age, we have the luxury of having everyone ignore the tone and timing of our wind passings and tummy functions, but a healthy bowel movement in the proper receptacle is cause for celebration when you've experienced a few of the unpleasant alternatives.

She doesn't complain, but now and then, she shows signs of wear. During a recent "serial enema" (the term itself is an appalling reminder of Bette Davis's assertion that "old age ain't no place for sissies"), Margo said to the nurse, "Darling, I love your work, but I'm not sure how much more I can take."

In general, Margo was always a progressive and good-humored pragmatist when it came to her personal health. (Her mother was the same. I remember my grandma Gigi quipping about feeling "half-assed" after her colostomy.) During the early years of their marriage, Margo and Frankie had hoped and tried, but years went by, and she didn't get pregnant. Quite ahead of her time, Margo refused to be discouraged. In a day and age when women were trained not to question their family practitioner, she researched the science and went from one doctor to the next until she found a fertility specialist.

*Frankie receives the happy news of my arrival on board
the Swoose in Italy, September 1944. But Margo forgot to
mention one small detail. (It's a girl!)*

They found out I was on the way just before Frankie left for the European Theater. He spent the summer flying missions out of Italy, I think. I can't recite the timeline chapter and verse, but it was a grueling stretch during which Frankie and his comrades pushed through airspace, strafing and bombing a pathway for ground forces, mile by mile and at great cost, while Hitler and Mussolini slaughtered Jews, gypsies and resistance fighters below.

They started at two in the morning, Margo wrote later, *with the briefings for the day's mission. Next the long flights over enemy land through skies set with traps of death, then back to the base and the time to turn an exhausted body and anxious mind to the hours at his desk, administrative duties, trips to higher headquarters, and finally, the effort to grab a few hours of sleep before another mission would begin . . .*

He had seen so much death today, he couldn't imagine a birth.

On a bright September afternoon in 1944, as Frankie climbed wearily from the cockpit, he was handed this telegram:

> DEAREST SWOOSIE SIX POUNDS SIX OUNCES
> YOUR BEAUTIFUL CABLES RECEIVED I LOVE YOU
> ABOVE ALL ELSE
> MARGO KURTZ

According to family lore, Charlie, the machine gunner, clapped Frankie on the back and said, "I'm going to write Red and Danny the news. I'll tell them you finally managed to do something without our help."

Frankie carefully folded the telegram away in his flight papers. When I found it in a box of papers and press clippings after

Margo came to live with me, I was so grateful that it had been informally but lovingly archived. Oh, I do love that telegram, love that she made room for the words *above all else* in the scant 106 characters (thirty-four less than one is allowed on Twitter): Forget the punctuation, but don't spare the poetry. That is classic Margoism.

Unfortunately, she neglected to mention whether their Swoosie was a boy or a girl, so Frankie dangled in suspense for another two days, happy but subdued by the gravity of this new assignment: fatherhood.

There are several apocryphal tales circulating about how I came to be named Swoosie. The Associated Press reported that I was christened Margo Junior and nicknamed Swoosie at the suggestion of an AP reporter at the hospital. Margo indulged that, but it's clear from letters and accounts in both her books that she and Frankie intended all along to call me Swoosie. My birth certificate says Swoosie. I have no memory of ever being called Margo Junior, and I certainly never felt pressured to be her Mini Me.

The rote "How I Came to Be Named Swoosie" explanation I learned to recite as early as I could recite the alphabet: "I was named after a B-17 my father flew during the War."

Looks fairly terse on paper, I see now, but I tried on various versions over the years, adjusting for length, pithiness and situational impact. At the end of the day, brevity is the soul of wit, isn't it? Keep it concise. Tweak delivery as appropriate for the audience. The backstory about how the namesake of my namesake was the subject of a Kay Kyser song, "Alexander the Swoose," or the wrap-up component about the Swoose ending up in the

Smithsonian—why go there? I held all that on reserve for the inevitable Q&A period that always followed introductions:

"Was your little sister not able to pronounce *Susie*?"

"What nationality is that?"

"Were your parents drunk?"

Other FAQs ranged from eastern European lineage to good-luck charm.

Apparently, my parents—sober or not—were the only two people in the entire Sally-Mary-Ethel-oriented universe who thought *Swoosie* was a proper name for a person. It was repeatedly made clear to me that they were mistaken and that Swoosie was, in fact, a ridiculous name, which I came to hate. I hated having to repeat it at social gatherings and spell it out every year on the first day of school. Hated the raised eyebrows and suppressed snickers. Hated how everyone from the playground to the Emmy Awards consistently mispronounced it, rhyming it with "woozy" and "floozy" instead of "juicy" and "you see."

"Swoosie," one of my many elementary school teachers enunciated. "Are you sure, dear?"

And for a terrible moment, I wasn't! For a moment, it actually seemed more logical to me that this name was the silly invention of my childish mind rather than a carefully considered, legally binding decision made by two responsible adults.

"Anything that sets you apart is an advantage," Margo tried to tell me, and this did prove true later on, during my career, but during my school years, it was agony. Ninety extra seconds as the center of attention feels like a gift on film; that same minute and a half is a prickly eternity in a classroom full of fourth-graders. And as an added bonus (my fellow military brats will testify for me here), I often had more than one first day of school per year as my family relocated, freely and frequently, from one state to another.

I finally embraced the *Swoosie* of it all when I was about forty. It probably has been an advantage, but more important: I just like it. I can't really specify a reason or catalyst. Don't really need to.

"Because it is my name!" cries John Proctor in *The Crucible*. "Because I may not have another in my life!" That's reason enough, I suppose. Anyway, somewhere along the line, I evolved into the nostalgic whimsy of it. These days, however, when I say, "I was named after a B-17 my father flew during the War," I have to specify "World War II" because *War* with a capital *W* has been eclipsed by decades of skirmishes and analogies. I clarify it as a "B-17 *airplane*" because the Swoose is not the newsmaker it was back then when people were seeing her in newsreel footage before the Saturday matinee. Even then, I doubt that people understood what the Swoose meant to my father personally.

Frankie's company had suffered terrible losses in the Philippines; more than 65 percent of his men were killed at Clark Field two days after the attack on Pearl Harbor. He'd watched a number of his comrades—his friends—burn to death on the tarmac, and he was forced to leave others behind when he and a strangled remnant of the 19th Bombardment Group eventually managed to escape to Australia. There they salvaged enough parts from an assortment of wrecked B-17s to cobble together a Flying Fortress. The Swoose. She was bulky but elegant with her grafted-on tail and riveted skin, their one chance at survival and only means of salvation. As long as they had her, they could fight back, and in that moment, fighting back was the only way to make those lost lives—and the almost certain loss of their own lives—mean something.

"Those scratches on her running gear were made by sand grains of Wake Island," it says in *Queens Die Proudly*. "That little dent on her wing was made by a spent-bomb fragment the day the war began . . . The battle paint on her wings was blistered by the sun in the high skies over Java and nicked by sandstorms over the Australian desert. Of the very few to escape Clark Field, she is the only one to come home."

California, 1934

When I was very small I was dreadfully afraid of horses. Then one day when I was five years old, my father picked me up and sat me in the saddle on top of a horse. I was as frightened as you would expect. But I stayed, and in time I rode, quite well, and loved it. At nineteen, it was all to do again. One quiet day Frank said: "Margo, I'm going to take you flying next week."

I was suddenly very dizzy even being only a few inches off the ground in his little open Ford roadster. Fly? Out home in Nebraska I had seen flying circuses. I had seen planes crash. The mere thought of going up in one myself—oh, no!

Less than a week later my shaking body with choking stomach was lifted into the front cockpit of a small green plane. It took off, it gained height; I was sitting on the peak of a pyramid heaved into the sky by a frightful explosion. But then we came above the overcast, and somehow the blindfold which is ignorance was lifted from my eyes, all my senses came to, just newly alive, and I was drinking in the exhilaration, the intoxicating air which only airmen breathe. The small robin who first gets the feel of his wings—what a surprised yet natural confidence! Now I could turn my head and look at Frank in the back cockpit—now I knew I could turn without "upsetting" the plane.

He was smiling, and in the clear blue of these heavens, the message came to me so truly. He was taking me into his life, and this blue sky set the stage of my new horizons, and the story unfolded so naturally. Nothing was a burden now. In this plane I had lifted above the details, the worries and distorted comparisons—had put them in place. There would be no easy routes into these new horizons. But here was my realm, and here my way.

So you see, this isn't the first time my mother has left the Earth.

Before they were married, my father taught her to fly. I have a photograph of her on the wing of Yankee Boy, the 120-horsepower aircraft in which Frankie—still a teenager—had already begun to make a name for himself as an aviator. Another photo shows her at the beach, lifted high above her brother's head. Margo's history is defined by an innate buoyancy that attracted and uplifted everyone around her.

A certain amount of credit for that belongs to my grandparents. Their house in Omaha was the epicenter we circled back to over the years as military life kept us nomadic, and that was good for me, but in the bigger picture, I think it was Daddy Art and Gigi who set the tone of joy, love and acceptance pervasive in my upbringing.

During most of my first year, and off and on through much of my childhood, Frankie was overseas. Often Margo and I stayed with Daddy Art and Gigi, and I stayed with them myself while Margo trooped around the country on book and war-bond tours. Among my earliest memories is the comfortable impression of being on Gigi's lap, circled in her arms, resting my head on her ample bosom while she played poker, chain-smoked Chesterfields and sipped Early Times bourbon from a tall glass tumbler. It's a little ironic—or perhaps plain hilarious—that we were being held up as a *Good Housekeeping*–anointed example of the All-American Family. We were definitely not shaped like one.

My grandparents' home was a comfortable two-story dwelling in a pleasant but not especially affluent neighborhood. If Omaha were L.A., this would have been Sherman Oaks, not Beverly Hills. Solidly middle class, but rich with stories. Family anecdotes were told and retold with great flare.

Among these was the tale of how my mother was born after Gigi (who had developed tumors, you see, after the birth of Mici, who was six weeks late, weighing in at a comic-strip-hippo-preposterous fourteen pounds) was told by Charlie Mayo of Mayo Clinic fame, "Grace, no more babies," but lo and behold, when Gigi went back to the Mayo Clinic a few years later for the purpose of a goiter operation, Charlie Mayo said, "Listen, Grace, we can't do the operation until after the baby is born," to which Grace replied with a shriek, *"Baby! What baby?"* loud enough that she was heard clear down the hall by people who are undoubtedly still talking about it.

"So I was an accident," Margo would say at that point.

"The happiest accident ever," Gigi would assure her with a squeeze. "And then along came Bob and Homer, so after that, well, I didn't pay much attention to the Mayo brothers."

It had to be a goiter. The very word sounded fantastically, exotically grotesque, and whenever I repeated this bit of family lore to an audience of new friends, I made sure they felt every thyroid-constricting throb.

What a great story! Colorful characters—Dr. Mayo was even a celebrity of sorts—hospital drama, building suspense, a mad twist of plot, a happy ending, and that modest hint at the ongoing romance between Daddy Art and Gigi. It's a great bit of theatre, as all good family anecdotes are, be they comedy or tragedy. I appreciated this as I went on to make my life and living among vibrant storytellers.

Frankie spoke to me very little about his childhood, and after he died, I was stricken by the realization that I'd missed my opportunity to question him about it. It's not that the subject was verboten; it just didn't seem to come up. Nothing was missing. There was no void where "his people" belonged, no occasion where their absence was felt. If anything, the two or three isolated side trips we made to visit Frankie's mother brought into bold relief how intensely estranged they were. I vaguely remember her posing for a few obligatory snapshots, taut-lipped and cool-handed. Some years later, there was a passing mention of her death, but we didn't go to her funeral.

Back then I knew only a few fragmented particulars about Frankie's early years. I'd heard something about two stepfathers who beat him with belts, and apparently no one did anything to pursue him when he ran away from home at age ten. There was an

anecdote about him selling fruitcakes that year during the holiday season; he wound up living off the stuff because he had nothing else to eat, and that was why, from that Christmas to his last,
he couldn't stand the sight, smell or mention of it.

Frankie related that anecdote as a funny fruitcake story. He
was hilarious when he wanted to be, and let's face it, fruitcake is
always good for a laugh, so it was easy to slide by the fact that this
was actually a story about a little boy who was hungry and homeless, thumbing rides with strangers, sleeping on athletic club
floors, placing a heart-stopping amount of trust in strangers and
scratching out his own little hardscrabble existence by dint of wit
and industry.

Margo chronicled Frankie's childhood and diving career in a
second book, but it was never published. I didn't even know
about it until eight or ten years ago. She found the manuscript
while she was moving or reorganizing or something and told me,
"I'm going to do something with this. It needs work, but it's pretty
good."

I encouraged her, but the weighty tome was well over four
hundred pages, typed on that friable old-school typing paper
people used after the war. Neither Margo nor I had any idea how
something like that would translate technically or artistically to
new-school publishing. The manuscript disappeared into the natural tides and eddies of household activity. When it resurfaced
not long ago, I waded through it, wishing Margo was still able to
answer questions about it.

The opening pages are kind of a treatise on the fact that we
never know what to do with our heroes when we're done with
them. After the war, it would seem, Frankie was struggling to
figure out where he belonged in the world. Perhaps this book

was Margo's way of helping him put all the embattled elements of his life story in perspective. She flashes back to his preteen years, during which he ran away from home and sold bicycles, magazine subscriptions and newspapers to finance shelter in flophouses and athletic clubs, where he met Johnny Weissmuller and others who mentored him as a diver. He traveled with aquatic exhibitions and "tumbling acts" and began to fly—all by the time he was fifteen.

Employing more spin than a turboprop, Margo let the harsh realities of Frankie's truncated childhood slip away between the lines and transformed his story into a *Fountainhead* of idealistic dramalogue: Huck Finn meets Dale Carnegie in one high-diving heroic journey. Kindly strangers and well-heeled benefactors were rendered in fine detail while drunk drivers, deviants and absentee responsible adults were wistfully—even poetically— reduced to little more than a footnote. She devoted minimal typeface to the people who'd abused and neglected little Frankie; they didn't deserve to be the subject of a sentence any more than he deserved to be the direct object.

I don't know what my father thought of this book or if he ever even read it. Given his enthusiastic support for Margo's magazine writing and for *My Rival*—and given how against nature it was for either of my parents to be discouraged—it seems odd that this second book was tucked in a drawer and never mentioned for fifty years. All I know is that Frankie chose not to share these memories with me, but he was undeniably scarred by his (*cough*) upbringing. From his perspective, the little boy in Margo's book probably felt more desperate than spunky, because spunk is an entirely different dynamic when you're the one schlepping your fruitcakes on the corner of Skid Row and Third.

In later years, Frankie did send money to his mother, but I remember that being done with a trudging sense of obligation— probably the same degree of concern he'd received from her during his childhood. Nothing good or bad was ever said about her as a human being, but her obituary offers a small keyhole. It was sent to Margo and Frankie by one of his older sisters (Vera, I think), who occasionally sent items she'd clipped from the local paper with obsessive precision, leaving not a millimeter of frivolous margin beyond the typeface.

Dora Fenton Kurtz, the obituary reports, died in 1975 at age ninety-five. She'd graduated from Palmer Chiropractic School, married Dr. Frank Kurtz in 1899 and had four children: a boy (deceased), the two sisters and "Col. Frank Kurtz of Los Angeles, who was the most decorated pilot of World War II, being pilot of the historic Boeing Bomber, 'the Swoose,' which is now in the Smithsonian Institute. He was also the only male Olympic medal winner to make three U.S. Olympic Diving Teams."

Not only does Dora's obituary say more about Frankie than it says about her, it says more about *his airplane* than it says about her! We're left to speculate about the story of her life other than a few basic stage directions ("Exit Dr. Kurtz; enter Stepfather One wielding belt."), but Dora Fenton Kurtz graduated college at a time when less than 3 percent of women went beyond high school. There was a starkly divided highway between motherhood and career. Palmer was the first chiropractic college in the world, and she would have studied with its founder, Dr. D. D. Palmer, who originated chiropractic care as a health science and began a blood feud with allopathic medicine, and doesn't that make you wonder which kind of doctor Dr. Kurtz was? Were they fierce competi-

Daddy Art and Gigi set the tone of joy, love and acceptance pervasive in my upbringing.

tors or ideological enemies? Apparently, there was enough chemistry between them to get her pregnant with four children neither one of them wanted to raise, but not enough to fend off the step-fathers.

No matter how you look at it, Dora's life was a study in contrarianism, and it seems that Margo's book did the best possible thing one could have done with all that. Perhaps it was her way of telling Frankie that if the people who should have loved you laded you with issues instead, you have to zip open that emotional baggage, unload the crap and spirit away whatever well-disguised blessings you can extract. If there's a lesson to be learned or a quality to be mined, you stuff it in your pocket and leave the rest by the side of the road. You stick out your thumb and hope that love comes along to offer you a lift.

Frankie is living proof that we're allowed to move on from the families that created us and create the families we need. I'll never know if his childhood was the casualty of a culture war or the product of a moxie-meets-moment; what matters is that he survived it, physically and emotionally, and that it instilled in him the very traits that would empower him to physically and emotionally survive a war. What I take from all of the above is a sense of awe about the depth of love and breadth of caring Frankie was capable of, despite the meager rations he grew up on.

But this is where Margo comes in, and with Margo came Daddy Art and Gigi, who embraced him as their son, and all my mother's siblings, and all my father's Band of Brothers. And then came me. There was no lack of love in Frankie's life, and that— *above all else*—is what defined my family.

Best-case scenario, one is born into a place of art and grace. Second best: one learns to rise above.

"My father was a remarkable man," Margo tells Antonio, the beautiful Brazilian man who has arrived to keep watch over her through the night. "We five children, three girls and two boys, we loved Omaha. The kind of really important people all grew up there, so Omaha became famous for what it could offer. And so my father got all of us on board and got us working, and so we all took our place there, and we learned to fly and do other things too. My father wanted his five children to know how to do anything they wanted to do."

It's heartening when she gets talkative like this. That old war-bond tour energy lights her eyes. She has a good audience. Perry and Antonio and I listen without patronizing her, nodding and softly commenting once in a while. "Wow. Amazing. That's very interesting."

"We all got crazy about flying. And I even learned to fly and had my part around it. I had been flying. I had been flying as a youngster, but I'm one of five children, and we all learned to fly, and we all grew up in Omaha, Nebraska, which is about halfway from here to New York. And we grew up there, but I grew up in Omaha, Nebraska, actually, which is a good place to grow up. It's good for people my age."

Candidly, I'm not sure who else in her family learned to fly, but it's quite clear in Margo's book that her first time flying was that moment with Frankie and Yankee Boy. These days, Margo's stories are a bit iffy on the facts, but they still have a lot of that old flare. In an odd way, the language of dementia seems to transcend the earthly bonds of the dictionary. The word "flying," for instance. In the well-oiled mind, it means airplanes; in Margo's story, it takes on the poetic connotation of a woman whose meta-physical feet rarely touched the earth.

One of the difficult dynamics for me to overcome as my mother aged was the compulsion to correct her when she called someone the wrong name, or forgot what year we were living in, or went off on a story that took a plot point from a book she read in 1958 and morphed it into an actual event that happened to her just this morning. Partly, I just like things that are correct, damn it, but moreover, I wanted her to stay with me in the here and now. I couldn't bear to lose my touchstone, my sounding board, my trusted advisor in all things from love and work to which dish soap is least chafing to the hands.

From my perspective, the Q&A portion of the program was nowhere close to over. I still had much to learn from my mother, and the bitter lesson in my father's decline was that I am not as talented a listener as I would like to be. I was convinced that conversations were made of words. If words lost their meaning and became malleable, communication was impossible. I didn't know then that words are the trees obscuring the proverbial forest that shifts with the wind, creating a language of its own.

The willingness to let go of all that was a mountain for me to climb, and it's a fundamental job requirement for anyone who comes into our home as a caregiver. This is one of the reasons I love Antonio; English is a distant second language for him, but he speaks fluent Margo. And I must admit, it doesn't pain me to have this gorgeous young man hanging out with us for the evening.

"My husband keeps himself very fit. He's a handsome man." Margo pats Antonio's well-muscled arm. "You seem to be in excellent health. You're quite attractive yourself!"

I heartily agree as I take our cups to the sink.

"Good night, Mommie." I lean in behind her, circle my arms around her shoulders.

"Good night, my darling angel," Margo says.

Then she slips off to her bedroom on the arm of the gorgeous Brazilian, and I head up the stairs with a good book, thinking, *What's wrong with this picture?*

Best-case scenario: one is born into a place of art and grace . . .

CHAPTER THREE

Imaginary Friends

California, 1939

Yankee Boy was a simple little fellow. He carried only 120 horsepower in his engine, and his instrument panel offered no complications—just a compass and a couple of engine instruments. What he lacked in equipment, he made up for in confidence. He had an upstart manner—like a redheaded, freckle-faced little boy, ready to fight on half a pretext, and not afraid of anything. He made a lot of noise for his size . . .

We had a small ten-cent-store airplane, the kind you buy your nephew the day you have offered to take him downtown. With this we would practice takeoffs and landings so I could absorb the angles of glide and climb. It helped sur-

prisingly. But sometimes it did seem that my whole life, like
that dime-store toy, had been turned into work.

Another reason I love my work: it brings out the best in me. In all
of us, I think. All ailments, grievances and trivialities are left at
home, and we bring our best selves to work. We primp our hair,
put together a nice outfit. I'll go all in with skinny jeans and boots
with heels—a far cry from the baggy yoga pants and sneakers I
sport at home. It's not that I love the people at work more than
I love the people at home; it's that I love *myself* more at work
than I do at home.

The Margo and Frankie I knew throughout my life were ener-
getically deft at both work and play, and to me as a child, there
wasn't an appreciable difference between the two. Like Yankee
Boy, I was rambunctious and technically uncomplicated; I knew
the drill—the job at hand—and joyfully undertook whatever that
might be. As much as I loved being in Omaha with Daddy Art
and Gigi, I was born and raised to go along for the ride; I loved
being on the move with my parents.

I would quiz them relentlessly on presidents and state capitals
from the back seat as we merrily rolled along in our sky blue '51
Ford. (This was the same car in which Frankie taught me to drive
a decade later. Hey, why run out and buy something on time
when you could fix this one to run just fine? "If it works, you stick
with it," was Frankie's credo.) Margo put me in charge of folding
the maps, and Frankie joined me in pretending I could actually
read them, so we all had our assignment: pilot, copilot and navi-
gator. Conversation was spirited and spirits were high. Endlessly

fascinating Americana streamed by outside the car window. Road trips had a ring of adventure more than agenda.

That said, Frankie was never anything other than Frankie. He had a plan: a carefully strategized route and realistically optimized timetable, which he executed with the inflexible good cheer of a supply convoy. No fuel was wasted on side trips to self-pity, petty differences or whining. There was really nothing to whine about; I was having fun most of the time. I never noticed that my parents expected me to comport myself like a trouper, never felt that I was being dragged along or baggage handled. It all made perfect sense to me: here was the first step, and there was the goal. Why would anyone *not* want to take the smartest, most efficacious route from here to there without hesitation, complaint or extraneous drama?

I wasn't mollycoddled in the car, but I was mightily entertained. In the wide backseat, I was surrounded by my dearest friends. Dolls and teddy bears never did a thing for me; my buddies were a diverse crew of unique beings with expressive faces and distinct personalities. D. B. Senior was a proper cocker spaniel who mentored D. B. Junior, a dog of some indiscernible fuzzy pink breed. I loved them dearly, but first and forever, there was Javitz, a small pink pup with big, floppy ears. She's very sarcastic, celebrates irony and can ring a little cynical before you really get to know her. She has a good shit detector. When we met, I was eight, and I named her Frosting because she looked like frosting. She quickly set me straight. No, her name was Javitz, and Javitz she remains, sixty years later. She should probably be in a museum, mounted in one of those glass boxes where oxygen can't get to you, but I keep her in my closet with her best friend, a hand towel named Mike, who was originally hired on as a blanket but devolved over the years into the Shroud of Turin. If Mike went missing, Javitz was beside herself.

Randall, accompanied by his tail, Big Red, joined me at my New York co-op while I was doing a series called *Love, Sidney*. So Randall was born with a silver spoon in his mouth. When Margo met Roland, he was draped over the cash register at Bullocks during their white sale. If you bought enough pillowcases, you got one of him, so Roland is self-deprecating and grateful while Randall is grasping and jealous and entitled.

"We consider the word 'stuffed' an epithet," Margo told a flight attendant on our way to Hawaii for Christmas several years ago.

"It's a racy remark is what it is," Randall huffed.

I tried to gently suggest that perhaps he'd be more comfortable in Margo's carry on, but he'd already engaged the flight attendant in a conversation about her dear friend, a blue poodle, and then the people seated on either side of us shared stories about their constant-hearted companions. (Margo has always had that effect on people. She drew stories out of them; a few minutes with her in an elevator, and they'd be proffering memories like baby pictures out of a wallet.)

Long before I came along, Frankie and Margo had a history of anthropomorphic friends. Like Yankee Boy. And *Nippu Ji Ji*, Margo's snub-nosed roadster, who sympathized with her aching loneliness when she was unbearably young and horrifically in love with a man who wasn't there. She gave Frankie a wily little koala that functioned as his wingman until well into World War II. Long before I ever thought about purposely creating characters for fun and profit, I was surrounded by characters who seemed to create themselves in whatever order they were called forth by the universe.

On long road trips, it often fell to Javitz to talk me to sleep with a rambling stream of consciousness that led to a rambling stream of dreams, and Frankie provided a throat for her endless, raspy patter.

"Tonight, as we are all slowly sinking into the depth, I want you to know that the principal, nay, the *star* of this entire performance is an old, well-known Far East figure named Harry Kreeshna of the Kreeshna Nobbos from the Ganges just off Calcutta. And we all have our *mon*-tras and *man*-tras and what not, but all we do is go from one Harry Kreeshna to another Harry, like Harry Belafonte . . . Harry Cohn . . . Bloomingdale's—"

"Bloomingdales?" Frankie interrupted. "How did that get in there?"

"All right, all right," Javitz would chide us back on track. "This sleep dust is totally effective. As you slowly sprinkle it, it is so insidious, you find yourself seized by a gentle paralysis. The eyelids go clunk. Just suddenly drop. That's the first drop before the head drops sideways—repeat, *sideways*—and then *plop* goes the head forward, and that's all she wrote. Dr. Sure couldn't put you to sleep any faster."

California, 1936

Soon Frank and I were making short cross-country hops together. To say these trips were heaven is too casual. It's closer to say they were a song, a love song without words, a song more of colors, of lights. You see, we couldn't talk—if we had an interphone, only Frank could talk to me, not I to him. But I could see his head above his cockpit, so I could hear those blue eyes.

Above me and in front of me, to the left and to the right, there is blue sky. It's clear and empty. I am completely free. But just as I am drinking this expansion into me, I do see something tangible and earthy; I can see the shadow of my airplane on the rolling white clouds underneath me. I can see it bumping along so relaxed and free.

Then way up here in the heavens, where I have been no-where and no-when for some while, I decide it is time to look at my watch, and check my time, and alter the lazy course of that shadow bumping along over white clouds. I'll take it someplace now. I've tasted real freedom up here, and it was pleasant and refreshing and joyful.

I've tasted freedom and it will somehow go along with me. With me because it's in me, I've breathed it in so deep.

Many of our long family drives were one-way trips; we moved seventeen times and lived in eight different states before I started high school. Norfolk, Virginia. Tampa, Florida. San Antonio, Texas. Mascoutah, Illinois. We hit all the glamour spots. Home was wherever the three of us were together; housing was whatever was available, so we lived in some very humble abodes, but once in a while, circumstances or serendipity placed us in swanky digs.

Margo used to tell the tale of a Washington cocktail party where she and Frankie bumped into Texas senator Lyndon John-

Happy traveling companions in 1949.

COURTESY OF THE AUTHOR/CARL WALDEN

son. On hearing that we'd been living out of suitcases, shuttling between hotels near my father's interim office at the Pentagon, LBJ boomed across the room, "Bird! These young folks need a place to live."

Before the evening was out, Lady Bird had us moved into their house across the cul de sac from J. Edgar Hoover. It was a lovely home for a little while. My best memory of it is a wonderfully squeaky step about halfway up the staircase. (I discovered this by jumping up and down until it squawked like an accordion.) Lady Bird said it always alerted them when LBJ's brother came home drunk.

Margo did her best to keep me current and comfortable in one new school after another. I was a happy and personable little girl, but I was shy, so those innumerable first days of school were daunting at best and at worst, excruciating. As an only child who was used to behaving like a miniature adult, I wasn't particularly adept at socializing with other kids, but I was savvy enough to know when I'd committed a faux pas.

When I was about seven, I went to a little classmate's birthday party, and I was very excited about the gift I had chosen for him: a miniature flashlight. I arrived to find the big birthday party table all set for us. Beside each paper plate was a party favor: the exact same miniature flashlight. Mortification!

You'd think that several decades of theatrical slings and arrows would have dimmed the memory of this irretrievable loss of face, but just thinking about it brings back the sting. I never had stage fright; I have *life* fright. Perhaps the backhanded gift in our nomadic existence was that, over the years, it honed my sensibilities about how each fresh audience was going to react. Certainly being thrown into a series of rooms filled with strangers laid a

Margo and me in one of the many backyards I grew up in.
I'm thinking San Antonio or Tampa about 1950.

foundation for my ability to face a new audience eight shows a week without a ripple of nerve. Most women of my generation learned to please people; I learned to entertain them.

I also learned (from my parents' powerful example) that wherever you go, kindness and generosity pave a much smoother road than fear and selfishness. Sooner or later you'll move on, and the only thing you take with you is who you are. Your failures follow you only if you fail to forgive yourself, and the people you grow to care about are left behind only if you forget them. The only consistent thing in one's life is one's self; every other variable is in constant flux.

This was perfect training for my life as an actor: a job where you go from one project to the next, never knowing how long you'll be there, hoping and praying—*throw salt! knock wood! sacrifice a virgin!*—that it'll go on for as much as a few months. To even whisper the possibility of employment that continues for *years* would be bad luck, a worse temptation of fate than redecorating your dressing room.

Generally, where Frankie went, Margo and I followed, but somewhere between the Allied occupation of Japan and the early stirring of the Korean War, he was stationed in Tokyo for eighteen months. He could have taken his family if he'd signed on for three years, but he opted for the shorter tour, and it was decided that Margo and I should stay in Omaha with Daddy Art and Gigi.

Frankie loved Japan. He made the effort to learn the language and came to appreciate Japanese art and history. Later I got the impression that he was frustrated by his work there and felt he could have been doing something more, and I remember some dark comments about his being sent there to fight the Korean

War. (I don't know how he felt about that war, but I do know he was adamantly opposed to Vietnam.) I was too young to under-stand it then, but it seemed to me in later years that Frankie's so-journ in Japan brought unexpected healing to both him and Margo. He strongly connected with the Japanese people, who warmly embraced him. That probably sounds rosy to some cyn-ics, and I completely understand, but Frankie was an honorable, self-disciplined man in a place and time where honor and self-discipline were greatly valued.

His assignment in Japan never smacked of a victory lap, but they knew who he was; during the War, Frankie was known and feared in Japan, just as Japanese and German flying aces were notorious by name in the United States and Europe. In the air, these men were doing their level best to kill each other. On the ground, political correctness hadn't been invented yet. Books like *Queens Die Proudly*, and even the wartime edition of *My Rival, the Sky*, referred to Japanese soldiers as "Japs"—not as a racial epithet applied to Japanese people but as tightly wound short-hand for the enemy who flew at them daily with relentless preci-sion. During the first year of their marriage, Margo and Frankie attended twenty-two funerals—and that toll doesn't even take into account the men rounded up for the Bataan Death March, which Frankie and the surviving shred of his company narrowly escaped.

When I was a child, I never heard about any of that. I knew what the War was, as much as any child can know what any war is, but I guess I had a comfortable vision of Frankie flying mis-sions over open fields, taking out a vacant bridge or an empty railroad trestle or perhaps an abandoned factory, but only if it was nighttime and all the workers had gone home. Even now, it's a struggle for me to think of it any other way, because the Frankie I knew all my life was so overwhelmingly gentle and kind.

They say no one prays for peace more than a soldier (though a soldier's lover might disagree); as far as I knew then or can decipher now, Frankie's prayers were answered. He made peace with it. He talked about the people of Japan with compassion and respect. I remember hearing about his efforts to help a little boy who was living in a cardboard box near his office. Knowing what I know now about Frankie's childhood, I suspect he felt he had more in common with that boy than he had with the little boys who lived in Daddy Art and Gigi's neighborhood in Omaha.

While he was in Tokyo, Margo had the opportunity to go over and visit him on one of the invitation-only maiden flights of the newly founded Japan Air Lines. She was on assignment to interview two Japanese princesses for a magazine article. (Atsuko Ikeda and Takako Shimazu, I think, but the article is gone with the fog.) Margo returned full of stories, poetry, music and art. They didn't bring back anything expensive or of museum quality. Most of what they brought was utilitarian—carved barrel tables, lamps, a chest of beautifully carved drawers with iron handles— but this is when the Japanese fisherman came to live with us, along with a number of other little presents and mementos. The stories that came with these items were more about the people of Kyoto. Margo loved how kind and gracious they were, more polite and less hurried than brusquely busy Americans.

Margo told me years later that as she boarded the airplane, she tripped and ran her stocking, and one of the JAL flight attendants discreetly gifted her a spare. It was a small thing, but the moment meant something to Margo. Of course, here again, I see cynical eyeballs rolling like billiard balls, but what I took from that as a little girl—from Margo's gratitude and the flight attendant's small kindness—was how little the warring of two countries has to do with any differences between the people who are most profoundly affected by war.

Margo and Frankie had only one regret about that time: they wished they'd taken me to Tokyo, and I wish that too, in retrospect. But at the time, I was happy camping in Omaha with Daddy Art and Gigi. Gigi recognized the creative in me and encouraged it, having come from a creative family herself. Her brother, Homer Conant, was famous for his fabulous art deco costumes and sets for the Ziegfeld Follies and for whimsical posters and magazine covers he did in the 1920s. While Gigi played piano, Margo's brothers, Homer and Bob, rendered gospel and opera standards in impressive bass and tenor. (Our favorites were "Home on the Range" and "Red Sails in the Sunset.")

Gigi enrolled me in ballet classes, which quickly illuminated the stunningly plain truth that I was born to be a prima ballerina. Having inherited the seemingly incongruous mix of Margo's poetic license and Frankie's straight spine, I was a natural dancer. I read a biography of Anna Pavlova and fell in love with her grace and hyperbole. "To tend, unfailingly, unflinchingly, towards a goal is the secret to success." This was on a Friday, and I determined that I would be able to do the splits by Monday. It actually took me a bit longer than one weekend, but I did it eventually and quite impressed my teacher.

I was cast in our winter recital as the Sugar Plum Fairy, my

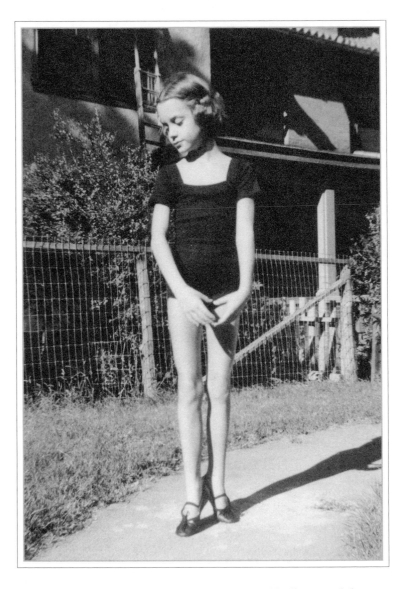

Gigi enrolled me in ballet classes, which quickly illuminated the stunningly plain truth that I was born to be a prima ballerina.

first starring role. I still have pictures. In my favorite one, all the snowflakes are prostrate on the floor, as if I've slain them. On Margo's return, Gigi reported to her that I had danced superbly. She was particularly impressed by the poise with which I held *attitude* between movements, never breaking character as I gracefully dished my finger through my nose and resumed my *bras croisé*. The prima ballerina at last! One singular sensation!

I took ballet very, very seriously. I'd performed in those aquacades with Frankie, remember. He took his performances very seriously, and I picked up on that, though I didn't understand the difference in what was at stake. Later on, I understood that for Frankie, a missed mark or faulty timing could mean disaster—paraplegia, even death—but that never crossed my mind back then. All I saw was that performance demanded discipline, an assiduous dedication to preparation and execution, and that the reward for this labor was ecstasy, defiance of gravity, and an outpouring of approval that definitely felt like love. I grew to love doing things that scared me—doing them in front of a lot of people. I learned that the more daunting the task, the sweeter the victory when you pulled it off.

Observing Frankie's meticulousness, I learned that God is in the details. Or the devil is—according to some people. My thinking is that the devil is in a *lack* of detail.

"If you're giving directions and there's one tiny wrong turn, well—where the hell are you?" I ask Perry whenever he gently suggests I do some homework on a homeopathic remedy for OCD. I drive myself crazy, feeling like Cassandra: How can people not see these potholes and paper cuts from which I try to protect them!

A few years ago, after I'd invested a few hours in reorganizing my cache of Post-its and other micromanaged office orts, Perry said (with great affection), "Swoose . . . why don't you go practice your expressions in the mirror?"

I keep hoping I'll settle down, but Frankie never did mellow. Toward the end of his life, his checklist had dwindled in import, but not in length. As items like "Arrive at Pentagon" disappeared, he replaced them with the daily tasks of his shrinking galaxy: shower, shave, exercise, haircut. He needed a structure to his day. Structure implied purpose.

I am my father's daughter, down to my marrow. During another Omaha sojourn, I slipped through a crack of bad timing and wasn't allowed to enroll in fourth grade. Margo tried to fight it, but to no avail. In my mind, the only thing worse than feeling like a misfit at yet another new school was not even having a school to not fit in at. The Frankie in me couldn't bear it. During school hours on a school day at any point during a school year, *there must be school*! I stoically commandeered a small writing desk and wooden chair from some cranny in Gigi's house, begged the curriculum from the inflexible public school administrators, mapped out an hourly schedule that included lunch and recess, and established my own classroom in a small spare room upstairs. It's not that I loved school. School was torture for me. But I wasn't going to fall behind, and it seemed to me that fifth grade would mean nothing if I hadn't paid my dues in fourth.

I don't recall any of the adults in the house helping me with this, but I was encouraged and uninterrupted. They let me do my own thing. This dynamic was a theme during my early years. Frankie often said, "He travels fastest who travels alone." It was possibly the most dangerous thing he could have said; I took it quite literally. The singleness of purpose was great for getting to your goal but also . . .

"To a certain extent," says my therapist, "being a lone wolf was a necessity in both his childhood and yours."

Oh, yes. I have a therapist. Of course, I do! Working in show business without a therapist would be like living in London without a good pair of Wellies. My therapist—we'll call her Ethel—is a lovely, insightful person with an expansive, Joan Baez vibe. She's a genius, an emotional intellectual, but very hard to reach. (What does it do for your abandonment issues when you feel abandoned by your therapist?) She's in her own world—not disorganized but in a different space. Just when I'm about to give up, she'll answer and say, "I always have time for you." She recently relocated to the high desert, so I communicate with her via Skype. I approach the computer in my dimly lit office like Leonidas to the Oracle, and if the neurotic gods of high-desert Internet are with me, she appears.

"What do you make of (such and such a thing)?" I ask her.

And Ethel the Oracle lays some lightning bolt of truth on me like: "It seems to me, the only thing missing from your childhood was a child."

Nora Ephron made her debut as a playwright with *Imaginary Friends* (a play with music by Marvin Hamlisch), in which Mary McCarthy and Lillian Hellman are assigned to be roommates in Hell. Cherry Jones and I did it on Broadway in 2002, and as an aside, I'd like to say here that Cherry is the only actress I've ever heard utter the words, "I think my part is too big."

Anyway, toward the end of the show, Cherry's Mary says, "What did we do to deserve each other?"

And my Lillian dryly replies, "Everything, apparently."

This is the perspective with which I now see my childhood. I see how my parents and I invented each other. If you ask a child psychologist, he or she would probably say it was a recipe for Hell, but for me, it was as close to Heaven as I could get without wings of my own.

Hollywood High was a bright bubble of innocence (much like my hair!).

CHAPTER FOUR

My Last First Day

---∞---

California, 1932

I was still going dancing with my list of swains, and I don't think any of them even knew I was dating Frank. I wonder whether they seemed quite real to me. Looking back, I think I had changed worlds, that autumn day when I walked over to him.

In the midst of good times with someone else, I could be thinking of a slim and slender-faced boy who was working. He might be working evenings now because the days were too full of just school. I would know he only had time and money enough to have a dinner of one hamburger and a glass of milk between a busy day and a busier night. Then for a moment it was hard for me to swallow.

And then I wanted to turn and yell at myself something like, "Why not just enjoy the dancing and the fun? Why be worrying about something anyone would say you shouldn't trouble your flippant blonde head about?" But that night, just before I closed my eyes to fall asleep, I would wonder— When will Frank get to sleep tonight?

All the same, he was a very rich poor young man. Between hamburgers, we had feasts of Southern California glamour. Frank was in great demand at every gay function which in any way centered at a swimming pool, to give exhibitions of diving. These were times when he could compete in the entertainment field with the most lavish of the solid-ground boys and walk off with an undisputed first, looking so playful and glamorous, you just wouldn't believe how often on the days before and after a 15-cent hamburger had to pinch-hit for dinner.

It was a lean life, and bright, and high. We'll never outlive it, never want to.

Margo has one foot in the timeline today. She's a seventeen-year-old student at USC. But she knows me. Somehow I fit into the old picture frames.

"You're off to New York?" she says when she sees me with my car keys.

"No, just a reading at the studio. I'll be back in a few hours."

"I'll just stay here and enjoy a last spray of life," she says, savoring it.

Margo was so free-spirited and fun-loving as a girl, it worried Gigi and Daddy Art that she ended up spending her late teens and half her twenties waiting for Frankie to finish flight school and wrap his head around the reality of marrying her. Family and friends disapproved. They needled and nudged her to date other men, get with the Glenn Miller and go dancing with someone who wouldn't squander her childbearing years, someone who wouldn't make her a war bride at best and at worst, a war widow and possibly a single mother—which (nodding respectfully to how tough that is now) was a lot tougher back then.

She had a broad selection of suitors to choose from, though she had high standards, including a strict rule about not getting in a car with a man who drank. According to family lore, she and her sister Mary Alice—Mici for short—both had opportunities to marry the heir to a large corporate fortune. Once Margo's heart and mind were set on Frankie, she could not be moved.

During the first decade of my life, for all practical purposes, Margo really was a single mother. Even when Frankie was there, she handled the logistical decisions while he called down the tactical ones from his thirty-thousand-foot view.

She says in *My Rival, the Sky* that her first magazine articles and the book itself were at Frankie's behest, but I don't remember him encouraging or discouraging her about working while I was growing up. The original contract for the book specifies an option on her next two books. Perhaps the publisher expected a novel or maybe the kind of literary essays that later came from Anne Morrow Lindbergh. Clearly, they believed in her talent. She had a place to go. It was a choice she made, for whatever reason, not to pursue it. Margo was constantly busy, but she never earned money for anything after the book went out of print.

"A woman should always keep a certain amount of her own money," she told me early and often. "A little stash off to the side her husband doesn't have to know about, from her family or her work or whatever. Just so she can have her own money."

In Margo's case, that money initially came from Gigi, who probably got it from her mother, Grandmother Conant, who'd established and run three hotels in Omaha. I'm sure Frankie did know about it, but Margo handled all their investments and banking and bill paying. She was a terrific businesswoman who wasn't afraid to come up with creative ideas if a financial bottleneck required some finesse. Warren Buffett joined our extended clan in 1952. (He married Susie Thompson, whose sister Dottie was married to Margo's brother Homer, which gives you some idea of the wide-branching family phone tree Margo activated every time I made an appearance on TV or big screen.) Margo adored him as a human being and admired the way his mind worked. She learned from their lively conversations and became a small but proud Berkshire Hathaway stockholder back in the 1960s. Frankie and Margo both attended annual stockholders' meetings, but Margo was unquestionably at the helm.

Now that I think of it, it was really quite progressive for Frankie to take the backseat on all that. He never felt the macho need to be in control of our household; she was indisputably in charge. Margo was quite a clotheshorse, but she was smart about it. If she said we were going to Saks to buy dresses, Frankie was all for it because he knew Margo would never do anything crazy. Margo's spending priorities went more toward cultural influences, which in Omaha meant museums, galleries, books and ballet.

We didn't go on typical family vacations, but starting when I was about ten, we made regular trips to New York. While Frankie tended to whatever official business needed tending to, Margo and I made the most of every minute. She was a savvy shopper who knew her way around the bargain basements and trunk sales, but as far as I was concerned, Broadway was New York's reason for being. We stayed at the Waldorf Astoria on the military rate. Margo would order a tureen of tomato soup from room service, and I'd lie on the bed with the *New Yorker*, reading the descriptions aloud, picking what I wanted to see.

"*West Side Story* . . . no. Sounds like something about Puerto Rican gangs."

My first Broadway show was *By the Beautiful Sea*, in which Shirley Booth played a woman who owns a boardinghouse full of vaudeville performers and falls in love with a Shakespearian actor or some such thing, and as hilarity and a big eleven o'clock number ensue—oh, you know. By the end of the third act, you're choking back tears, and you'd swear to Molière these were people you'd known all your life.

I was infatuated with the *liveness*—the immediacy of it—the characters were people, not images on a screen. Their love, struggle and hope were as real as the sweat on their temples and the sound of their feet on the wooden floor. This was something much more akin to Frankie's performances on the high dive; poised at opening places, then springing to life, hurtling toward earth, flying, flipping, spinning, slicing into the safe water. So much could go wrong, it kept your stomach in a tense knot until—*oh, thank God!*—so much went right. Everything was at stake, right here, right now. This was a real moment, an actual place populated by sensationally exotic creatures who came out only at night. And Wednesday matinees.

On another early trip, we went to see Burgess Meredith in a matinee performance of *Teahouse of the August Moon*. We went to Sardi's afterward, and they must have been having a particularly slow day because we sat in a coveted corner booth. My heart did a butterfly loop when I realized that seated right next to us—right next to *me*—was Mr. Meredith! I was too starstruck to hear anything but my own pulse ringing in my ears, but Margo chatted him up and got him to sign my Playbill, which he did with his unforgettable gravely laugh and crinkle-eyed smile.

We saw Anthony Perkins in *Look Homeward, Angel* at the Ethel Barrymore Theatre and waited in the alley afterward so we could ask for an autograph. Seeing the actors emerge from the stage door felt miraculous. I could hardly speak as he signed my program. A vivid memory of that moment washed over me one night as I walked out the same stage door after a performance of *Imaginary Friends*, and people were waiting for my autograph. I had another flashback when I saw Imogene Coca's revival of her cabaret act with Sid Caesar in 1990, but I kept that to myself. It would never do to tell another actress, "I saw you on Broadway when I was just a child!" (Especially after she paid me a stellar sideways compliment: "Jerry Zaks tells me you're a genius.")

Right about this time (the mid-1950s) I started to suspect that Plan A—my quest to become a prima ballerina—might be unworkable; our frequent relocation made it impossible to maintain any kind of continuity in my training. I also began to understand that Omaha wasn't exactly the cultural Mecca it looked like from the perspective of a military base in West Texas. Nonetheless, I was happy to decamp there with Margo while Frankie went to jet school in Wichita. After Frankie came back, and we were on our way to wherever it was we went after that, Frankie made a point of stopping early one evening at a tiny motel somewhere in Kansas so I could see Elvis Presley on the *Ed Sullivan Show*.

It was a big deal for the American television audience in general and for twelve-year-old me in particular, but when we arrived in the seedy motel lobby where the TV was located, there was a cadre of elderly people, several in wheelchairs, gathered around watching a quiz show. Frankie busted out the jaunty airman charm and talked them into changing the channel, which they immediately and vocally regretted when the world-famous pelvis went to work. (In *Swoosie!: The Musical*, this moment would be a big production number with wheelchairs spinning in formation and a tap solo for the scrawny night clerk.)

Honestly, it's laughable now—CBS was so nervous about the whole thing, they arranged the cameras to crop the shot at Elvis's rib cage most of the time, briefly cutting in with strategic shots of the Jordanaires bop-bopping in the background, dedicated to protecting my innocent eyes from the lurid image. Now I'm working for them on a show that routinely talks about vaginas, penises and orgasms.

But mostly, I look back on that, and I love Margo and Frankie for making it a priority on this and many other occasions to indulge me in this type of cultural watershed moment.

Years before Elvis came along, I was smitten with Tommy Edwards, the smooth singer of "It's All in the Game," my favorite song of that moment.

"Many a tear has to fall . . ." I could croon the whole thing by heart with great interpretive flair. *"All in the wonderful game that we know as love . . ."*

As we were traveling on one of our many Point A to Point B car trips, I read in a local paper that he was appearing near our route. I begged Margo and Frankie to take me, and they made it happen, agenda be damned. We ended up cruising a questionable area of Chicago till we found a parking space near the concert venue, an Apollo-like theater, where we stood out—two painfully white people and their pale, skinny princess—amongst the large, entirely African American audience. (This didn't stop us from going backstage afterward to wait for an autograph. I was forever smitten with the gracious Mr. Edwards.)

It was an interesting progression from Glenn Miller to Tommy Edwards to Elvis; the world beyond the car windows was spinning faster, and I was beginning to sense that. But suddenly none of it mattered. Daddy Art died in 1956.

It felt like the unmerciful turn of a page. He had leukemia, but he hadn't known it long and wasn't very sick at all, so we were stunned and brokenhearted. I was twelve, and this was my first experience of death. Margo and Frankie had become accustomed to loss and grieving during the war, but this was different. Devastating. And our poor darling Gigi—she began to hit the bottle a bit. Understandable, but after a few months it got worrisome.

Margo told me later, "The hardest thing I've ever done in my life was drive away and leave Gigi in that house all by herself."

One year after Daddy Art died, almost to the day, Gigi died of those natural causes that stop the heart of a lover who's lost her lifelong significant other. The rambling house in Omaha was sold, and we drove away from the only modicum of permanence I'd ever known.

Frankie retired from the air force in 1959, and it was decided that we should return to Southern California. It seems to me he was at a crossroads, struggling somewhat with the politics of the military, which kept him from advancing in rank despite his many medals, vast accomplishments and commanding officer experience. My father wasn't the sort of hawk who ascended the ranks during the Cold War, but it wasn't in his biology to roll over or aim low. The question lingered: What do we do with a hero once we're done with him?

He went to work for John Jewett "Jack" Garland, whose father, real estate developer William May Garland, was instrumental in building the city of Los Angeles and bringing the Summer Olympics to L.A. in 1932. Frankie won a bronze medal for the ten-meter dive that year and remained connected to the Olympic community throughout his military career. Meanwhile, Margo had remained connected to Jack Garland and his wife Helen all those years, not because she thought it might be a good connection but because she was (and is) Margo.

When Frankie left the air force, Margo wanted us to settle in Southern California. She reached out to plant the seed of an idea that Frankie might fit in nicely with the other executives at the Garland Building, and in fact, he did. There may have been some adrenaline lacking in the world of real estate management as opposed to the world of high flight, but he rolled with the changes. Margo was happy to have a place to call home, and I was thrilled to know that this would be my last first day at a new school.

My parents bought a house across the street from Bob Hope and his wife in a pleasant but not ostentatious neighborhood in Toluca Lake.

"A *tiny, little house* across the street from Bob Hope," Margo and Frankie always emphasized so as not to leave the impression we were living in some kind of mansion. "The smallest house in the neighborhood." Which it was. Possibly the best example ever of *location, location, location.*

Their wandering days were over. They put down roots, and that house remained my home base until I bought the house where we live now in 1994. I eventually had an apartment in New York, of course, but when I was in L.A., I was at Frankie and Margo's, nodding off over my script and falling asleep on a fold-out bed in the same room where I'd nodded off over my homework in tenth grade.

With high school looming, Margo and I set to work on my style. She was judiciously clothes conscious—not vain, but always aware—and she taught me all the tricks of the trade. The art of hair was very important to Margo and me because we hardly had forty strands between the two of us. I was also less than blessed in the area of décolletage. My archrival in Mascoutah was Donna Wolf, whose impeccable sweater sets filled me with covetous wonder. Margo made it her mission to bring my wardrobe up to that bar, even though my sweater sets never filled in the way Donna's did, and it was becoming apparent that they never would.

As a child, I'd been swan and goose by turns—a burly spark-plug at three, a graceful Sugarplum Fairy at seven, a knobby-kneed pony at eleven—now there was no denying it: instead of Margo's hourglass chic, I had inherited Frankie's physique, lean and utilitarian as a swizzle stick. Nonetheless, I was under the delusion that when my hair was piled on top of my head just so, I bore a striking resemblance to Brigitte Bardot. (I mention this only because it is a tribute to the self-esteem Margo nurtured in me.)

Margo rose to that challenge as well as any costumer who has since followed in her footsteps. With the help of sturdy undergarments and wise wardrobe choices, I started Hollywood High looking like a *Mad Men* extra with a lower-caliber bullet bra. My shoulder-length, wren-brown hair was bobbed, bleached and teased into a blond Sandra Dee helmet (appropriate to my crush on Troy Donahue); my brows were plucked and trained with bonsai precision. Girls weren't wearing pants to school yet, so there was the issue of shoes, but shoes were Margo's forte. She hooked up a nice selection of serviceable pumps, plus a natty pair of bright red sneakers, which I wore with my Toluca Nixonette uniform.

Oh, don't misconstrue. I was completely oblivious about politics, but the Nixonettes had adorable hats. And pom-poms! In 1968, I was politically aware enough to know that Frankie was for Nixon because he was against the war in Vietnam, but in 1960 it was all about the pom-poms. We entertained the rally crowd in the parking lot at Alfonse's Diner and had our picture in the paper, which certainly fulfilled the Nixon-Lodge promise of a better America, as far as I was concerned.

Hollywood High was a bright bubble of innocence (much like my hair); I was blissfully ignorant about the struggle for civil rights, women's issues, wars and rumors of wars in the world. I wouldn't have dreamed of smoking or drinking, and my understanding of sex was based on the innocuous misinformation in health class films. As a preteen I used to scan the list of articles on the front of *Reader's Digest.* Anything with "premarital intercourse" (which I mentally pronounced "pre-marshal") was pretty well guaranteed to be hot stuff. Even with this wealth of information at my disposal, it was years before I understood why Margo and Gigi used to giggle themselves silly whenever they bought cucumbers at the grocery store.

"Don't forget to get one for the salad," Gigi always said.

When I finally got the joke, I was profoundly embarrassed for both of them, but looking back, I realize my mother's quietly un-apologetic sexuality—the way she always applied a dash of red lipstick and dotted perfume between her thighs before Frankie came home—it reassured me that I was not depraved as my own sexuality evolved.

Not that I was in a rush. I've always been far more enthusiastic about men in theory than empirical practice. I loved the idea of being Sandra Dee, dating a parade of suitors like Margo had at my age, dishing with clique sisters, but my first great love and constant preoccupation was what we then called "play practice." Initially, I was supposed to go to North Hollywood High, because before we moved into the house across from the Hopes, we lived in a little rental place several miles away. I had heard about the legendary drama teacher at Hollywood High, John Ingle, and I just had a compelling feeling that this was where I belonged. Without questioning the validity or importance of my calling, Frankie (who'd gone to Hollywood High himself) went to the mat for me and managed to get me in.

My instincts were right. Of course, none of these names would have registered on my radar in 1960, but in classes behind and ahead of mine, Mr. Ingle taught Richard Dreyfuss, Barbara Hershey, Albert Brooks, Joanna Gleason, Stefanie Powers, Julie Kavner, Nicolas Cage and many other remarkable actors, and given the chance, any and all of us will sing his praises. In the 1980s, he retired from teaching and had a pretty grand acting career himself, playing Edward Quartermaine on *General Hospital* and popping up in hundreds of wonderfully odd and Ingle-ish character roles, including the preacher in David Byrne's *True Stories*, which I was in too. I was overjoyed to see him but couldn't bring myself to call him John. He would always be Mr. Ingle to me.

Gotten up in true Mad Men *style (with my trusty ballerina flats close at hand) in Mascoutah, Illinois, 1958.*

But getting back to 1960 . . . Play practice. Mr. Ingle had a strong, square jaw and a grand theatrical voice. His wife was an opera singer, which somehow made him even more magnificent. He saw some spark in me and fanned it with high ideals about acting as a discipline, an offering of self, never a selfish catharsis.

My sophomore year, he assigned me a monologue from *Dark Victory*. A woman dying of a malignant brain tumor. Well, my dears, there are three things I can play the hell out of: a cancer patient, a mental patient and a hooker. (Basically, anything you don't want in life is what actors crave in a role. During a meeting with the writers of *Sisters*, making a case for Alex as more than comic relief, I actually heard myself pleading, "C'mon, guys, why couldn't *my* daughter get leukemia?") I tell you, something happened to me as I was delivering that monologue. The lowering of the lights. The intake of breath, pulling in silence and energy from the small audience. Mr. Ingle schooled us with strong mandates about the compelling obligation we must feel when we stand before an audience and ask for a piece of their time. This is an irreplaceable sliver of their lives. He wanted us to ask ourselves, "What am I offering that is worthy of that?" And for the first time I felt the answer. It was a true *Eureka!* in the bathtub moment. In this moment, when I realized I had the power to become someone else, I suddenly became myself.

That day after school, I told Margo all about it, breathless, elated, certain she couldn't possibly understand. But she did, and now I understand why. She was flittering around USC, happily dating her swains and dancing her shoes to pieces, when something came along and left her thunderstruck. From that moment forward, all other pursuits paled in comparison. She understood the singleness of purpose that took hold of me when I found my identity in Mr. Ingle's class. She wasn't alarmed at the sudden and dramatic change in me.

In his book *Talking to Myself*, Studs Terkel wrote about seeing Billie Holiday sing: "Something was still there, that something that distinguishes an artist from a performer: a revealing of self. *Here I be.* Not for long, but here I be."

I loved Studs. He became a buddy of mine after a backstage visit when I was doing *The Philanthropist* in Chicago. His unsullied moral compass, that pragmatic midwestern wisdom, reminded me of Daddy Art, and what he said there about Billie Holiday reminds me of what Margo wrote after watching Frankie dive. *Here I be.* Indeed. I wasn't there yet, but I'd caught a glimpse of it. Once I knew what it was—what it could be—everything else fell away. I didn't care about gossip or trivial pursuits or being Sandra Dee. Metaphorically, I went into the black tights and character shoes of a drama student. (Corporeally, I was still in my *Mad Men* pencil skirts and pumps for a few more years.)

The following year, we did Thornton Wilder's *Skin of Our Teeth*, and after the show one night, Mr. Ingle told me, "There's a gentleman here to see you." It was Eddie Foy III—one of the "Seven Little Foys" of Vaudeville fame. He'd grown up to be a casting agent. I could hardly breathe. This was it! I was being *discovered* in one of those "discovered in the Hollywood malt shop" moments.

"You were wonderful!" Mr. Foy said. "There's a small role coming up on *The Donna Reed Show*. I'd like you to consider it."

This did not take a great deal of consideration. Are you serious? Consider winning the lottery! Consider attending the ball in a pumpkin carriage! Consider entering Heaven without the inconvenience of being dead!

Mr. Ingle was almost as proud of me as Margo and Frankie were. I got out of school for a day to shoot the scenes. I got my SAG card, a lottery prize in itself. I was entirely professional on the set and cool as a Dilly Bar when I returned to school, big girl on campus.

"Oh, there was a pop quiz in social studies? I wouldn't know. I was filming all day yesterday."

My role was Party Guest, but my main scene was a split-screen phone call with Shelley Fabares, who played Donna Reed's daughter. The shoot went fantastically well. Everyone was lovely to me and made me feel fabulous about my performance. I was a hit! Who's to say what this could lead to?

Of course, Margo and Frankie told all the relatives, so the entire extended family and hoards of friends all over the country had been mobilized by the time the episode aired. Everyone was glued to the TV at the appointed moment. The party scene commenced. There was a fleeting glimpse of a frothy blond bubble that may have been the back of my head. The phone call had been reduced to one line, my voice on the other end of the telephone while both sides of the screen were wholly inhabited by Miss Shelley Fabares.

Rule number one when working in film and TV: don't count your chickens until the final cut. A career in show biz is a never-ending rotation of moments when you think you've made it and moments when you know you haven't.

I knew I'd made it when I was eight years old, and Margo took me to a taping of the *Ed Sullivan Show* and he had us stand up with Rocky Graziano. I knew I'd made it when S. J. Perelman took me out for a cheeseburger and gave me a copy of *Chicken Inspector No. 23*, which he'd inscribed: "For Swoosie Kurtz, the

*One of the moments I felt I'd made it. On the red carpet in 1990,
collecting an Emmy for* Carol & Company *with the
incomparable Carol Burnett.*

only logical one to succeed Eleanora Duse, Constance Collier, and Ethel Barrymore. 15 Sept 1966." And when I was made an honorary Rockette. And when I was an answer in the *New York Times* crossword puzzle. Seven down.

I knew I had not made it when the script called for a "Swoosie Kurtz type" and the director told me I was wrong for the part. I thought I'd made it but found out otherwise one evening as I waited for friends at Joe Allen's Restaurant. I'd recently received rave reviews and a Tony for my work in *Fifth of July*, so I was feeling like Melba the Toast of Broadway, and Joe Allen's is a popular après-theatre spot, so I rather expected to turn a few heads when I walked in. But as I sipped my Perrier, it seemed like a lot of people were downright staring—even pointing!—in my direction. I felt they were entitled to see the Many Sides of Swoosie. Pensive: chin lightly resting on the heel of my hand. Enigmatic: with a *Mona Lisa* smile. Industrious: rummaging my bag purposefully, applying lipstick without a mirror.

The preening and shenanigans went on for several minutes before I realized that people were actually checking out the evening specials printed on a blackboard directly over my head. All that was missing was a little toy flashlight next to each table setting.

In a 1962 issue of Time *magazine:*
"SWOOSIE & PARENTS: At 17, all swan."

ASSOCIATED PRESS

CHAPTER FIVE

Why I Wasn't at Woodstock

Yesterday, Margo slept until two, got up and ate a bit of breakfast, then went back to bed. When I tried to rouse her at dinnertime, she shook her head.

"I think I'm dying," she said before she drifted back to sleep.

But today, when the home health nurse arrives, Margo is up, bright and happy, taking in an episode of *Breaking Bad*, which she likes to watch with the subtitles turned on so she can do the dialogue along with Walter White/Heisenberg and Jesse Pinkman.

"If you believe that there is hell, I don't know if you are into that. But we're already pretty much going there, right? Well, I'm not going to lie down until I get there," says Margo Heisenberg, and Margo Pinkman retorts, "What, just because I don't want to cook meth anymore, I'm lying down?"

"Sorry for asking you to make an extra trip," I tell the nurse. "When I called last night, she seemed very low."

She smiles an understanding smile. "It's like a roller coaster. Only you're not on the ride."

But I do feel like I'm on the ride.

"No one else is gonna get killed," Margo tells the television. "Yeah, you keep saying that, and it's bullshit every time."

"Hello, Margo." The nurse gives her a warm hug. "Shall we check your vitals?"

"Oh! Aren't you wonderful to think of that?" Margo hugs her back. "That would be a terrific thing for us all to participate in."

"All right. You first, then Swoosie."

"You know my daughter? Swoosie Kurtz? She's beloved. Or beloved. That would be another way to state the fact."

The nurse takes Margo's temperature, pulse and blood pressure, then takes mine, and then she does Perry, who has arrived with his dog Boo.

Margo grasps my hand and says, "This is your husband?"

"Almost," says Perry.

"Margo, I don't have a husband," I remind her.

"Oh, no . . . darling. Tell me he hasn't died."

"No, I've never been married." But then I see that her eyes are on the door down the hall, and I wonder if perhaps she means Frankie.

"Interesting," she says after a moment. "I thought maybe you'd like someone in your area."

Twelve off-color comebacks cross my mind. Things that Joyce, my character on *Mike & Molly*, would say without hesitation.

There's been a lot of speculation about my romantic life over the years, why I've never been married, and whether my sexual orientation is straight, gay or ambidextrous. In the minds of many, if a woman never marries, it means she was never wanted, or (if she was wanted but failed to appreciate it) she must be a lesbian. I was an attractive young woman, eminently credible as a suburban wife and mother onstage and on-screen, and I aged without much need for surgery—cosmetic or catastrophic. These days, I am a woman of a certain age who's kept herself fit and healthy and turns out a good pony show on the red carpet. I have good teeth and some money.

Well, then, people wonder, *what is wrong with her?*

I know it would be terrific for the sales of this book if I were to come out as a lesbian in the next paragraph, so right here on this ten-meter platform of tell-all truth, I'd like to say that I am . . .

Sorry. I got nuthin'.

We all know there is no such thing as a tell-all, nor should there be, but the unfortunate whole-wheat truth here is: I am both straight and narrow. I haven't been a nun, but I am almost that married to my work. And I tend to dress in black most of the time. (That's what theatre people do; you won't find a community that wears more black and watches less television unless your car breaks down in Amish country.)

I always knew that I did not want to have children and never felt compelled to analyze or articulate why. Getting married wasn't something I actively did *not* want, but I was never fully available for it at any given moment. I was never fully available for anything that took me away from my work, and suddenly forty years went by, and I just sort of . . . forgot to get married. It seems to me that if one has to set a reminder on the calendar ("Pick up dry cleaning and get married before menopause!"), one is doing a disservice to the person being penciled in.

My mother had a choice, and she chose to make marriage and motherhood her life's work. I followed in the career-consumed footsteps of my father. Candidly, it might have made things easier if I had been born a lesbian, because what I really needed was a wife like Margo. Do you have any idea the percentage of my income that has gone to the agents, managers, housekeeping staff, shrinks and stylists who do for me what Margo did for Frankie? I'm not complaining. Just reporting. It's significant. Between my work schedule, my OCD/hermetic tendencies, the towering memory of my father and my ongoing devotion to my mother, I think I'd be a high-maintenance wife by conventional standards. I have periodically been an excellent girlfriend, however. I've been told by the best that I do a hell of a second date.

One of the many things I love about Margo is that she never questioned my choices, never pressured me to accommodate a man or the rote expectations of society. She has always known me so well; she must have realized early on that I was a better candidate for prima ballerina than I was for suburban housewife. She never pined for a grandchild or hinted that my biological clock was ticking. Or that it wasn't ticking loudly enough.

My going out into the world as an artist required no act of rebellion; I never felt I had anything to rebel *against*. But I did go out into the world, God knows. I did go out into the world.

I graduated high school with honors onstage at the Hollywood Bowl and went off to USC, still a nonsmoking Sandra Dee prototype with a full-ride scholarship in place and my virginity intact. *Time* magazine ran a lovely photo of me striding across campus flanked by Margo and Frankie. The accompanying article, a few column inches under a piece about Marilyn Monroe's will being filed for probate and just to the left of a breezy account of Jackie Kennedy's recent yachting adventure in Capri, is mostly about the historic significance of the Swoose, how the Swoose got its name, and I subsequently got mine. The photo is captioned: "SWOOSIE & PARENTS: At 17, all swan."

In that moment, I was an apt poster girl for women of my generation, suspended in glossy black and white between Marilyn's cautionary tale and Jackie's fairy tale. Not long after the photo was taken, I met Josh White, and he transformed my life.

Omaha, 1938

Before another Christmas came round, I had gone miles off our course. The weather aloft was too much for me, I'd come out of it, down, and goodbye forever to flying. The rough weather consisted of friendly voices, queerly misguided friendly voices saying over and over, "Margo, you are wrong to spend all your youth waiting for someone who isn't ever going to do anything about it."

"Margo, you're not being fair to yourself—you owe yourself some fun, you should be dating some of these boys. You know, you're only young once."

"Margo, he'll always put work, flying, everything ahead of you. Now, there is this young man, Bill, you know, he would always be so wonderful to you, and he would give you such security."

I'd known how to fly above that weather for nearly four years; but somehow, now, it began to be too much. You see, the time was nearing June of 1938, when Frank would become a second lieutenant, a June that would be just perfect for getting married in, and why didn't he ever speak of these things in letters?

Well, there came a letter, and it did have a June thought in it, an absolutely unlooked-for June proposal.

"I am going to request permission from the War Department for some special study when I graduate this June. I believe I can swing it. Of course, darling, there is the one bad point—it will keep us separated another year. But I know you won't mind—it will be a wonderful foundation."

It was enough to wither a girl's heart.

For a while I dated the boys, but in the midst of the friendly voices, all so approving now, there was a kind of silence making me feel jumpy. Like when the hum of a motor has suddenly died, and you keep waiting for it to come on again.

I thought a typewriter might fill up this silence, and so I got a secretary job, but there were loopholes for silence even there. Then I thought the noisiest job in the world would be a kindergarten. I went back to college to study to be a teacher, and I went around in sober dresses and flat-heeled shoes, and thought about nothing except child psychology, for months.

Home for Christmas, and there was a warmth and coziness about the fireplace, and the family all around, and a tree with presents. It was a nice outside warmth, and that was all. I didn't care—I didn't care about anything.

On a cold afternoon I came home from a cocktail party, chilled through in spite of all the gaiety. And as I walked in the door, there in front of me was a burning red bouquet of three dozen roses, the kind Fred Astaire sends in the movies, and someone was handing me a card—"I'll be with you this evening"—and I didn't understand this card, but there was a little pinprick against my heart, and perhaps I did feel a little warmth beginning, inside.

I thought, well, it is a holiday, and why don't I make myself look a little brighter? The sleigh and reindeer—that was an army bomber, and the "gift" which arrived with, oh, such a jingle-bell ring of the doorbell was a tall, handsome Air Corps lieutenant—how the silver wings shone!—whom I'd never seen before, and with whom I'd been at home forever.

It was nice to sit by the fire and feel really warm. After a while, Frank was looking into the fire pretty seriously, and saying: "I've tried all the ways I knew, to tell you, Margo, I love you, and if you don't believe it now—just ask my Commanding Officer. He said, 'For God's sake, Kurtz, take a plane, and go back to Omaha and marry that girl so I can get some work out of you!'"

Except in cases like Frankie and Margo—those rare instances where one's First Great Love actually sticks—I think the function of a first great love is to introduce us to ourselves, and then initiate us into the world of the brokenhearted. We go into it not even suspecting what we're capable of and come out of it amazed at what we've already done. A first great love, if you're lucky, follows the Bonnie and Clyde triptych: mutual cahoots-inducing sexual chemistry, a long spree of behavior that feels like getting away with murder, and a blaze-of-glory finish that leaves you both full of holes on the roadside. Josh

White and I enjoyed all but the last of these, and two out of three, as they say, ain't bad.

Josh came to the cinema department at USC after studying theatre and design at Carnegie Tech (Carnegie Mellon, in modern parlance). He was a native New Yorker with a very New York sensibility about theatre. He was wryly adorable with his Woody Allen glasses and Jewish idioms. He wasn't much taller than me but was far more worldly and had a very urbane fashion sense. He didn't mince words about my airy hair and cashmere twinsets.

"You're very blond," he said bluntly. "You might want to tone that down."

One of my strengths as an actor, if I do say so myself, is that I appreciate good direction. I developed a thick skin and learned the difference between an ad hominem tear-down and a genuinely constructive critique. This was the best kind of criticism: the kind that confirms what you already know and challenges you to be true to yourself. When I tell people that Josh helped me shop for clothes, decorated my apartment, hooked me up with a haircut at Vidal Sassoon and bought me a black Rudi Gernreich swimsuit, they assume he was gay and I was deluding myself, but in fact, he was just one of the early 1960s avant-garde. He was interested in cutting edge art of all kinds, and the work of both Vidal Sassoon and Rudi Gernreich (who changed the world by inventing the monokini) certainly fell under that heading.

Margo enjoyed Josh's quick wit and bookish brilliance and respected him as a curator of chic. They had in common a fabulous fashion sense. Frankie, on the other hand, had very little use for Josh and, in fact, persisted in calling him "Jeff" throughout the six years that we were an item. Josh (in Frankie's mind) had never had to work for anything. Strike one. Josh was a political liberal. Strike two. Strike three always seemed to be lurking on the tip of someone's tongue, which made it stressful to have the two of them in the same room.

Basically, they came from two different universes. Josh's family was wealthy, and his father (a television producer) fully supported Josh's varied artistic endeavors as worthwhile occupation. Frankie was a self-made man who perceived Josh as silver-spoon-fed, and while Frankie always backed me in my own artistic endeavors, he was profoundly uncomfortable with the fact that Josh took me on expensive vacations and bought me things, which might give the impression we were "shacking up," and I was one tap shoe away from being a kept woman. I, of course, went all *West Side Story*—"But I love him! Nothing else should matter!"—which did nothing to ease the tension. It was the first of the very few times in my life when Frankie and I were at loggerheads over anything.

I convinced myself that my parents didn't know that when I went to New York with Josh, I gave it up at the Waldorf (which is really not a bad spot to forfeit one's virtue), because back then, the assumption was that a nice girl was a virgin until she got married. I certainly assumed Margo was a virgin until she got married. I'm not sure why we never confided in each other about this detail of our lives. All Margo told me about their wedding night was that she and Frankie checked into their hotel and realized they didn't have a key for their suitcase, so Frankie had to call down and ask the front desk to please send a bellman to the honeymoon suite with a hammer and screwdriver.

(Get out of my head with the double entendres, Joyce. I mean it.)

They asked the elderly bellman to hang out with them and

have a glass or two of champagne; so apparently, they weren't exactly in a frenzy to be alone. In her book, Margo was appropriately circumspect about her sexuality, but she was candid about her longing when Frankie was away and her attempts to seduce him when he was too exhausted to seduce her. To me, in personal conversations, she added the detail that in their early months together, she lay in bed beside him, wide-eyed with fear she'd pass gas.

Josh wanted to photograph me in the black Gernreich monokini; I was as wisp-thin as a French model and a lot more pleasant to be around. He staged the photos in the backyard at my parents' home in Toluca Lake, but from the look on my face, you'd think I was in Biarritz. There's one where I'm sitting in a white rattan peacock chair with my legs crossed and toes pointed exactly the way they were in that photo of the four-year-old me on a white bench at the aquacade—except the sunny look on my face in that photo says "lucky me." The sultry look on my face in Josh's photo says "lucky *you*." His presence is as evident as a tourist's thumb in a snapshot of the Grand Canyon. If Margo didn't know what was up when I got back from the Waldorf, she had to have known it when she saw that photo.

"If you want to do real theatre, Swoosie, you have to be in New York," Josh told me, and here again, it was nothing I didn't already know, but I had a full-ride scholarship at USC, where my parents were celebrated alumni. The suggestion that I might be better off on the other side of the country wasn't well received. Josh helped me set up an audition at Carnegie Tech and went with me to New York. I was accepted, but I couldn't feel any more enthusiasm about going there than I felt about staying in L.A.

It's funny that Margo and I both came to a turning point after

Josh wanted to photograph me in the black
Gernreich monokini; I was as wisp-thin as a French
model and a lot more pleasant to be around.
JOSHUA WHITE

two years at USC. We both left to be with our one true love. She left to follow Frankie; I went to the London Academy of Music and Dramatic Arts.

"Swoose, why not finish your degree here first?" Frankie pleaded. "You've got two years in, a full scholarship. This doesn't make good sense."

But it made perfect sense to me. (At least as much sense as it made for Margo to ignore all those well-meaning voices telling her she was crazy for waiting six years to marry someone who was likely to fly away and get himself killed.) But as the time of LAMDA's Los Angeles auditions approached, I got very nervous—nauseous nervous, which was very unlike me—and I think Frankie saw that this was extremely important to me. As a friend says about her daughter's tattoos, "It's a part of her, therefore I love it." Frankie turned that same sort of corner, seeing that this was the path from which I would not be swayed. He and Margo let me know they were ready to help me do what I needed to do.

Facing me at the audition was a tall, gaunt English actor, Alan Napier, who'd been onstage with Sir John Gielgud in the Oxford Players and on film with Orson Welles in *Macbeth* and would later play Alfred, Batman's stalwart butler, on television. He was lovely, very encouraging, and I had a good feeling even before I got the letter. When I was accepted, it was like a dream. Or maybe like waking from a dream into real life.

My friend Dolly and I came up with a plan to see Europe on the cheap before school started. We bummed hither and yon, stayed in hostels and drank too much. Then Josh flew over to help me set up housekeeping, and I rented a pretty little flat where the lovely landlady looked just like Peggy Ashcroft.

"No wild parties," she said curtly as I was moving in. "And of course, no blacks."

I decided to move down the street to a place on Earl's Court Road that was half the size and not as pretty, but also much cheaper and not as bum-stuffed (as they say). I was much happier there. Margo and Frankie never harped on it, but I was very conscious about spending their money. They were paying my tuition, and sometimes Margo would send me $20 in a letter, knowing I wouldn't ask for it and could really enjoy nonessentials only if I earned them for myself.

Wherever I go in my career, I'll probably never experience a paycheck that made me feel as rich as the $100 or so that I'd received for my blink-and-you'll-miss-it on *The Donna Reed Show*. I just wasn't good at spending anyone else's money after that. I'm not extravagant by nature, and I liked being organized about my home and school budgets. My new apartment had a grand old claw-foot bathtub, but it didn't have automatic hot water. You had to put in several two-shilling pieces and hope for the best, always emotionally prepared to shampoo under a lukewarm tap and rinse with ice cold. A few hours of power also required an infusion of two-shilling pieces, so I'd often wake up frozen to the bone because my electric blanket had gone cold, or I'd have to go off to class with only one side of my hair done.

All that aside, I was in my element and loving every day. The American Course was only one year, so I lobbied to take the English Full Course, which was two years. I'd left USC without graduating, but I hadn't traveled all the way to London to go to school with Americans. I was elated when it was decided I'd be allowed to do the two-year, deep-dive into all the nuances of elocution, the grammatical structure of Shakespeare, all the guts and bones and feathers of the craft.

Michael Macowan was the artistic director at LAMDA back then, and he reminded me a lot of Mr. Ingle with his pugnacious energy and appetite for characters. One small exercise that made a strong impression on me early on: Working on Chekhov's *Cherry Orchard*, one of the actresses was required to slap someone, but each time we came to that moment, she couldn't bring herself to do more than sort of apologetically smack the guy.

"Look, just slap your own hand," Macowan told her. "Give it all you've got."

She tepidly clapped one hand to the other.

"Commit to the physical act," he urged. "Go there. See what fuels it."

She raised her left hand to the level of the actor's face and slapped it hard. I could see the connection in her eyes, like lights turning on in an attic, and that spark of electricity arced for an instant with the actor facing her. She slapped him, and he felt it—not just physically, but truly, emotionally, viscerally. Not because it was a real slap, but because it was real theatre. The physical act did take her there, and she took her cast mate with her.

"Right then," said Macowan. "Because we can't wait around for you to feel it eight shows a week, can we?"

This simple truth has stayed with me throughout my career. Years later, during a table read for the movie *A Shock to the System* with Sir Michael Caine, a young castmate (who hadn't yet learned that a hole is to dig and a table read is to read) kept pausing to ask endless questions about motivation and subtext. Finally, gently and gentlemanly, Michael said, "Tell you what, luv, it will all be revealed at the premiere."

With all due respect to the Stanislavski purists, there are times when we're onstage, and someone's Uncle Horace is hacking up a lung in the second row, or a fire truck is screaming down the alley, or the person you're in bed with smells like a bag of old hams, and you just don't feel what your character is supposed to be feeling. Sometimes you feel like an actor who has sprained her ankle or lost her lover or heard some hideously funny remark made backstage.

Really, this is applicable to daily life as well. Isn't so much of what we do based on a willingness to commit our presence to a given moment? The most challenging role I've ever played is the Unflappable Daughter who remains calm in any given crisis, even as my stomach crumbles into the rubble of suppressed panic. I can't make things all right for Margo, and I can't feel fine and philosophical about her decline; I can only commit to be here with her, and on good days, my willingness to do that creates an arc of energy. The lights go on in Margo's attic, her joy reflects mine, and my joy becomes genuine.

To this day, so much of what I learned at LAMDA enters into my work (not to mention my daily workout), because it simply made sense to me. We were taught to engage both the physical center of the body, near the tailbone, and the emotional core of the body, the solar plexus. We stretched. We strengthened. We tightened down and loosened up every muscle including our vocal cords. We immersed ourselves in words, learning to deconstruct sentences in search of a playwright's nuanced meaning, changing dialects as easily as we could change a hat.

For me, there was the added luxury of the British dialects that surrounded me. I was endlessly fascinated and entertained by the idioms and classically British understatement. My singing teacher, for example, used to tell the class, "That didn't exactly ravish me." (So many uses for that one!) One Friday evening, I was standing on the platform in the Earl's Court tube station with my classmate Maureen Lipman, who became a very successful actress in the West End and on British telly. We had our heads together over a newspaper, deciding which movie to see, when a phone rang in a nearby phone booth. We looked at each other. Shrugged an unspoken *what the hell?* and Maureen stepped inside, picked up the phone and said in her inimitable British accent, "Earl's Court Tube Station, may I help you?"

A brazen voice inquired if she'd like to suck his you know what.

"No, thanks," she said. "I've just put one out."

How could I not love such people?

My first year in London, Josh came over to see me during Christmas break, and we went skiing with his parents, who were welcoming and warm. They had a house in Klosters, Switzerland. I had not been skiing before that, and I have not been skiing since, but I wasn't about to be the one left behind on the bunny hill.

The second year, I went with him to the Venice Film Festival, where his short film, *The Sunflower*, was being featured. We stayed at the Lido Excelsior Hotel, and he photographed me in my bikini on the grand staircase after I won third place in the Excelsior Guest Beauty Contest.

We didn't talk about anything that had happened in the past or would happen in the future. We were in love when we were together, and when we weren't together, I was in love with whatever play I was in. I dated here and there, but wasn't particularly bowled over by the Brits when it came to the romance depart-

Josh and me in Europe, probably 1964 or so. Dig those Nehrus!

JOSHUA WHITE

ment. I graduated from LAMDA with a general idea of who I was as a human being, in command of all that I had learned, and in awe of all that I had yet to learn.

"You need to come to New York," Josh told me again, but he didn't need to. I was already scoping out auditions and querying agents. While I looked for an apartment, it made sense for me to stay with Josh at his place in a great old brownstone owned by his father. So we were together again, together meaning *together*, as far as I knew, and that didn't change when I moved into my own place just two blocks away. It was perfect. Josh was at 33 East 63rd, and I was at 33 East 61st, which meant we could see each other every day, but lights out would always find me comfortably tucked in with Javitz and whatever script I was studying.

New York had changed since I was a little girl swooning at the stage door. John F. Kennedy was dead; John Lennon was alive. Josh had started his strange and wonderful Joshua Light Show, combining all his strange and wonderful sensibilities—theatre, film, art, music, magic tricks, puppetry. Josh and his merry band called it "arcane arts" and "mixing the Druid fluid." He burned and melted things in pots and pans, dribbled ink down a broken windowpane. He shot footage of my eyeball and projected it fifteen feet tall. The goal was to suck audiences and performers into one psychedelic surreality, a pitch-perfect chaos.

After three weeks at the Anderson Yiddish Theater with Moby Grape, Procul Harum, B. B. King and Big Brother and the Holding Company, the Joshua Light Show moved to the Fillmore East as resident artists, producing four culture-shifting shows a week for more than two years. A 1969 *New York Times* article marveled at their "Mondrianesque checkerboards, strawberry fields, orchards of lime, antique jewels, galaxies of light over pure black void and, often, abstract, erotic, totally absorbing shapes and colors for the joy of it."

That article was headlined "You Don't Have to Be High"— and believe it or not, we weren't. I was usually doing a workshop or show off-off-Broadway. Sometimes as far off as Cincinnati. I did a lot of schlepping around to regional theaters during those years. But during the happy stretches of being home in New York, most weekend evenings, I'd arrive in Josh's scaffolded kingdom backstage at the Fillmore East at half past eleven. The crowded space was populated with roadies, bandmates and icons: Jimi Hendrix, Janis Joplin, Jefferson Airplane, The Byrds, Grateful Dead, The Doors. The air was an asthma-inducing mélange of dope smoke, dust, mildew from the old seats, and fumes from the overheating airplane headlights and Franken-rigged slide projectors. While most people were trick-or-treating for whiskey and acid blotters, Josh and I sat on barstools near the control board, a couple of squares sharing a bottle of Coke and a box of onion crackers. Art was everything in our hardworking but adequately funded *la vie bohème* existence. We were utterly in love with each other and with our work.

The Prime of Miss Jean Brodie, a marvelous play based on the novel by Muriel Spark, opened in London just before I left and quickly migrated to New York. I was cast as Monica in a summer tour. Our Miss Jean was played by Betsy Palmer, and we followed her from the Poconos to the Jersey Shore, staying in miserable digs that could hardly even be called hotels or even motels— these were summer camp shacks calling themselves cottages, often too ramshackle for real guests but plenty fine for us.

Every night, Miss Jean Brodie instructed her Little Girls: "Miss Mackay retains a picture of the former Prime Minister on the wall because she believes in the slogan, 'Safety First.' But Safety does not come first! Goodness, Truth and Beauty come first! . . . Benito Mussolini is a man of action, he has made Capri a sanctuary for birds. Thousands of birds live and sing today that might well have ended their careers on a piece of toast."

And that—long story short—is why I was not at Woodstock with Josh, who was in his element, projecting his spectacular vision. I suppose I missed Woodstock for the same reason I forgot to get married: I had a show to do, and I was so happy doing it, truly, I never gave much thought to anything I might be missing. And now that I have given it some thought, I can honestly say, I don't regret a thing. It's fairly revelatory that in our six years together, Josh and I never once discussed the possibility of getting married. I saw it as one or the other: have my life absorbed by my work or have my life absorbed by another person. Those were the two role models that had been set before me. If I'd ever met someone I couldn't resist marrying, I might well have ended my own career on a piece of toast.

I returned from the tour, exhausted but elated. I was so happy to wake up in Josh's rumpled bed. But when I went into the bathroom, I discovered a cache of pink plastic rollers. The kind that gave a girl that purposefully messy Brigitte Bardot coif—a stunningly slutty version of Sandra Dee.

Blah blah confrontation, blah blah tears, blah blah *I love you, but she's easier to be around because you're so* blah blah blah. What does any of that ever mean? Especially when you're in your twenties, and you think you know what *complicated* is, but in truth, you haven't a clue. Sob story short, Josh broke up with me. Not to be with roller girl. Just to not be with me. All in the game, I guess. Many a tear has to fall and all that rot.

*1968: Jimi Hendrix onstage with my all-seeing eyeball
projected by the Joshua Light Show at the Fillmore East.*

THE JOSHUA LIGHT SHOW

I continued working in another off-off-Broadway show. Josh called and called, but I wouldn't answer. I was grateful to lose myself in eight shows a week. Standing in the dark, waiting for the time the stage manager calls places, I could feel my splintered heart beating. By curtain call, it even felt like love.

About a year later, while I was doing *The Effect of Gamma Rays on Man-in-the-Moon Marigolds*, I ran into Josh one night, and he looked good. He was still everything I had fallen in love with, and there was a brief panicky moment when I thought he wanted to get back together, but as minutes dragged by, we just made a little pile of small talk between us, the way you make a little pile of crumbs and dog hair on the kitchen floor before you sweep it into a dust pan or whisk it out the back door.

"What are they paying you?" he asked.

"Sixty-five a week before taxes," I said.

To his credit, he did not point out that I would have gotten more on unemployment. I didn't care. The truth is, most of us weren't even thinking beyond the next time the stage manager calls places. Any of us would have done that gem of a show for free if we'd been asked.

That's how actors are hard-wired. "It's worth it," we tell ourselves, "You never know. Someone might see me. It might lead to something else." I still tell myself that every time I do a table read in exchange for a swag bag or an animation voiceover just to run it up the flagpole of an interesting producer. As grateful as I am for all the opportunities that have come my way, I'm not sure I'll ever shake off the feeling that I'm waiting for my big break.

Last year, during a spring pilgrimage to New York, I had dinner with Josh. He looked like a gently aged Harry Potter with his black-rimmed glasses and undiminished desire to do magical things. We talked about Margo and how our lives are now. Josh had become estranged from his parents; his mother was in an assisted living situation since his father had died. His wife of thirty-five years had died as well, but he'd reconnected with a woman he knew in his Carnegie days and was planning to marry her. He seemed happy, and I was happy for him.

"I came across the negatives for those nude pictures," he told me over dessert.

"*Nude pictures?*" I coughed. "Nude pictures of *me?*"

"Don't you remember? I sent you the contact sheet decades ago."

"Oh, my God . . . those. Right, right."

I'd stuck the contact sheet in a drawer and tried to forget. Now I focused on my fork and plate so I wouldn't see in his face what he'd forgotten or not.

"I'll send the negatives," he said. "Just so you know there's no funny business."

A few weeks later, he sent them, enclosing several other photographs as well, including one of Jimi Hendrix onstage in sweaty ecstasy beneath an enormous projection of my eyeball.

Josh had taken me to Woodstock after all.

"Perfect Moment."

JOSHUA WHITE

CHAPTER SIX

Love and Squalor

March Air Force Base, 1940

Our house seemed to be nearly as full of books as it was of us, and nearly as busy with studying as with billing and cooing.

Daytimes, while the groom was flying, the bride in her new clothes was being shown to the other wives at breakfasts and luncheons; and evenings there were dinner parties so she could meet the officers. These Air Corps people turned out to be just human beings, such nice ones I found myself forgetting I was in a strange land.

When exams were finished, Frank was given a whole month's leave, for a real honeymoon. So one noonday in

June the new *Nippu*, polished high blue, stood packed and ready for a trip. This warm, very warm Saturday spelled a two-week anniversary, and Frank arrived in his sweaty damp khaki uniform carrying a dozen long-stemmed red roses. There was no place to put them, and they didn't last long, those red roses on my lap in the sun, but I can see them so well even now.

Nippu lapped up the miles along the coast beside the ocean. There were lovely long days and nights of driving, swimming, diving, sunning, mooning, and then we walked miles over the World's Fair, and our bride ate the one bad hot dog on all of Treasure Island, and a husband who had so recently promised to guard and protect his beloved "in sickness and in health," did.

March Field days were made of love and fun and hard work and learning the hard way. It was like living in a nutshell and being king and queen of infinite space. The nutshell was our house—really it didn't seem much bigger than that—everyone in the kitchen together in pajamas and negligees having milk and cookies.

According to legend, Diana Barrymore killed herself in my apartment building on East 61st Street, and after living there for a year or so, I understood why. The place was horrifically maintained with a consumptive elevator and rusty pipes that offered just enough hot water to inspire a moment of tormented hope at the beginning of an inevitably cold shower. To be honest, all this made me love it even more.

"I like stories about squalor," says the girl in J. D. Salinger's

"For Esmé—with Love and Squalor." "I am extremely interested in squalor."

My quaint little studio on the fourth floor was just seedy enough to make a good story without actually being dangerous, and it was in a wonderful neighborhood. Across the street was Madame Romaine de Lyon, a bistro that served only omelets, which was perfect for me, because I have a severe peanut allergy and must be very careful.

I was blue for a while after Josh and I parted company, and after *Marigolds* closed, I was unemployed, but being my mother's daughter, I was not one to sit around feeling sorry for myself. I decided a typing class would be a wonderful way to meet some new people and hone a safety skill, because—let's face it—two things desperately needed by every aspiring artist are good friends and something to fall back on between jobs.

The first day, I arrived for class ten minutes early. No one else was there yet, so I had my choice of typewriters, and I chose one smack in the center of the room, optimally positioned to scope out my fellow students. The second person to arrive was the instructor, who said, "Well. Let's begin." She turned off the lights, fired up a little projector, and left me sitting there by myself, in a dark room in New York City, watching a flickerish film about the QWERTY keyboard—a sad reprise of my self-made schoolroom at Gigi's house. I picked up my bag and left, thinking I'd have better luck making friends in the unemployment line, and if I'd needed something to fall back on, I had my ass.

Fortunately, work picked up, and Margo and Frankie (still and always my best friends) came to visit regularly. We'd sit on crooked barstools at Mme. Romaine's, laughing and talking, and doing the purposeful New York non-gawk if Mel Brooks and

Anne Bancroft strolled in for brunch. Paul Simon had his office in the building next door, and after we were introduced by Israel Horovitz, we'd occasionally wave to each other from our respective windows. I was now, indisputably, a New Yorker.

Jack Garland had died the previous year, and the niche he'd created for Frankie was phased out, so Frankie was facing another terrible moment of Post-Ticker-Tape-Parade Syndrome. It took some time, but in his inventive, indefatigable way, when the right job did not present itself, Frankie created a job for himself, something for which he had a natural talent and a lot of unpaid experience: motivational speaking. Supported by a corporate sponsor, he traveled all over the country, speaking to Kiwanis and Rotary groups, educational and industrial conferences, and anyone else who needed a stern but positive talking to.

"For Esmé—with Love & Squalor" was Salinger's comment on what was called "battle fatigue" after World War II and later identified as post-traumatic stress disorder. He focused on the inglorious and took America to task for romanticizing the war. Margo and Frankie were the very romantics Salinger was talking about, of course, and I was just beginning to understand that as I watched Frankie's continuing struggle to adjust to life on earth. The story first appeared in the *New Yorker* in 1950, but we'd moved on to a whole different war by the time I created stage adaptations of *Love and Squalor*, *A Perfect Day for Bananafish* and *Franny and Zooey* at LAMDA in the 1960s.

Anytime he had a speaking engagement on the East Coast, Frankie would come to see me, and he never left without hanging a picture or replacing a broken lock or picking up something from the hardware store to spruce the place up. He and Margo made a point of seeing any show I was in as many times as possible. They never stayed in a hotel. Frankie slept on the sofa, and Margo and I shared the queen-size bed that occupied the center of the room. Usually, I had trouble sleeping when I came home late at night, still wired from performing. It was comforting to snuggle in with Margo and listen to Frankie snore, just like when we were three happy vagabonds catching a nap at a rest area off in the middle of nowhere.

I was lucky enough to be employed for two years in my first off-Broadway show, *The Effect of Gamma Rays on Man-in-the-Moon Marigolds*, the heart-twisting story of two sisters under the thumb of a tyrannical nightmare of a mother (I always thought of her as the anti-Margo) and how each of them is affected by their spectacularly dysfunctional home life.

The younger sister, Tillie, has this stunning monologue about how her science teacher explained the origins of life:

"He told me to look at my hand, for a part of it came from a star that exploded too long ago to imagine. This part of me was formed from a tongue of fire that screamed through the heavens until there was our sun . . . And this small part of me was then a whisper of the earth. When there was life, perhaps this part of me got lost in a fern that was crushed and covered until it was coal. And then it was a diamond millions of years later—it must have been a diamond as beautiful as the star from which it had first come . . . And he called this bit of me an atom. And when he wrote the word, I fell in love with it. Atom. Atom. What a beautiful word."

Oh, I so understood that overwhelming shyness, and I so loved Tillie's willingness to focus on the miraculous, her ability to live this shabby, abusive existence and still see the coal turning into the diamond. That eureka moment with her science teacher was exactly the sort of epiphany Mr. Ingle had handed to me at Hollywood High.

Mine, was my first thought when I read that monologue, and my second thought was, *Mine! Mine! Mine! I love it. I want it. I need it.*

"So get it," said Frankie. It was that simple in motivational speaker parlance. At twenty-six, I was a bit long in the tooth to be playing a little girl raising marigolds for a junior high science fair. But I was small, and I knew I could pull it off vocally—which is really the hard part—because I'd done *Love and Squalor* and *Bananafish* at LAMDA and *Miss Jean Brodie* after that.

I knew the director, Melvin Bernhardt, and he told me later he was going to call me to come in and read, but I didn't want to presume, so I went to a cattle call audition, agonized through two or three callbacks and was cast in a tiny but tasty role: a girl whose science project is a blanched cat skeleton. I was also one of two understudies, standing by for the actresses cast as the two sisters. On unemployment (thanks to *Miss Jean*, a Downy fabric softener commercial, and a couple of grim nights watching paint dry as an extra in a forgotten Dustin Hoffman film), I'd received $65 a week, which was not taxed. Off-Broadway scale was $60 a week, from which taxes were withheld, so I took a pay cut of about 20 percent, which I was thrilled to do. I'd been holding my breath since I saw Paul Zindel's brilliant script.

Marigolds turned out to be the little engine that could. With Melvin Bernhardt directing, Sada Thompson as the horrific mother (Beatrice), and Pamela Payton-Wright as Tillie, we opened off-Broadway in the spring of 1970 at the Mercer-O'Casey Theatre, part of Broadway Central Hotel where Diamond Jim Brady was shot. This was a year before the theater underwent renovations, and it was so run down, the floors above us had been made into a welfare hotel. The catwalks and backstage spaces were redolent with multinational cuisine being cooked out on the fire escapes. The plumbing leaked like it was made of chicken wire. Every night when the stage manager called places, Sada started the show in a particularly unlucky spot with water dripping down the back of her neck.

Because I'd originally been cast in the smallest part in the show, the not-so-coveted role of Equity Deputy had also been assigned to me. It was my responsibility to file a report on the substandard conditions of the theater, which meant I had to go through the welfare hotel, knocking on the doors of the impoverished families with their hot plates on the fire escape and mattresses on the floor and toilet down the hall, collecting affidavits testifying that the place was uninhabitable for theatre folk. The irony was not lost on me, and I was stricken with compassion for the people living there, but this was the only way we'd be released to another venue, so I dutifully trudged those dank hallways day after day, dodging rats, stepping over derelicts, and becoming less interested in squalor with each passing moment.

In the midst of all this came thrilling news that *The Effect of Gamma Rays on Man-in-the-Moon Marigolds* had won the Pulitzer Prize for drama. The next night after the half hour and five minute marks, the stage manager called, "Ladies, will you take your Pulitzer places?"

We moved uptown to a nice new theater where I could walk to work, and I was gainfully employed for two years. *Bliss.* It was one of those shows with all the elusive alchemy you hope for but

Over two creatively decadent years, I played three different characters (not at the same time) in The Effect of Gamma Rays on Man-in-the-Moon Marigolds *(1970–72).*

learn not to expect. A Pulitzer-caliber script. A director who got it. Actors who revered it. A crew who delivered it to the stage eight times a week.

We went through a series of mothers, working our way up to Joan Blondell. I moved into the role of Ruth and eventually graduated to that maraschino cherry of a character, Tillie, after Pam left the show. I got the call a little after six in the evening. The stage manager said, "Get down here. The understudy is defrosting her fridge." (Moral of the story in my twenty-something mind: Never defrost the refrigerator again! Dreams could be coming true while you're going at it with an ice pick.) Sixty seconds after I hung up the phone, I was on my way to the theater, my feet barely touching the sidewalk. Tillie and I were perfect for each other, despite the difference in our ages, which disappeared onstage so credibly that audience members were occasionally stunned to see me out drinking champagne with the grown-ups after the show.

Meanwhile, Joan Blondell wanted to basically rewrite the character of Beatrice. Sada had made her entrance costumed in a ratty old robe; Joan wanted to be fully coifed, made up and outfitted in a peignoir from Bergdorf's. She wanted to stand under a wash of pink-gelled lights. She wanted the audience to have more sympathy for the horrific mother.

"I don't think I should kill the rabbit," she said. "People can't like me if I kill a rabbit."

"Miss Blondell, setting aside that the script as is has won a Pulitzer," Melvin said patiently, "Beatrice is the one killing the rabbit. And no rabbit is actually killed."

"The impression is given. And it's very unlikable."

She was a terrific lady—lots of fun and very good in the

part—and this is how it is sometimes when Hollywood comes to New York theatre, but Melvin was at critical mass. He left and took his name off the play. The producers had the lights gelled, Joan gave us all vaporizers for Christmas, and the theoretical rabbit took one for the team. All in all, it was a tremendously educational and overwhelmingly happy introduction to the world of New York theatre.

Margo came to see *Marigolds* so many times, everyone began treating her like part of the crew. It drove me a little bit crazy how she was always talking to everyone, the life of the party, no topic taboo—the antithesis of shy. She struck up a friendship with Jimbo, the house manager, and he is still my deeply cherished friend who slays me with his offbeat sense of humor. By the end of the run, we were a typically loving and dysfunctional off-Broadway family. It was hard to say good-bye to everyone—and even harder to say hello to my old pals at the unemployment office.

This is where Frankie, who knew too well what it felt like to be displaced, was a good man to have around. There was no wallowing in *what-if*s or resting on one's laurels.

"It's nice to imagine that it'll be easier to get work after a resounding success," he told me, "and to a certain extent work does beget work, but in between those resounding successes, there's a lot of pavement-pounding. You can't get around it."

This was before I had an agent. Or at least, I think it was. I've had so many come and go, after a while I lost track. I've tried them all: CAA, ICM, Sam Cohn—tried William Morris three times—before I finally landed with my present crew, whom I love as human beings, which makes loving them as agents easy. I also have a wonderful manager now—Konrad Leh—and I'm all the more grateful having kissed a number of frogs before meeting these princes.

Changing agents, they say, is like changing deck chairs on the *Titanic*, but of course, you couldn't have told me that back then. All anyone wanted was an agent, because we had this ridiculously crooning "Someone to Watch Over Me" idea of what an agent was and needed to believe that not having an agent was the reason we didn't have work.

I landed a one-shot thing on *As the World Turns*, and it actually turned into a recurring character—Ellie, an ugly duckling trembling on the verge of being noticed. I'd get a call for that once every two or three months, and one of the principals was kind enough to set up a meeting with her agents, a husband and wife team. When I arrived, the husband half of the team sat me down and we talked at great length about where I hoped to go with my career and what he thought they could do for me.

"How do you feel about nudity?" he asked.

"It would depend on the material," I said. "If it's part of the story."

"Of course," he readily agreed. "But if I'm gonna be out there selling a product, I gotta know what I'm representing. Know what I mean?"

"Of course . . ." Truthfully, it took a moment to dawn on me. "*Oh.* I see. So. Um, I'm not really interested in that . . . but I do so appreciate your time."

Agents are difficult. I always used to feel bad and inadequate after I talked to an agent. Sleazy agents make you want to take a hot shower, and great agents make you wish you could be Big Box Office or the sugarplum fairy or whatever it takes to set their little eyes alight. Back then, even the ones who weren't asking for a peep show were staring with unforgiving professionalism at my skinny legs and elf hair, mentally shuffling me and fifty-one other girls like a deck of cards. For the time being, it was less demoralizing to take myself around to all the open auditions and obsessively check in with the answering service afterward.

Hayes Registry fielded calls for hundreds of hopeful actors, which meant they were extremely well practiced in letting people down easy. You'd call in and give your name and number, and the operator would say, "Nothing *yet*." You'd thank them, and they'd wish you a pleasant day, knowing you'd call back every few hours until you got cast in something, fell asleep on a park bench or killed yourself. God love them for tempering that brutal "nothing" with that optimistic "*yet*." A one-word motivational speech.

Finally, I got a call for a big TV commercial—a national ad campaign for Sure Antiperspirant. They were looking for a new face and after a number of callbacks had narrowed it down to two or three actresses. The catch phrase for the ad campaign was: "Don't take my word for it. You've got two arms. Try it yourself!" I practiced this several dozen times in the bathroom mirror and found my various interpretations very compelling.

"*You*'ve got two arms. Try it. For yourself!"

"You've got two arms? Try it for *yourself*!"

At the final callback, I was ushered into a corporate office, all plush and mahogany, overstuffed chairs, underfed secretaries. Hellos, welcomes, handshakes. *What sort of a name is Swoosie?* Swan, goose, WWII. *Oh, really? How interesting!* Chortle chortle, okay, show us whatcha got.

"Can I just say something before I begin?" I said. "Not everyone out there has two arms, and I just feel that—you know—we should be sensitive to that."

Konrad, who does not mince motivational speaker parlance, would refer to this as "shitting on the table," but for whatever reason, I felt the need to stick up for all those one-armed men out there. This was pre-*Fugitive*, I guess. The one-armed man wasn't on-trend yet. I don't know. Needless to say, it didn't work out with the deodorant gig, but I had made my point.

I auditioned at a cattle call for the original cast of *Hair* and managed to keep up as they taught the dance combinations, but for all its blissfully ignorant exuberance, my rousing a capella rendition of Bob Dylan's "It Ain't Me, Babe" was met with a terse, disembodied "thank you" from the dark seat bank. I auditioned for the role of a corpse on a gurney, lying there with all my force of will trained on my motionless diaphragm, but the production assistant handed me my headshot and said, "We're looking for someone less animated." I was slightly longer-lived on *Kojak*, though I never did understand the plot of that episode. Something involving the Twin Towers. So when it was time to do my scene, they stood me in front of this big window with the towers behind me. Telly Savalas said, "Did you know I can see through your skirt?" And then I got murdered.

Brian Murray was doing *The Philanthropist* in Chicago—that's when Studs Terkel came backstage to see us—and we were such a hit, the show went to National Theatre in DC for a month. We had a nice big opening night with almost all of the 1,200 seats inhabited by big brass politicos and Washington names. Reviews were okay, but we found ourselves playing to audiences of 120, then a school group of several dozen children. They'd put us in the Wardman Park Hotel where we lived when I was four and Frankie was working at the Pentagon. We each had a lavish suite with a dishwasher in the kitchenette, so we laded in tons of groceries the day we arrived and closed three days later.

Another lesson in "Don't buy new carpet for your dressing room": I did an off-Broadway play with a movie star leading man above the title. We opened at the Martinique at the Edison Hotel on the 4th of July and celebrated our independence when the show was closed less than a week later. As I was cleaning out my dressing room, the movie star came over to me and bluntly suggested—well, let's call it dinner and a show. And for the sake of moving forward, let's pretend I said, "No thanks, I've just put one out."

It's not that I was a prude; it just wasn't the appropriate time or place. Candidly, the theatre community dating pool isn't that deep for heterosexual women. We end up falling in love with gay men (I'd marry Nathan Lane next Saturday if he asked me), or we give in to a romantic recidivism that brings us back to men who've already been disqualified for one reason or another.

I can't remember why I shelved my favorite English guy. I met him during a play in Canada, and we had a recurring fling over the next few years. He's a terrific English stage actor who's also worked a lot in American film and television, usually playing, well, The English Guy. He was wonderfully tall and lanky with a melodious voice, and he had that whole aristocratic Royal Shakespeare thing going for him. He called me "dahling." As I recall, I was terribly turned on by that.

Anyway, English Guy and I happened to cross paths in New York, and he asked me out for cocktails at the Rainbow Room above Rockefeller Center. Very classy. Very romantic. We sat there talking about Shaw and gazing into each other's eyes. I was so deeply involved in whatever he was saying (or perhaps deeply involved in looking like I was deeply involved in whatever he was saying), I didn't notice that he was absently noshing on peanuts from a little silver dish.

The moment we got in the cab, we fell into each other's arms. My head reeled as he kissed my burning lips.

No, seriously—my lips were kind of burning. Never mind.

To the elevator!

Oh, damn it. That decrepit thing was never working when it was most desperately needed.

To the stairway!

By the time we reached my apartment and settled on the sofa, things had gotten pretty intense, and I was starting to feel a bit strange. My lips and cheeks were beginning to feel oddly prosthetic, and I heard myself acquiring what sounded like a Portuguese accent when I said, "Um, excoosh me for just a tiny second, pleezh."

"Hurry back," English Guy smiled slyly.

"Absolooly. Hold dat thought."

When I flipped on the light above the bathroom mirror, I was confronted with a scene from *The Elephant Man.* An angry little nose protruded hotly between my ballooning cheeks. My bottom lip sagged like an old handbag.

"*Ho-wee shid!*"

I knew immediately what the trouble was. A fleeting thought about the emergency room was quickly discarded for a better idea: *Keep calm and carry on.* I rummaged my medicine cabinet, popped half a dozen antihistamines, scooping water from the tap to my grotesque mouth, put out the light, and stumbled back to the sofa in the dark.

Things get a little murky after that, but I seem to remember my eyelids turning to wet cement and my paramour asking, "Dahling, are you all right?"

"Sure, sure. Fine. Go ahead," I said, but English Guy finally sat up and turned on the light, horrifying us both.

"Good God! Swoosie, what's happened to you?"

"I'm gedding very shleepy," said the Portuguese whaler who'd taken over my face. "I think I better call it a night."

This brave man made a half-hearted attempt at shining armor, but I sent him on his way and conked out, hoping this wasn't how it all went down for Diana Barrymore.

I heard that unmistakable melodious voice across the room not long ago at a book party for Jack O'Brien, who was launching his memoir, *Jack Be Nimble.* Jack had directed Cherry and me in *Imaginary Friends* and so many other people in so many other shows; the party was the sort of grand Broadway family reunion that happens, but not nearly often enough. My old friend and I exchanged a warm embrace and makeup-respectful kiss. After a little banter about work and the world in general, I asked him about his family, and he told me his wife had died. At the edge of his flawless cocktail party deportment, I could see how enormously he had loved her.

Back home in my office in L.A., I mention the more recent encounter to Perry, who says, "That could be interesting."

"We've exchanged a few emails," I shrug. "I wouldn't want to mislead him, but I'd love to be in a play with him. He's aged well."

"Who's aged well?" Margo pipes up from the sofa.

"A guy I used to see. Remember that English fellow?"

"Oh, I love the English!" she exclaims. "Such a wonderful people."

"That's something you'd like to say to people sometimes, isn't it? 'You've aged well.' Because we all worry," I ponder aloud. "But how do you phrase that without sounding backhanded? 'Still standing, I see. Good on you, old chap. Most people your age are dead or look like they've been taxidermied, but my goodness, you've aged well!'"

"Who's aged well?" Margo asks.

"That English fellow, Mommie. The Englishman."

"Oh, I love the English!" she exclaims. "Wonderful people. You should do it."

"What?"

"Tell him he's aged well," says Margo. "A person should be told."

I set Randall aside and take her hands between mine.

"You've aged well, Margo darling."

"Oh, precious girl. Do you really think so?"

"Yes," I tell her honestly. "You've aged beautifully."

"So have you, dear," she says. "We have every reason to hope."

The off-Broadway sorority of Uncommon Women and Others, *1977: (Back row left to right) Ellen Parker, Cynthia Herman, Meryl Streep, Anna Levine and me. (Front row) Jill Eikenberry, Ann McDonough and Alma Cuervo.*

CHAPTER SEVEN

Uncommon Women

—∞—

California, 1941

I sit huddled and cold in *Nippu* (my little roadster). Frank is walking into the infinite black night. Army olive drab doesn't last long in the dark, so now you can't see anything, anything but the blue flame spouting out of four engines of a ship a long way down the field. You are the most alone girl in the whole world, and you wonder why you left so much warmth and so many people at home to be alone like this. This kind of wondering makes tears come to your eyes—they've been in your throat a long time.

But you have hold of the steering wheel, and you're lifting yourself up a little in the seat, lifting toward the sound of a plane revving up for the takeoff. The moment it leaves the ground—you can tell by the sound of the motors—you're all alone again.

Still, you watch it bank and turn and fly over the field and head east. Just as it is over the field, a tiny little light on it, the green one, blinks on and off three times. Now only the pilot could do this, and he would do it for only one reason . . . for someone on the ground.

So you are alone, even the plane's motors are quiet now, and the airport is so big and dark and strange, and you are actually afraid of the quiet.

Margo is restless tonight. From the corner of my eye, I can see the lights on the baby monitor we've placed in her bedroom. They blink in a little row whenever she stirs.

A busy day (by our present paradigm) seems to have taken a lot out of her. She has been insistently worried about this little girl who comes and goes. Someone has to take the little girl somewhere or tuck the little girl in, feed the little girl some dinner, find the little girl's cat. Perry and Angela and I speculate on who the little girl is: me as a child, Margo as a child, a ghost, an angel or simply a character created by Margo's need to care rather than be cared for. We try not to quiz her about it simply for the sake of our own curiosity. But we are curious. It's as if Margo's visceral concern has endowed the little girl with skin and bone; none of us would be completely surprised to see her sitting on a chair in Margo's room.

"Perhaps the hallucination is a metaphor for the child in both of you," Ethel the Oracle speculates.

This works for me. I've always had a propinquity to the child characters I played onstage long into my adult years, a closeness I couldn't quite explain but could always count on to make the character ring true. Arthur Rimbaud said, "Genius is the recovery of childhood at will." Naturally, I'd love to embrace that explanation. In truth, it's the flat chest and chicken legs I inherited from Frankie, and the vocal control I learned at LAMDA. The rest I'll have to ask about if I ever catch up with the specter of the little girl.

At the time, if anyone asked me about it in an interview, I said, "Part of me has never grown up and doesn't intend to." If asked to articulate it from my present perspective, however, I would say that playing a child is *child's play*, which is to say it is the purest form of abandon. There's utter joy in it for me—returning to a childhood I largely missed out on, seeing it through a different prism, the way Margo sees it on those mornings when she wakes up and is thirteen for a few delicious minutes.

At twenty-eight, in Edna O'Brien's *A Pagan Place*, I played Della, a fourteen-year-old girl dying of TB but possessed of a great, defiant spirit, which made the role worthwhile, even though I had to drink raw eggs onstage eight shows a week. At twenty-nine, in Truman Capote's *Other Voices, Other Rooms*, I played Idabel Thompkins, a churlish thirteen-year-old tomboy based on Capote's childhood friend, Harper Lee, who grew up to write *To Kill a Mockingbird*. We thought this show was going to Broadway, but it didn't pan out, which was a crushing disappointment, but Idabel left me with a gift I intend to keep for the rest of my days: red hair.

The moment Idabel and I laid eyes on each other, I met my inner redhead and would never look back. I felt like I'd come home. In character, in costume, this hair was tomboy red; when I walked out the stage door in a leather jacket and jeans, it was *statement* red and quickly became *Swoosie* red, a personal trademark that simultaneously defined and defied type. It's not the color; it's the way the color works with the rest of me, so it has to be done right. (Perry, a man of many talents, honed his hairdressing skills at Vidal Sassoon and has been keeping me fiercely red to the roots for many years. At some point, he gently shepherded Margo away from her strawberry blond, luring her to the dark side so he could do us both with the same brew.)

That Swoosie Red—the mindset, not the hue—may be part of the casting karma that enabled me to play characters much younger than my real age. In 1975, I was thirty-one, playing fifteen-year-old Muriel in *Ah, Wilderness!* on Broadway. It's a sweet gig. Muriel doesn't make her entrance until the third act, which meant I didn't have to be at the theater until nine. While the curtain was going up, I was at home eating the plain broiled chicken breast I always eat right before I do a show. The only downside was that by the time I arrived at Circle in the Square, everyone else had been on already. If there was a notable person in the audience, they knew about it and never spared my nerves; they always insisted on telling me.

"Olivier is in the audience tonight. Second row on the center aisle."

This isn't something you want to hear right before you step out on the dark stage, searching for your glow tape mark. In the best circumstance, that moment is very akin to standing still at the tip of the ten-meter diving board. Knowing in advance that Olivier or Jackie Kennedy will be sitting there when the lights come up raises the platform at least another seven meters. (That said, Olivier came backstage after and gave me a nice "Lovely scene, darling!" with a robust hug I can still feel every time I think about it.)

That hopeful Hayes Registry *"yet"* had finally lived up to its promise. I was a steadily working actress. This was the moment in New York that spawned *That Girl*, the Precambrian forerunner to *Sex and the City*. I was the spunky heroine making my way in the city that never slept. (I hardly slept myself.) In *My Rival, the Sky*, Margo said that for her, with Frankie on the far side of the globe, the city was the loneliest place in the world, but it never felt like that for me. It served me, suited the singleness of purpose I'd learned from Frankie.

"You train yourself to do one thing really well," he always told me, "and you make your life doing it, and if you have to move on to something else, you move on and give that the same hundred-ten-percent focus."

I couldn't imagine (and still can't) doing anything but exactly what I was doing. I didn't have time to imagine it. If I wasn't performing, I was rehearsing, and if I wasn't rehearsing, I was auditioning, or being fitted for costumes, or keeping up my voice and dance lessons. Most days, I was doing at least three of those and studying a script when I fell into bed at night.

There's a caste system of sorts that places stage actors above film actors and film actors above television actors, even though film actors generally made more money and television actors generally became more famous. Back in the 1970s, there were fewer people attempting to do it all, because being in television meant that, when awards season rolled around, you'd be snubbed in favor of "serious" actors from the stage or big screen. I wasn't really thinking of anything but doing the work, so I was choosier than I had any business being, but I chose to be busy. There have been only a few times in my life that I was working on only one thing. (These days, in addition to *Mike & Molly*, I do the occasional voiceover, including Seth McFarlane's mother on *American Dad*, but I'm trying to pace myself to be here with Margo as much as I can. It's hard sometimes to feel the world spinning by just beyond my reach, and I imagine this must be how a young parent feels when she or he steps away from work to stay at home with a child.)

It was a big deal for me to get a tiny part in *Slap Shot*, a Paul Newman movie about Rustbelt hockey players. We shot on location in Johnstown, Pennsylvania, whose business district consisted of a religious bookstore and a tool shop, and whose claim to fame is that it was once destroyed by a flood. I checked into a horrendous little motel, sat down with my script and cried. (I won't lie: this was not an uncommon occurrence.) I'm not an obsessive line-counter in an ensemble situation, and I was comfortable in a supporting role, but this was hardly even an athletic supporter. This was a lot more slap than shot, and I'd wrangled an early release from a terrific play in order to do it.

"Well, you're there," Frankie calmly counseled me through a pay phone. "Be there. Be grateful. Do your best. You don't know how it might work out."

It worked out well. The next day, I sat in the stands in the bitter cold, wearing huge hair and a jacket that looked like it was made from unborn Kleenex, cheering enthusiastically for Mr. Newman and the other hockey players brawling on the ice. As the bloodthirsty crowd cheered on the brawlers, I was supposed to say to my fellow hockey wives, "Good crowd." Between takes, Paul Newman said to the director, "She's got the best goddamn line in the whole goddamn movie. We gotta come up with more

Inexplicably, Melissa McCarthy has this photo of me posted on the door of her dressing room on the Mike & Molly *set, which makes me feel very honored, Melissa being a quintessential uncommon woman of her generation.*

for her to say." The screenwriter came up with some additional zingers to give me a bit more reason for being, and my unborn Kleenex jacket even got some exposure in the movie trailer.

Floating around the Internet, there's a snapshot of me draped sideways on Paul Newman's chair, nonchalant but respectfully so, wearing a Yale baseball shirt that I bought at the Yale gift shop just to amuse Margo, who had not-so-secretly wanted me to go there. Inexplicably, Melissa McCarthy has this photo posted on the door of her dressing room on the *Mike & Molly* set, which makes me feel very honored, Melissa being a quintessential uncommon woman of her generation.

We finished shooting, and I went to Washington to do *A History of the American Film*, then back to Broadway to do *Tartuffe* with Tammy Grimes and Victor Garber and Mildred Dunnock, whom I'd been in awe of since *Death of a Salesman*. (I couldn't believe I was onstage with the woman who said, "Attention must be paid!") As I was performing *Tartuffe* at night, I was rehearsing *Uncommon Women and Others* during the day, and we got the news that *A History of the American Film* was going to Broadway.

History . . . is like a sumptuous feast Christopher Durang cooked up for the actors lucky enough to be cast in it. I played a Bette Davis prototype with side trips as Cagney's moll, Ida Lupino, a hooker, a husband stealer, a crazy lady, Liz Taylor (à la *Who's Afraid of Virginia Woolf*), the wheelchair-bound Peter Sellers from *Dr. Strangelove*. Basically, everything but an ingénue, which was fine by me. I can always sink my teeth into a character who's up for chemo, electroshock therapy or a solicitation conviction.

Also in the cast—as Hank, a Henry Fonda prototype—was Brent Spiner.

"He's from Houston," I told Margo. "He's tall and lean. Long-ish hair. Wry smile. Kind of a wonderful sculpted face with good bones and a prominent nose."

It's not my way to share delicate details, even with Margo, but I gave him high marks for faithful yoga practice.

"Most important," I said, "he's *funny*. But also very evolved. Very smart. He was born on Groundhog's Day."

"Portentous," Margo said. "For six weeks, anyway."

"Well, I told him right up front, 'Just so you know, I'm not interested in a relationship. I don't want to get involved with anyone.'"

"To which he replied . . . ?"

"He said, 'That's cool. No pressure.'"

The magic words. We were together for six years, nine of which I was very much in love with him.

Omaha, 1942

"Pardon me, Sergeant, I'd like to help you with this typing if I may."

He looked up at me the way the people must have looked at Joan of Arc. And in just the time it takes a hundred pounds to plunk itself down in a seat, I was typing, with stacks of papers beside me. As fast as I made the pile shorter, he built it up again.

When an office is as busy as this Air Force Headquarters, there isn't much time to gaze around. But I noticed some of the girl secretaries were giving me a good looking over. I was their new competition with the boys in the office, and they weren't going to let me in too easy.

The Colonel walked in looking straight ahead and puffing a cigar, and concentrating the way colonels do. But at my typewriter he stopped concentrating and said: "Well, for—Hrrrrmph, for goodness' sakes. Are you here?"

When I had offered to come, he had said he couldn't pay me anything because he already had his quota of personnel, and when I answered that I wanted to be a volunteer worker, to give my time so that I could help build the Air Forces in ever so little a way, and be helping Frank—maybe he was too busy to realize just how much I meant it. Or maybe I looked too small to make much of a dent in all their stacks of work.

I think the Colonel was amused to see me on the job now, but he figured if I'd always wear a pretty red dress like this, I'd at least be ornamental.

"This is Mrs. Kurtz, whose husband is fighting in the Philippines," he announced.

It made a new feeling in the room. I think everyone was glad to be able to feel more real about their work—almost as if they could reach out and shake hands with one of the boys over there fighting, and you just automatically hold your head a little higher because today you've dropped a pebble in the pool of war.

I began to notice how the applicants for aviation cadet training were coming in, but there wasn't anyone to answer their questions and take their papers. So one morning I put the nice big stack of typing-to-be-done right back on the

Sergeant's desk and told him: "I have just been promoted to receptionist."

I set up a desk, and I snared everyone who came in.

"Hello, beautiful, trying to show off those pretty dresses out here in the front office?" the Colonel remarked.

"No, and besides, you should get around more, Colonel. I went over to the Navy recruiting office for air cadets. They treat their 'customers' much better than we do here. We were losing lots to them, but I think I have the situation in hand now. I may ask for a Coke machine next week."

It was hard for me to appreciate when I was younger how truly extraordinary Margo was in the context of her youth because in the context of my own youth, she was a housewife. Or, as they're more commonly known, "*just* a housewife." Frankie and I were not low-maintenance people, so believe me when I tell you this was a full-time job—just not a job with lavish benefits like minimum wages and respect. Margo was never particularly political or outspoken about feminism—or "women's lib" as we called it in the 1970s; she simply went about doing whatever she wanted to do, no liberation required, and she wanted me to be equally true to my own path.

Frankie was an accidental feminist. To his dying day, he was an avowed Republican with typically Republican things to say (how did you think I got roped into the Nixonette gig?), and people always assumed he was a real hawk by nature. But he was adamantly against the Vietnam War and surprisingly evolved in his views on a woman's place. His woman's place was at his side, and he was grateful to have found someone who could hold her own, who asked him for an opinion instead of permission. He had a genuine respect for women and loved having a strong woman to play off of—two strong women once I was grown up enough to butt heads with him—but he never played the patriarch. He never laid down the law, so I had little to rebel against. He never had to push me; his high expectations pulled me like a magnet.

In her play *Uncommon Women and Others*, Wendy Wasserstein drew from the 1957 inaugural address given by Richard Glenn Gettell, President of Mount Holyoke College: "A Plea for the Uncommon Woman."

> *Who are the best, what is the best education for them, how much and in what manner the College should adapt to the changing needs of succeeding generations, and what is the uncommon woman—these are questions to which unanimous answers cannot be expected. But they are questions which deserve frequent discussion and reexamination . . . The concept of the role of women is vastly outdated—particularly for the uncommon woman.*

I was introduced to this marvelous play in 1977 at the Eugene O'Neill National Playwrights Conference, which is the equivalent of summer camp for actors, writers, directors and dramaturges. We all boarded the bus leaving Broadway and 53rd at noon on a Sunday. They fed us on the porch. People were constantly falling in and out of love and sneaking off to meet in the woods. Creative energy crackled. Mosquitoes enjoyed a banquet of bare legs and sweaty necks. Agents circled like pelicans, ready to scoop up the biggest talent. The first time I went, I was twenty-nine—the same age Margo was when she had me—and I was baptized by fire,

At the Eugene O'Neill Theater Center. Pure joy!

thrown headfirst into a play in which I made my entrance with a Kotex on my head. Instead of my customary monastic chicken breast, I had wine before every performance. I thought I was wonderful, but who knows? In any case, it was an enchanted summer, and it got better each year.

Wendy was in residence. And I do not exaggerate when I say that she looked like a pile of clothing thrown into a basket with a wild black Jewfro on top. When she giggled, everyone giggled, and she giggled frequently. She was sharp, witty and generous, and probably the most connected person I'll ever know—right up there with Nora Ephron. Everybody knew her—and they enjoyed her.

She'd brought a raft of scenes—some hilarious, others heartbreaking, and all buoyantly, irreverently genius. We worked and debated and slept on and reworked these pages until she'd brought them together in what we all were certain was a groundbreaking play. *Uncommon Women and Others* had a wonderful run off-Broadway, and later, PBS filmed it for Great Performances. It was a landmark moment for me professionally. The role of Rita showcased every strength I had in my creative creel. Those lines—*those Wasserstein lines!*—fit me like a glove and dovetailed perfectly with who I was as an actor at that moment.

"I've tasted my menstrual blood!"

"Timmy's not gay. He's going to be my Leonard Woolf."

"This entire society is based on cocks."

Some of the language had to be watered down for television ("There's no penis in PBS," Brent quipped), but the irony and absurdity struck true.

"It never occurred to me that someone might not want me to be so uncommon."

What a kick in the head that line was for me. I'd never quite figured out what it meant when I found the rollers in the bathroom drawer, and Josh told me, "I love you, but I *like* her. She's so much easier to be with." Now that distinction made sense to me.

Wendy was free of ego as she rewrote whole chunks of the script and generously gave credit for a few funny lines I kicked in. I felt like the leader of the pack—not that I was; the feeling just spilled over from Rita's sense of herself as the expert on everything. She's her own worst enemy, but that frenetic self-assurance is the engine that keeps her absurdist world turning. The need and determination are palpable. Rita's bravado and desire to shock and get attention make us laugh, but there's vulnerability there, along with a certain brand of sadness they all share. Jill Eikenberry's Kate has all this certitude, but it's weighted with a perfectly played joylessness. Meryl Streep's Leilah has tenacity, but it's tinged with envy. What's endearing about these girls, then and now, is the hope.

"When I'm thirty," Rita keeps saying, "I'll be pretty fucking amazing."

Wendy was the first playwright to express the burgeoning expectations that came with that particular wave of feminism, and so many of those issues haven't changed. We feel free to do as we please, but others still feel free to judge. We're free to have both career and family, but if you choose one or the other, it's assumed you're lacking half a life. I recently told one of the writers on *Mike & Molly*, "Bring on the dick jokes. I'm fine with that. But I want to be the first person on broadcast television to say *clitoris*. Just asking for equal time."

That hasn't happened yet.

Most profoundly, *Uncommon Women* was a life-changing experience for me personally. For one thing, it's the only time in my life I'll ever have a bigger part than Meryl Streep. Beyond that, it was one of those moments in life when I consciously felt myself grow.

I was *better* because of this play. My brain got bigger. My heart got wiser. My soul got older. My ability to become friends with other women matured, and my ability to remain friends with other women was born. Before this play, I had plenty of gal pal acquaintances, but my true friends had always been boys and men. I don't know why I thought a lot of women had some sort of agenda (I'm not blaming Margo, but I can't help noticing now how she projected that agenda on the other women in the typing pool), but this play changed my mind about that.

To this day, Jill Eikenberry and her husband, Michael Tucker, are among my dearest friends. Judith Light was there in the beginning, but had to go back to her steady job on *One Life to Live*. Glenn Close did the off-Broadway production, and Meryl Streep came on board for the PBS version. I cherish each one of them, and whenever we cross paths, there's this injected memory of how we used to be college roomies. Margo had worried that I'd missed out on that sorority experience, but now, in a way, I hadn't.

The saddest possible cause for reunion was Wendy's death in 2006.

The news knocked the wind out of me. I'd heard rumors that she wasn't well, but I had no idea she was quietly preparing to leave us. I wasn't ready to say good-bye to Wendy my friend or to lose Wendy Wasserstein the artist. She gave away a great deal of herself in her plays, but kept her private life private. A standing joke between us whenever we spoke: "How's your personal life?"

one of us would ask, and the other would broadly play it off, "Moving on!"

I was always prodding Wendy to do a sequel. *Uncommon Women* in their fifties. Oh, how I wish that could have been. Five of us from the original cast did a long scene from the play at her memorial service. Meryl did a piece from *American Daughter*. Christopher Durang got up and killed us all, saying, "I got on my computer and realized I needed to delete her email address."

But because of the uncommon woman Wendy had always been, over the subsequent months—years even—what echoed between people who knew her were all the small stories, the disparate scene work that made up her offstage life. She died in January, and in April, I got an email from Josh White:

> Alice told me you ran into each other at Wendy's memorial celebration. That was very sad news. For a while, Wendy and I went to the same therapist. One day our therapist said she needed to rush home (a block away), pick up and mail her taxes. Her concern was not being there to let Wendy in. I volunteered to wait. When Wendy got there, I told her, "The doctor said you should go in and start without her." Wendy, being Wendy, laughed that wonderful laugh.

My body of work is important to me, and it's built on words that are set down in scripts. When the words are there, I am deeply, humbly grateful. When the words aren't there, I appreciate them even harder.

The script in front of me tonight is funny—delightfully so—but I have very few words to say in it. (Paul Newman, where are you when I need you?) A familiar restlessness begins to buzz at the back of my neck. It's been too long since I did a play, a movie, something more than just one thing. But my place is here right now. With Margo. It's a womanly place. I don't mind saying so.

Be there. Be grateful, I hear Frankie tell me, but the lack of activity we endure some days would have driven him wild with nervous energy. Tonight, there's not the slightest tick of a clock in the resounding silence of my house. On days I don't work, if not for the quiet comings and goings of the caregivers, the hour hand would have no purpose at all. Sometimes it seems that we are clinging to each other on a life raft, Margo and I, waving frantically to a passing cruise ship, and that cruise ship is *time*. It's the clock and the calendar that everyone else lives by while we seem to have gone adrift with our childhoods and motherhoods entirely out of order.

"When I hit forty, I'll be pretty fucking amazing," I said when I picked up my Obie for *Uncommon Women and Others*. In the thrill of the moment, it slipped my mind that PBS was broadcasting the awards show live. (I wouldn't presume to take credit for it, but the Obies were never televised again.)

"When you're a hundred, you'll be pretty fucking amazing," I tell Margo.

And I'm starting to think, *When I'm seventy . . .*

I don't know quite how to complete the sentence. I want to believe I'll enter a Jessica Tandy phase. She never slowed down. Hume Cronyn once told me she'd go crazy if she was out of work for six months. I was actually up against her for a Tony in 1981, she for *Rose* and me for *Fifth of July*. (No one was more stunned than I when I won.) At the same time, we were both playing small but luscious character roles in the movie *The World According to*

Garp, so at four a.m., right about the time most Tony-goers were stumbling home to bed, we were arriving on set to shoot all day. Glenn Close and I continued on into the frigid night, huddled next to each other in big coats, sipping Courvoisier and trying to stay warm between takes. I stumbled home to my own bed around ten the following morning after promising the *Fifth of July* stage manager I'd be there, bright-eyed and bushy-tailed, for the two o'clock matinee.

Anyway, Jessica Tandy was seventy-three that year—four years older than I am now—and the best part of her film career was just beginning. She won her first Oscar at age eighty, which I think we can all agree is pretty fucking amazing.

Gwen from Fifth of July *by Al Hirschfeld 1980*

AL HIRSCHFELD

CHAPTER EIGHT

Like a Beach House at the Winter Olympics

The first guy to tell me he loved me was Bill Ganz of Mascoutah, Illinois. We were in seventh grade, he a sandy-haired 4-H kid, me, a sunburned army brat. He took me to a junior high prom and was very sweet and respectful the entire evening. When he walked me to the front door, he opened his heart and said, "I love you, Swoosie. You are as important to me as my hogs."

We moved to Tampa shortly thereafter, and as we drove away, he was there to see me off. I craned my neck to look out the back window, watching him get smaller and smaller, waving, waving, thinking, "I am leaving the only boy I will ever love."

I was deeply moved by that hog thing. It meant a lot, and in the back of my head, it settled as a sort of litmus test for men in my life: *Do I mean as much to him as his hogs?* Not more than the hogs, mind you. I'm not asking for that. Only as much. But he has to understand what my own hogs mean to me.

As a rule, Frankie had never intimidated or grilled my boy-friends. He was always warm and welcoming. (With the exception of Josh, who will readily admit that he was an arrogant little nabob who rather enjoyed needling my father.) Frankie and Margo loved Brent Spiner in particular. Brent made them laugh, which is paramount in my family. He was easy-going and supportive, which is paramount in show biz. They could see I was crazy about him and he treated me well, always cracking me up, never allowing me to take the business or myself too seriously.

Brent and I were pals. Companions at arms. He understood the vagaries and vicissitudes of the industry, so he could effectively reality check whatever drama was going on, and he gently dismantled some of my uptight personal regulations. I was reluctant to stay over at Brent's apartment because of a persistent roach problem, but he frequently stayed with me at the Diana Barrymore suicide manse and was understanding when I had to kick him out. I had time alone with him when I wanted it, time alone with a script when I needed it. I was in hog heaven, so to speak.

Of course, I can see now how this wore thin for Brent. Not many people would list "self-involved and unavailable 92 percent of the time" as desirable traits in a romantic partner. (I would, actually, and I firmly believe that Nathan Lane and I could still be that for each other.) I did try my best to do right by Brent, and we did have some great times.

We cooked at my apartment with Tommy Schlamme, who'd grown up with Brent in Texas and was on his way to becoming an A-list director and producer, and Tommy's girlfriend (later his wife), Christine Lahti. We walked over to Central Park to hear Springsteen on a summer night. We talked about art and theatre and books, smoking pot and sleeping in. (No offense to the Temperance League; for a while I found that a little weed went a long way in the causes of better sex followed by better sleep, but I was a lightweight who came to it late. God knows, I could have been pulling all kinds of shenanigans backstage at the Fillmore; I chose to work eight shows a week instead. *Je ne regrette rien.*)

Christine's star was on the rise; she'd just done . . . *And Justice for All* with Al Pacino and, during the years we were all hanging out together, scored an Oscar nomination for *Swing Shift* with Goldie Hawn. She inspired me to be more outspoken and better informed. I wanted to hold my own the way she did whenever she and Tommy got into heated political debates, usually about gender bias and sexual politics. They were going at it one night in a crowded restaurant, and through an unfortunate lull in the noise level, Tommy blasted: "I think I know more about the vagina than you do!"

In *My Rival, the Sky*, Margo describes a particularly happy and hardworking time in her life as lean and high and bright. This was exactly that for me. I'd scored my first Tony nomination for *Tartuffe* and won my first Obie for *Uncommon Women* and my first Drama Desk Award for *A History of the American Film*. Al Hirschfeld drew a caricature of me to go with an interview in the *Times* (another major first for anyone on Broadway), and my agent was fielding a variety of interesting offers.

The cherry on top of all this was my best East Coast girlfriend, Charlotte Moore, who now runs the Irish Repertory Theatre. We met in the late '70s, doing a reading for Joseph Papp. Without full lights up, stages and rehearsal spaces tend to take on the environment of a meat locker. I finally asked, "Am I the only one who's freezing?"

Charlotte parried, "I haven't been warm since July of '64."

A steadfast friendship was born. As we soldiered through another reading a few years later, it became impossible not to notice a strong odor of human origin in the room. Charlotte furtively handed me a note that said, "Just wanted you to know, it's not me."

I love Charlotte because she is valiant and kind, but I won't deny it: whenever we go out, we're as giddy and good-timing as a couple of eighteen-year-olds on the town with our fake IDs, and when Frankie and Margo were in the mix, we were even worse. They loved Charlotte, and she adored them. To this day, whenever I get a good review or some award or other, she'll always call me up and say, "Thank you for once again ruining my day." (That's Charlotte, sophisticated and consummately wiseass, then and still.) She understands that I've always been about the work; the awards and rave reviews were meaningful to me primarily because I wanted to make Frankie and Margo proud. And I wanted to work more.

My parents' home in Toluca Lake was still my home base on the West Coast, and before Perry and Konrad came into my life, Margo and Frankie handled most of the insurance, investments, taxes and other official paperwork involved with the chore of being Swoosie Kurtz. I was chronically overcommitted, and for the most part, I loved that, but when I was too crying tired, I would ask Margo to take over and intercept phone calls, which she did happily and efficiently, identifying herself as "Miss Rogers in Swoosie Kurtz's office." Unfortunately, her voice and mine were so alike, that didn't always go smoothly.

"Yes, this is Miss Rogers calling on behalf of Swoosie Kurtz. I'm sorry, but Miss Kurtz has a prior commitment and won't be able to attend the charity luncheon."

"Swoosie? Is that you?"

"No, Miss Kurtz isn't available right now."

"Oh, knock it off, Swoosie. I know it's you."

"No, no! This is her mother!"

(In case you're wondering, that doesn't go down very well either.)

"Everyone needs help being self-reliant," Margo maintained, and the truth is, if Margo and Frankie hadn't helped me, there's no way I could have done what I did during those make-it-or-break-it years. If I'd been the self-destructive type, they wouldn't have enabled that; they empowered me by helping me keep my head on straight.

While Brent and I were doing *A History of the American Film*, I was cast in Mary Tyler Moore's one-hour musical comedy sketch show (à la *The Carol Burnett Show*), produced by Grant Tinker and succinctly called *Mary*. This was a pretty gutsy move in the wake of her legendary success with *The Mary Tyler Moore Show*, but Mary had started out as a dancer, and we all knew how funny she was, and, for God's sake—what's not to love about Mary Tyler Moore? This was a thrilling opportunity. The promising cast included David Letterman, Michael Keaton, Judy Kahan, and Dick Shawn.

David warmed up the live audience, and he was hilarious. At the first show, thinking it was hyperbole, I remarked to Michael, "He's amazing. He could replace Carson."

If there's any doubt in your mind that we were willing to do *anything* Mary asked us to do (or if you enjoy a little schadenfreude with your morning coffee), I encourage you to get on YouTube and type in "Mary Tyler Moore SINGS with David Letterman, Michael Keaton and Swoosie Kurtz!"

If you enjoy a little schadenfreude with your morning coffee, get on YouTube and type in "Mary Tyler Moore SINGS with David Letterman, Michael Keaton and Swoosie Kurtz!" (Back row left to right) Judy Kahan, David Letterman and Michael Keaton. (Second row left to right) Jim Hampton, Mary Tyler Moore and Dick Shawn. (Front right) Me with my arms crossed.

Go ahead. I'll wait.

It's okay to laugh. Laughter is healthy. Given the healing balm of three decades plus a couple of dry martinis, I'm able to laugh with you.

Yes, that is me with the pigtails. And that is David Letterman, cynic savant, dressed like a cheerleader, desperately trying to sort out his right foot and left arm as he joins in the chorus of Paul McCartney's "With a Little Luck" as rendered by a marching band. And yes, that is one of the most important women ever to grace the television industry, torturously chipper, executing choreography that looks like . . . bossa-nova-meets-yeast-infection. Years later, Dick Shawn actually died onstage during his one-man show—writhing on the floor in the grip of a massive coronary as the audience roared, thinking it was part of his act—and I think Dick would approve of me saying that the *Mary* McCheerleader production number was, in fact, more painful. We also did "The Rat Musical" in which we emerged from cages to sing and dance in rat costumes with long tails.

But here's my only regret about this show: I spent most of the time whining about the writing instead of enjoying one of the most entertaining companies I've ever had the privilege to be in. We'd all go to lunch together at the Jewish deli on Fairfax near the CBS studio, and if only there had been cameras there! I couldn't fathom why the most hilarious people in the Jewish deli were agonizing for a few thin laughs under the aegis of this mediocre material. Coming from the theatre, where the written word is god, I hadn't yet learned that with sketch comedy (à la *SNL*), the writing breathes and evolves, and you really don't know if it's going to work until you trot it out in front of an audience.

"Give it a minute," Mary tried to tell me. "It'll get better."

But a minute was more than we had. We shot thirteen episodes and went on hiatus. I was at Margo and Frankie's when the third one aired. Frankie knocked on the bathroom door early in the morning and said, "Swoose. You better see this."

The *Variety* headline blared: "Mary Show Axed."

About an hour later, I got the don't-let-the-door-hitcha phone call from Grant Tinker, who was as kind as anyone could be under the circumstances, if a little late.

Dick, who was outrageously funny and dear, onstage and off, had actually written some great material that never aired.

"My homeless bit," I mourned to Frankie. "The best thing I had."

Another regret is that I didn't immediately pick up the phone and call Mary to thank her for including me in her bold experiment. This show was an act of sheer balls on her part, and I was lucky to be part of it. It's hard to know what to say when people have poured so much love, sweat and chutzpah into something that goes off the rails. It's like the aftermath of a brutal review in the *Times*. If you run into each other on the street the next day, there's this elephant of misfortune in the room. Etiquette demands that you pretend not to notice the stench. Personally, I'd rather acknowledge the enormity of it in some way, say the sort of thing one would say to a friend who's been in a car accident or gone over the handlebars of a bike: "My God, I'm so sorry! Are you all right? Can I bring soup?" But that's not done.

Unless you're Margo.

She's the person who grasps the hand of an amputee on the subway and says, "Oh, dear. How awful for you. How did this happen?" It makes me feel small-hearted that I can't climb over my shyness and do that for people.

A few years later, Mary did *Whose Life Is It Anyway?* on Broadway and was magnificent. I went backstage after the show one night, and from across the room, she lobbed me my cue from one of the sketches that had died quietly.

"Martha!"

"Blanche!" I lobbed back, and I hugged her, and she hugged me, and there was no elephant. These things happen, and we get past them. What I took away from that experience was a determination to never again miss out on the joy of the company I was in, and that has come in handy on many occasions.

In fact, just after taping those last doomed episodes of *Mary* in L.A., I did an off-Broadway play called *Wine Untouched*. It was originally in Norwegian and perhaps intended to be sort of a lutefisk-fueled *Uncommon Women of the Fjords*. The script, I fear, had lost something in translation, but the company of five included Glenn Close, Donna McKechnie, Patricia Elliott, and Susan Slavin—all wonderful women to work with—so I eagerly signed on. (With a little luck, we'll make this whole darn thing work out, right?)

I said to Frankie, "If Glenn is doing it, how bad could it be?"

It was actually a lot of fun. Glenn and I and a rotation of our castmates went to Sardi's most nights after rehearsal. We'd been given these horrid cabbage cigarettes to smoke during the performance, so we'd light 'em up with our drinks and talk lively girl talk. There was much to discuss. Donna and I had a mutual interest in homeopathic medicine. Glenn and I were both reading this wonderful book called *The World According to Garp*. We all had interesting men in our lives. Surely the intelligent energy of these vibrant conversations could carry the play, I thought, even if the script was a bit *fakakta*.

The Norwegian playwright came to see the show the night before the final preview, to which all the critics would be coming. After a subdued curtain call, the audience filed out, leaving her alone in her fur coat toward the back of the house. As the five of us came out to greet her, she stood up and raised a trembling fist.

"Yoo hef ruined my play. *Ruined it!*"

As she picked up her bag from the box office and headed out to hail a cab to JFK for her flight back to Oslo, Patricia followed her, tearfully castigating, "You can't do that! You can't lay that on actors who are about to face the critics!"

The critics came, and they were not kind. But we faced them together. Afterward, Glenn and I sat at Sardi's, dragging on our pungent cabbage cigarettes.

"One thing I don't understand," I said to Glenn. "How the hell did they get you to do this play?"

"They told me you were doing it," she said. "I figured, if Swoosie's doing it, how bad could it be?"

"But . . . they told me *you* were—"

"Ladies." The maître d' approached our table and sniffed sharply. "I'll have to ask you to leave. Customers are complaining that someone in this corner is smoking marijuana."

"If only," says I.

The show ran for fourteen performances, and I went home every night knowing I'd have to get up early and go to a rehearsal or taping. Brent was good about leaving me alone on school nights, but late one evening Frankie showed up just after I'd settled in to study my script with an après-theatre joint, which provided my best hope of sleep. Frankie knew sleep was an ongoing struggle for me. He could fall asleep seemingly on command. If Margo said we were leaving the house in nine minutes, he'd prop his feet up and catch an eight-and-a-half-minute nap. Not me. I can't quiet the mind chatter.

Without trying to disguise the doobie, I vented my Norwegian woes. Frankie hated smoke in general because he was an athlete as a young man and a health nut later on, but he listened sympathetically. Pouring himself a glass of milk, he noticed old Javitz at the end of the sofa and had the clever idea that while Javitz talked me to sleep, we could record the lengthy monologue so I'd have it on a cassette tape the next time I had trouble drifting off.

Recently, I got someone to transfer the recording onto a CD, and—*oh, God, what a gift!*—right here on the computer in my office are Javitz and Frankie, together again, riffing like Nichols and May, returning me to the Ganges where mystical sleeping sand is mined and bottled for distribution.

"We put it in the hands of Harry Kreeshna," says Javitz. "And Harry says we roll the longest, biggest joint we can, and it's the flourish with which you hand it back and forth—that's the important thing of the whole thing."

Javitz clowns an exaggerated whistle-toothed toke, which, of course, has me giggling uncontrollably, then and now.

"I am the majordomo honcho that's known as the honcho hippo," says Javitz. "My mission is heaven sent. I have to put you to sleep." Javitz pauses to yawn, and it's contagious. In the here and now, I close my eyes.

"I'll be asleep before my audience," she mutters. "It's almost impossible to get these little chipmunks to sleep. I do my best, and in ten minutes they're up, running around, paying no attention."

"Hey, I do my best," stoned Swoosie says.

"That's right, Swoosie," says Javitz. "You do your best, and then you say, 'Now that's behind me. The day is over, and it's time for a wonderful night's sleep.' Because what we're sleeping for is not today or yesterday, but for tomorrow. We are looking forward, onward, upward. And isn't that, Swoosie, what life is all about?"

"Oh, Javitz, bravo," Frankie says. "You're really laying it on 'em today."

"Sleep now," Javitz whispers, ignoring him. *"Sleep, sleep, sleep . . ."*

Berlin, 1936

Frank won his place on the (diving) team and sailed for Berlin.

He wrote to me: "This is the most extravagant beautiful layout I have ever seen, this Olympic village. Not a detail is lacking for comfort and convenience. Every athletic installation is perfect in every way.

"Last night, Mr. Hitler put on a show for all the visiting countries. You know, like Fourth of July night in the States, when we watch the pretty Roman candles break into the sky. Well, it was to be this kind of show.

"But, Margo, it was a night of war. This Olympic arena in Berlin gave us war, and I didn't see one pretty Roman candle. The earth shook for miles in every direction, and each of us from every country sat there frozen to the seats, frozen by cold fear, while all Hell burst into the sky from that arena.

"I couldn't sleep all night, and I find this morning none of the boys could stop shaking long enough to sleep.

"If the purpose of these 'fireworks' was to scare us—Mr. Hitler has accomplished his mission—he has scared me."

Frankie was thrown enough that he tore up his shoulder on a practice dive. He went on to win a bronze medal anyway. He'd competed in Los Angeles in 1932 and made the U.S. diving team again in 1940, but the Helsinki Olympics were cancelled. After the War, Frankie dove in aquacades and exhibitions, but he didn't compete again.

Jack Garland, Frankie's boss after he left the military, was a member of the International Olympic Committee, so Frankie went with him to Rome in 1960. Margo and I went along with them to Mexico City and Grenoble in 1968, and though it was a lot of fun, she and I were chafing by the end. I have a comically morose photo Frankie took as Margo and I sat at the counter in an airport diner, looking like the B story in a Russian play.

Frankie was in Munich in 1972 when the massacre took place, and it broke his heart; it was a moment so antithetical to the spirit of this global community he had always believed in. In 1976, Margo and I went with him to Montreal, determined to help him recover the joy, and in 1980, I was delighted to hear that a play I'd recently done at the Long Wharf Theatre would be included in the Olympic Village attractions at Lake Placid.

It didn't really occur to me that a play called *The Beach House* might not be the most natural fit for the Winter Olympics or that, while this was a wonderful play that had gotten terrific reviews at the Long Wharf, people had not come to Lake Placid's wonder-land of ice and snow to sit still in a dark theater. Audiences stayed away in droves, as they say. It was a debacle. My castmates and I trudged around in special boots, which turned out to be less than waterproof, and I promptly came down with a rotten cold, so right away, my voice was going. We started asking each other: What's the Equity rule? If there are more people onstage than in the house, you get to go home? And if that's the case, how many of us would compulsively do the show anyway?

This was a terrific role in a really lovely play, but when the show was canceled, we were all profoundly relieved. It's not al-ways about what's good; it's about what fits. (A precept that ap-plies equally well to breast implants, men, and little black dresses.)

While I was doing *The Beach House* at the Long Wharf in New Haven, I learned that a production of Edward Albee's *Who's Afraid of Virginia Woolf?* was in the works there with Arvin Brown directing and Mike Nichols and Elaine May as George and Martha. In 1963, when I was fresh on fire from Mr. Ingle's drama class, I'd seen the original Broadway production starring Uta Hagen and Arthur Hill, and it left a scar. In 1980, at the Long Wharf, I felt like I'd seen it two weeks ago. I still feel the same way now.

"I'd sacrifice a finger to do that show," I told Brent, "but I don't think they've even thought of me for Honey."

"You have to speak up," he said. "Plant the seed while *Beach House* is fresh in their minds."

"I don't know. That's not really my style. I'd rather be asked. And I'm standing right there in front of them every night. How can they *not* think of me?"

"Very easily," he said bluntly. "No doubt a lot of actresses

Mike Nichols, Elaine May, James Naughton and me in Who's Afraid
of Virginia Woolf? *at the Long Wharf in 1980. I crouched offstage
thinking, "It doesn't get any better than this."*

MARTHA SWOPE

have already volunteered a finger. Or their agents have volunteered one on their behalf."

This turned out to be one of the great gifts Brent gave me. The next day, eating lunch at Howard Johnson's (where you eat three meals a day when you work at the Long Wharf), I gathered my courage and sat down across the table from the powers that be.

I was cast opposite James Naughton and learned something every day of rehearsal. As we drilled down into this blistering piece of theatre, I realized I could never fully wrap my head around how to play a character until I felt compassion for her. During the rehearsal process, I'm doing all the right things, executing my blocking, speaking my lines. Then something suddenly moves me, opens up an ocean of feeling, insight, empathy. I'm not like Honey at all; even when I was younger, I would have known better than to drink out of a bottle on an empty stomach. But her husband is so dictatorial, the night so terrible—the tension gathers like an orchestra tuning.

Mike (who had honed a decadently sardonic brand of passive aggression) didn't like the set from the beginning. Keeping in the spirit of the play, he made dry observations like, "She's the daughter of the college president. He's an academic. And they have *two* bookshelves? Hmm . . . four people . . . three places to sit . . . interesting."

The first night of previews, Naughton and I entered, and I said my line:

"Oh, isn't this lovely!"

"We've done the best we could since the fire," said Mike.

I clutched Jimmy's arm, trying not to crack up, thinking, *Oh, dear, this could get wild*, but from that moment on, Nichols and May disappeared into the *50 Shades of Intellectual Sadomasochism* that is George and Martha, reminding us that no one has greater dramatic chops than those who are capable of delivering great comedy.

Brent came to New Haven to see the show with Tommy.

"May I offer you one note?" he asked, hastily adding, "One note in an otherwise *flawless* performance."

"Of course," I said. "Let's hear it."

"When you walk in the door, remember how you look—the blond pageboy, pink party dress. We're getting a strong visual. You don't have to tell us who you are."

That's the kind of surgically right note I love, whether it comes from the director, a fellow actor, or the last usher on the left. Mentally I stepped back and saw how it applied to every entrance I made in that play. Later I saw how it applies to any entrance in any play. Right now, I'm stepping back and seeing how it applies to life. (So often we feel this need to announce and explain ourselves when the right thing to do is simply be there, letting our bones stand unspoken.)

The production was a hot ticket without hype, so it was meant to fly under the critical radar. Mike (who'd directed Burton and Taylor in the movie) had nothing to prove; he and Elaine specifically requested that no comp tickets be made available to the media, but I'm told that Frank Rich, who was fairly new at the *Times*, bought a ticket and came anyway, probably thinking he'd be seeing the legendary comedy team of Nichols and May screwball Albee's shop-worn masterpiece. He was forced to admit that our little company had put our own sick twist on this play that is an icon for sick twists and said Jimmy Naughton and I were "the Nick and Honey of one's dreams." It was a victory and a challenge and a revelation and spring break at the beach, all rolled into one.

Elaine and I shared a big dressing room and a lot of laughs. Mike always called her Arlene or Irene or Eileen. He called me Angel Tits—and has forever after—because that's what the boorish professor calls hapless Honey in the play. ("You want to dance with me, Angel Tits?") We all stayed at Colony Inn in New Haven. The play let out too late for room service, but I was always desperate for something to eat, so before the restaurant closed, they'd send up chicken breasts to Mike's room, which was the only one with a refrigerator. I didn't eat them fast enough, though, and they collected in Mike's mini-fridge until he finally bellowed, "Stop the chickens!" and that became our unofficial motto, applicable to a variety of causes.

Every night at the top of Act II, as Mike and I crouched together in a small dark nook offstage, waiting to make our entrance, I was piercingly, consciously aware: *Who needs sunlight? It doesn't get any better than this.* Nothing in *An Actor Prepares* could prepare an actor for that.

One evening about three weeks into the run, we were told Mike had a high fever and the performance that night was canceled. We didn't know we'd already done the last show. Poor Mike had come down with pneumonia, and it was bad; there was no way he'd make it back before the show was scheduled to close, no way we'd do it without him, and no way to extend the run because we all had other jobs waiting. I wasn't the only one burning the candle at both ends, but that entire year is a blur of rehearsing, performing, and shooting. I don't think I made a single trip

Quick comebacks and tough love. Gwen was like a joyfully oblivious Joan of Arc . . . if Joan of Arc had been a dope-smoking, pill-popping copper heiress. (Fifth of July *on Broadway with Chris Reeve in 1980.*)

MARTHA SWOPE

to see Frankie and Margo in Toluca Lake. I was in that phase of a young person's life when the center of gravity shifts; your parents are suddenly required to come and visit you for the holidays.

After *Virginia Woolf*, I performed in a production of Hugh Leonard's *Summer* while I was rehearsing *Fifth of July* for Broadway. The playwright, Lanford Wilson, was an amazing guy. When he died in 2011, his obituary in the *Times* said he "wrote like a wounded angel," which is also how he lived. He smoked hard and drank too much red wine and was very much like my character, Gwen. While we were working, he'd toss out some line of dialogue, or I'd spy some moment of attitude, his way of throwing away a remark, some physical angle with the cigarette that, all gathered together, created this wonderfully visceral picture of Gwen. I reveled in her quick comebacks and unabashedly selfish version of tough love; she's like an obliviously tuneful Joan of Arc—if Joan of Arc was a dope-smoking, pill-popping copper heiress.

Fifth of July opened at the New Apollo Theater in 1980, and to my knowledge, it was the first time two men kissed on a Broadway stage. Most of the cast had done the show while it was downtown at Circle Rep the year before—everyone except me, Mary Carver and our big gun: Christopher Reeve. This was to be his post-*Superman*, name-above-the-title vehicle demonstrating his chops as a serious actor playing a gay, paraplegic Vietnam vet. It was an act of valor—you've got to hand it to the guy—because the role had already been done masterfully off-Broadway by William Hurt, and let's be real, Reeve could have laid it down like Olivier and a certain percentage of the audience would have still stumbled out into the alley saying, "Whoa, did I just see Superman kiss a dude?"

Taking home a Tony for Fifth of July *in 1981.*
A girl never forgets her first time.

We opened after less than two weeks of rehearsal. The critics had good things to say about my performance and the play in general—but some other cast members, Christopher in particular, didn't fare so well. (When a critic says you've stolen the show, it feels pretty good, until you have to hang out backstage with a castmate who feels he's been robbed.) Nonetheless, the show found its feet. Eventually Richard Thomas came in to replace Christopher Reeve, and then we really caught fire. Frank Rich came to see us again, and wrote that "the full beauty of this comedy has finally been uncorked"—which is exactly how it felt. *Fifth of July* got a Tony nomination for Best Play but lost to *Amadeus*. (Damn you, Mozart!) I won a Tony, however, along with Drama Desk and Outer Critics Circle awards—Broadway's Triple Crown, as we say—but Margo and Frankie were almost beside themselves when I told them my caricature would be hung at Sardi's.

I was invited to make my first appearance on the *Today* show that December. The night before—a Monday, so it was a dark night for Broadway theaters—I sent Brent home early and went to bed, prepared to get up at four thirty a.m. to do my own hair and makeup. When my alarm went off, I could see my breath in the freezing cold air in my apartment. No heat. I turned on the shower. No hot water. Cursing the ghost of Diana Barrymore, as I frequently did during my fourteen years in that place, I took an ice cold bath but couldn't bring myself to get my hair wet. My hair was a tangled mop. I'd have to work with it, I decided, but before I set about that, I turned on the TV to see if I was being mentioned in the *Today* show promos.

The air was cluttered with news bulletins. John Lennon had been killed during the night. I sat there blinking back tears, not knowing if anything would happen as scheduled that day or why the hell it should. When I arrived at 30 Rockefeller Center, the crew milled quietly with ashen faces, up all night, still in shock.

"I'm assuming you need to cancel the interview," I said to a producer, but she said, "No, no! Don't go away. You're on in a minute."

I withered. *Oh, God. Great.* Because right now, America really, really wanted to see me sitting there talking to Gene Shalit about my blossoming career. I swallowed hard, and a PA wired me with a mic. *The Mating Season*, a TV movie starring Lucie Arnaz, Lawrence Luckenbill and me, was going to be on that night, so there was no putting this off until tomorrow. It was my job to get out there and . . . be there. And be grateful. I suppose we could try to invest it with some corned beef about why the show must go on or how we honor the dead by stalwartly executing the mundane tasks of life, but the truth is, there are times when nothing you do is going to feel right, so you just do the next thing on the list, and the next thing, and the next thing, until your knees feel solid again.

"Keep chopping wood," Frankie always said.

Shalit and I were able lumberjacks. The interview went well. We weren't morose, just a bit wistful, as one should be at the unfairly abrupt end of an era.

While I was still doing *Fifth of July*, I started work on *Love, Sidney*, Tony Randall's NBC sitcom. This was to be a groundbreaker about a gay man sharing his home with a single mother and her five-year-old daughter. The first taping was set for Margo's birthday, a good omen, but my heart sank at the first table read. I wasn't used to the idea that in television, the script can change radically overnight, and what you see the first day is almost never the finished product. Your character's occupation can change. Your neighbor could morph into your uncle or your ex-wife. Even if I'd known this, I was steeped in the hyper-literary, elitist New York theatre thing and felt like I'd sold my artistic soul to Lucifer.

Mike Nichols called me to do a reading of a play, and I confided my despair. "What have I done? I feel like I've signed my life away. This isn't a pilot. It's thirteen episodes, and if it gets picked up, I've signed for five years."

"I get where you're coming from. A few years back, Hollywood called, come on out and do this show, Nichols and May, and we went, thinking, 'Hey, what's the harm?' But we're sitting at the table, literally about to sign, and we looked at each other and put down the pens. We said, 'Sorry to have wasted your time.' In our hearts, we both knew."

"Oh, God." I covered my face with my hands. "You're not helping."

"Calm down, Angel Tits. If Tony Randall's doing it, how bad can it be?"

Most of my friends said, "You're out of your mind. This is a great job." And Mike was right about Tony; we were the Even Couple instead of the Odd Couple, a pair of Felixes with our Broadway work ethics and vaguely OCD exactitude. He had exacting standards and an impeccable sense of story structure, and he broke with tradition, sitting in on writing sessions and ruling the roost in general, which didn't endear him to a lot of people. I loved what he did for the show, which ended up being a wonderful gig. The writers hit their stride, and Tony's wide circle of friends made for amazing guest stars, including Betty White,

Myrna Loy and Helen Hayes. Prima ballerina Suzanne Farrell turned us all inside out, and Itzhak Perlman, who was a raunchy jokester, let me hold his Stradivarius. (And yes, he would make a lewd one-liner out of that.)

Taping a television show in front of a live audience actually feels a lot like doing a play. You get a chance to rehearse entire scenes, which you rarely get to do when filming a television show (like *Sisters* or *Pushing Daisies*), which is like a lean, mean version of shooting a movie. When you're filming, you work on the material at home—little or no rehearsal on the set. You get into full makeup and costume, and the continuity, the sound—everything is coming and going, and the adrenaline is flowing, and the molecules in the air change, and you do this thing, and then you sit and wait. And you wait. And you wait, making sure that you don't disturb a hair on your head or lose an iota of energy between takes.

As publicity ramped up and the first airdate approached, word was spreading that Tony Randall was doing a sitcom about a gay man. Affiliates began to pull out without even seeing the first episode. We were descended upon by the gods of Standards and Practices, whose job was to make sure the impressionable minds of TV-topia remain untainted by expletives, high-cut leotards and love that dared not speak its name. Tony had not set out to make a political statement; he just wanted to do a show about a different sort of family, a show with great heart, integrity and intelligence. He fought the good fight, but ultimately Sidney was watered down to a "happy bachelor" with only a few vague euphemisms and in-jokes referring to his sexuality until the very end of the last show of the second season (which turned out to be the very end of the show) when Sidney mentions a long-lost love, and the camera pans to the mantel where we see the photograph of a young man.

Brent came to every taping of *Love, Sidney* and helped me with material at home, going over scripts with me and making valuable suggestions, as he had during *Mary*. The night of the Tony Awards, when I was nominated for *Fifth of July*, he went all in on the tux and the red carpet and the whole routine. ("You're more nervous than I am," I teased just before my category was announced, and Brent wondered grimly, "You think anyone in the green room does shiatsu?")

He came to every play I was in, shored me up when things went badly and was genuinely glad for me when things went well. Before I moved from the Diana Barrymore suicide joint to a semi-swanky Upper West Side apartment, Brent gamely schlepped thirty uncomplaining blocks to be with me. He was amazing about a lot of things for a long time.

"I'm not smoking dope anymore," I told him one night. "I feel like it's depressing my energy. And it makes me cough."

Brent said he'd been thinking about making some changes as well. He was so good, and we both knew it, but he couldn't seem to catch a break. He wanted to cast off the negative influences in his life, reorder his priorities, get his shit together. I thought this was a great idea until I realized he was breaking up with me.

"Everything is copy," Nora Ephron used to say, meaning an artist should take whatever exquisite agonies life deals us and use it to make art, but as I sobbed in a ball on my bathroom floor, hating love, it didn't feel like anything I'd ever want to connect with or exploit.

Margo knew the whole story the moment she heard my

Tony Randall and me in Love, Sidney *before we were descended upon by the gods of Standards and Practices, whose job was to make sure the impressionable minds of TV-topia remain untainted by expletives, high-cut leotards and love that dared not speak its name.*

choked voice on the phone. She and Frankie were sad to see Brent go and heartsick to see me so shattered.

"Can't say I'm totally surprised," Frankie said gently, and in retrospect, of course, I'm not either.

Had the roles been reversed, if I'd been the one struggling while Brent's career was on the ascendant, I doubt I could have been the mensch he was. I know exactly who I was in those days; I would have been jealous and competitive. Looking back, I can't resent him for choosing the work over me, because I'd have chosen the work over him if I'd been put to the test. One of the reasons I loved this man is that he knew all this about me and never made me feel ashamed of it.

Shortly after we broke up, he scored a supporting role in *Sunday in the Park with George* on Broadway. On opening night, I sat toward the back of the house, grateful for the dark, hand clamped tight over my mouth, my heart breaking all over again as Bernadette Peters sang "Move On."

Anything you do, let it come from you . . . give us more to see. Look at all the things you gave to me.

Eventually Brent moved to L.A. Most people know him from seven seasons and four feature films as Commander Data in *Star Trek: The Next Generation.* We weren't in touch for a long time, but inevitably, a few years later, I ran into him at a party, and he looked good. Healthy. Happy. I teased him about being immortalized in an action figure, and he took it in his good-natured stride.

"Hey," he said, "if it's good enough for Alec Guinness . . ."

When I was a little girl and Frankie was stationed in Tampa, I had an enormous crush on a little boy named Charlie. I was the fastest runner of the girls; he was fastest of the boys. Match made in Heaven. Daddy Art and Gigi happened to be visiting, and Daddy Art drove Charlie and me out on a date—movie and burgers—after which he dropped me off first so Charlie could see me home. I leaped out of the car and said, "Race ya!" and beat him to the door, where he promptly broke up with me.

"Swoose," Daddy Art said when he came home to find me weeping, "you can't race your boyfriend and win."

Apply as needed to sex, television and Sundays in the park with Springsteen.

"The sound reeled out of me. I have no idea where it came from."
Bananas in PBS Great Performances: The House of Blue Leaves, *1987.*

CHAPTER NINE

Singing, Dancing and Schizophrenia

∞

Omaha, 1941

So Christmas came. And on that day the headlines said: Manila Surrounded.

I knew, then, that there could be no call. So on Christmas day I drove around town and called on friends. I'd pop into a house here, and the family would all be together. They had just finished Christmas turkey and their belts were loosened. They sat around the tree while the children played with dolls. I knew each time I got inside one of these houses I shouldn't have come. They were content before I arrived. Then the mother would nervously smoke cigarettes, and the father just sat there smoking his pipe. The girl would keep looking at her young husband, like she had something she shouldn't have. And he was very uncomfortable.

It didn't matter what we talked about, I could feel each one thinking, "She doesn't even know if her husband is alive, but here she is on Christmas day so calm."

I could know they were thinking this because not one could look at me straight in the eyes.

So I was an outcast everywhere I went on Christmas day. Finally I just went to my own room, our room with the K on the door. I spent the day writing Frank. And at night I drove past all the windows with the Christmas lights coming through in green and red shapes. We drove to the Post Office, alone, me and my letter. The corridors were very quiet tonight and dark.

Why is it that people are so uncomfortable with the thought of a woman who is, by choice or not, alone? It seems to waffle between suspicion and sympathy. Is she the witch or the widow? Or just waiting for Mr. Right? A solitary gentleman can be a confirmed old bachelor—or he can be the charmingly tardy Mr. Right—but a solitary woman must be Miss Havisham. I know the day is not far away when I'll be living alone again, and I'm trying to be honest with myself about the period of adjustment, the painful reality of learning to live without Margo and our ad hoc family, but for many years, I've always been perfectly happy living by myself in New York, and I expect I will continue to be.

I love my New York apartment—the first place I'd purchased on my own. The building is an art deco monument, where you half expect to see Dorothy Parker step out of the ornate elevator.

All the trims, tiles and inlays of the original design have been lovingly preserved or beautifully restored, an ongoing process that's had its up and downs since Frankie found this place for me in 1982. Employing the wisdom of all his years in the real estate business, he marched me all over the Upper West Side, measuring square footage, testing pipes and grilling hapless superintendents. While Frankie skeptically clicked the feeble light switches in the dark hallway and pointed out cracks in the plaster, I opened the tall living room and bedroom windows, looking down on Central Park. I had no trouble envisioning my life here, and even though that original vision included Brent and *Love, Sidney*—neither of which remained when the plaster dust had settled—it wasn't far from the life that in fact unfolded over the decades.

The neighborhood wasn't as gentrified as it is now, and the apartment needed a lot of work, so the price was right. There wasn't time to take a breath between *Fifth of July* and *Love, Sidney*. I was on set by day, trying to sort and pack the contents of the Diana Barrymore suicide chateau by night. Frankie stayed at the New York Athletic Club, where he still had privileges, and spent his days at my new place, barking orders at the housekeeper, measuring things, lecturing the workmen when they didn't come up to his exacting standards, castigating the movers to be more careful with my things, even though I really had nothing of any great value. After a few days of this, I was ready to throttle him.

"Do you really have to make this so unpleasant, Frankie?"

"There's a right way and a wrong way to get things done."

"No there's *your* way. Always. For everyone. Even if you have to shove it down our throats."

I suppose we were ready to throttle each other, really. As I came into my own, I became more and more like him, and sometimes it seemed there weren't enough cubic inches in the room for both of us. But he did get things done. With guilty relief, I'd show up every evening and see that another impossible task had been made possible: the plumbing, the wiring, the floors. He systematically transformed a crumbling mausoleum into a modern, well-kempt domicile where the kitchen cupboards were the correct height for my coffee cups, and the bathroom fixtures were the correct height for me.

Just as it all came together, we saw the announcement on *Entertainment Tonight* that *Love, Sidney* had been canceled. I remembered what a joyful surprise party it had been to see that *Marigolds* had won the Pulitzer. This was the evil twin of that moment. (It's nice now that we have text messaging, which delivers unpleasant news like a surgical scalpel instead of a chainsaw.) We'd started so well. Cover of *TV Guide*. Great reviews. I was nominated for an Emmy both seasons. But, so it goes.

The Emmy Awards show was a much bigger production than the Tonys back then. We were shooting in New York, so I flew to L.A. for Emmy night. Margo helped me get ready, and my agent served as my date. Afterward, I flew home to my beautifully finished Upper West Side apartment and checked in with the answering service. Somewhere in the years since I'd first moved to New York, my paradigm had shifted from *nothing yet* to *what's next*, and I was consciously grateful for that. Margo and Frankie joined me for a busy holiday in New York, then it was back to work in the new year. The fact that it was 1984 didn't strike me as portentous at all. And when the answering service told me, "Mike Bennett called for you," it didn't even occur to me that they meant Michael Bennett the choreographer and director—Michael Bennett the revolutionary—who'd forever changed both the process and the form of the Broadway musical with *A Chorus Line* and *Dreamgirls*. I'd done a reading of a two-woman play for him several years before, so I recognized his gravelly voice when I returned the call.

"I'm working on this new play with music," he said. "I'd like you to come down and do a staged reading of it. It's called *Scandal*."

He told me the script, written by Treva Silverman, who'd written for *The Mary Tyler Moore Show*, was "the best book written for a musical since *My Fair Lady*."

"That's huge," I said, silently adding, *if it's true*.

He believed it to be true in that moment; that was very clear.

"It's about this woman—Claudia—her husband divorces her. Says she's not worldly, not sexually sophisticated. So she goes around the world to educate herself. Goes to Paris, gets with a French waiter, there's a Swiss lesbian, a *ménage à trois* in Italy, and the brilliant thing is, every sexual encounter is a big production number—singing, dancers, the whole thing—because this is how it feels to her as she discovers all these new aspects of herself. But in the end, she realizes that she still loves the husband. And the husband, who has a parallel journey, realizes he loves her, so ultimately, it's a love story, but it hinges on the arc of Claudia's personal evolution. Would you be interested?"

"Absolutely," I said. "Who would I be playing?"

Michael laughed and said, "Claudia."

I sat there for a moment, waiting for the apostrophe to drop. *Claudia . . . 's sister. Claudia . . . 's best friend. Claudia . . . 's bridesmaid who is never a bride.* Truth be told, I was already calculating the comic potential of that Swiss lesbian. The last thing I expected when I picked up the phone—or pretty much any moment of my life prior to this one—was to be cast as the leading lady in the next Michael Bennett musical. I have a good ear and good pitch. I'd taken years of lessons and done plays with music. I could sing. But true Broadway divas like Patti Lupone and Kristin Chenoweth can *sing*. Different thing. I was closer to the Rex Harrison school; I sang like an actor. If critics compared me to the divas of Bennett's world—or if I allowed *myself* to compare me to the singing divas of any world—well, as Ethel the Oracle says: "Compare and despair." But to be in the room with true genius, I told myself, that was worth any amount of heartbreak.

"We'll have a rehearsal day and do the reading that evening," he said.

I usually think just about any show is great when I'm in the middle of it, but this show really was an unbelievable dream. Claudia is sharp, intelligent, funny, self-deprecating—not a Swoosie prototype, but a kindred spirit, and I knew I could joyfully play the hell out of her. Michael was as brilliant as I remembered, and here he was even more in his element, chain-smoking, striding around in jeans and sneakers with his shoulder-hunched gait, laughing his seductively abrasive laugh. We worked at 890 Broadway, Bennett's legendary incubator. The tall windows were always full of lights, day and night, but the energy in the room palpably thrummed when he walked in and drained away when he walked out.

We powered through the long rehearsal day. I went home exhausted and got up the next morning with the flu. Distraught, I called Margo. "I can't believe this. This is one of the greatest opportunities of my life."

"Did you take your temp?" she asked, as a mother does.

"It's over 102."

"Okay," she said without a trace of panic, "that's not good. But you've performed sick many times. It's part of the game. You'll get a good kick of adrenaline. That'll help."

She talked me through all the voodoo we actors perform—vitamin B, gargling vodka—and our fervent little company performed the reading in front of the core people: Michael, his trusted advisors, lawyers, money daemons. Then I went home and collapsed into bed, utterly exhausted.

Michael called me later that night, and said, "Your reviews are in, and they're raves."

"Do you think they're going to do it?" I asked.

"Honey," he gently reminded me. "I *am* they."

During the first six-week workshop, we focused on the book. Future workshops would focus on songs, dances, staging and putting it all together. It paid almost nothing and took up all my time. A lot of people were doing it just for the opportunity to work with Michael. Everyone in the world of New York theatre was well acquainted with the lore: his genius, his passion, his drug use, men and women he slept with, the gifts of prospect and gouts of verbal abuse he heaped on dancers in equal measure.

Michael Bennett never did anything the ordinary way, and it felt like an extraordinary privilege to be around him. The working hours felt rarified: pure artistic motive, diamond insight, moment-to-moment challenge that left us wrung with sweat and satisfaction. His methodology (which you get a small glimpse of in *A Chorus Line*) was a total immersion that turned the rehearsal process into an all-consuming love affair with the show. I was infatuated with him and with Claudia and with the corps of beautiful young dancers—the best dancers in NY and therefore the

Rehearsing for Michael Bennett's Scandal *in 1984. I was infatuated with Michael and with the corps of beautiful young dancers.*

best dancers in the world—who bore me aloft and passed me overhead. I was tossed in the air and caught with abandon, the way you'd toss and catch a toddler. I trusted them completely and loved being in their company. It was like hanging out with a herd of charmingly clever gazelles. Treva showed up with new pages and rewrites every day. During our time off (and by "off" I mean working on our own instead of on the clock), she and I spent many hours talking about the story, the characters, the nature of this beast we were giving birth to.

Almost every night, Michael would call me, smoking, talking hyperbole, saying intoxicating things like, "Watching you work today, I wanted to propose to you. You have *line*, love. A dancer has to be born with that."

Fine, I told myself. *Be smitten. But get it.*

I knew what he was, and he knew that I knew; I wasn't going to get sucked into the cult of Michael. But these were deep conversations that went on for hours. From May through December, as the workshops went on and our relationship deepened, I gave myself to the hyperbole, heart and soul.

After a few months of this, I went all Claudia and dove into a brief, tantalizing affair—this producer who sparked momentary fantasies about a show biz power couple with a house in Connecticut—so I was less than gracious when Frankie showed up unannounced one night. The sight of him in my space made me feel earthbound again. This was the part of the script where the sophisticated woman meets her unavailable lover in a dimly lit bar, not the part where the grinning ex-war-hero father drops by to change out the ballcock in her toilet tank. There was no way to explain to him that I was *breathing* differently at the moment, or that what I was doing every day felt like spinning straw into gold, and I didn't need him coming around uninvited and ballcocking it up with a tank of reality.

"How long are you planning to stay?" I asked with a bit of an edge.

"Oh, a few days," he said. "Maybe a week."

"Well, which is it? I need to know."

Frankie was no amateur with the verbal jabs, and he certainly didn't spare my feelings when he was expressing his own, but in this moment, he just regarded me quietly and nodded.

"Okay. I'll let you know."

I disappeared in a puff of diva smoke, and when I came back, he'd gone, leaving a note that said, "I'll be at the NY Athletic Club if you need me. Love, Dubby."

"I feel horrible," I told Margo on the phone. "I'm sorry. I just . . . I don't know. I felt the need to speak up for myself."

Margo was always the consummate Libra. Growing up, she was the middle child of five, and there were times she probably felt like the middle child still, masterfully finessing Frankie on one hand and me on the other in an effort to preserve the peace. She understood without judgment that I was feeling very important, at the center of this great endeavor. The buzzing had begun. Everywhere I went, people would honey up to me, wanting to be a part of Michael's in-crowd of theatre elites, dying to know what was going on behind that closed door at 890 Broadway.

More important, I was doing some of the best acting of my life and dancing my ass off. Coached by Cleavant Derricks, I was singing this amazing Jimmy Webb music that had been specifically tooled to make the most of my voice. Michael didn't hear me sing until Cleavant said I was ready, so it was a huge day when he finally came to hear me blow the doors off the Eleven O'Clock

Number (as we say in musical theatre) "The Most Important Thing."

Michael was revved on top of the world to have been proven right. He kept saying, "My Tony-winning actress—she can *sing*."

I'd never been in better shape, vocally or athletically, and I'd never been so completely happy. Michael could be harsh; I'd hear him hamstring dancers with cruel remarks, but he treated me like a jewel on a pedestal. Like a star.

I feel a bit chagrined now. Perhaps, up there on my pedestal, I wasn't getting enough oxygen to the brain. I was oblivious to any friction between Treva and Michael, largely unaware of all the little fights and love affairs that were constantly brewing and breaking up within the company. Some people thrive on all that backstage drama, but I usually forget to pay attention. When it becomes impossible to ignore—when it's more than a good, healthy argument over creative difference, when it becomes sadistic or cruel or a power struggle—I flee to a neutral corner. Frankie and I chafed each other's nerves at times, but I wasn't raised in an atmosphere where people shriek and flail at each other. Personally, I find it disturbing, and professionally, I think it's an annoying waste of time. The work is challenging enough when everyone stays unruffled.

Given a few weeks off during a chorus workshop, I went to San Francisco to shoot *Guilty Conscience*, a television movie starring Anthony Hopkins and Blythe Danner, who multitasks as one of my favorite people in the world and one of the finest actresses on the planet. This adroit little script was faithfully adapted from the play, a psychological suspense three-hander about a man, his wife and his mistress and their twisting plots to kill one another. It was a relief to earn a bit of money, and for the most part, it was great fun. There were a few episodes between Anthony Hopkins and the director, who was Welsh, I think, so maybe he reminded Tony of his father or something—I don't know. The two of them would start thundering away, Blythe and I would look at each other, and one of us would whisper, "Let's smoke."

The movie was being filmed almost entirely on location in an enormous two-story house. Blythe and I cowered at the top of the ornate staircase, like children whose parents are fighting. We lit up cigarettes and chatted amiably while Tony and the director tore into each other below, Welsh accents echoing off the woodwork. I confided in Blythe about the heady world I was working in back home in New York. The *Times* had been preparing a piece on Michael for their Genius series. Treat Williams and I had been written up by Liz Smith and pictured *in flagrante delicto* in a *People* magazine spread.

"This is life-changing," I told her. "I will never be the same."

Famous last words.

Scandal was finally coming to full flower with sets, lighting and costumes. Costume fittings always make a show feel real to me; you don't get to the point of fitting costumes until the production is an imminently happening thing. Michael's shows were always designed by the great Theoni Aldredge, and I loved the miracles she did for my body. I was elated, finally standing there in Claudia's skin. I was ready.

We knew we were going to be working very hard for a very long time, so a few of the dancers and I decided to go to Saint Bart's together in January, and I invited Margo to come along. The weather was perfect, and we had a perfectly wonderful time the first few days. The fourth day, we were all lying on the beach, and one of the dancers went in to check with his answering service.

He came out to us, ashen, shaking. "You guys better check in. They told me *Scandal* is postponed indefinitely."

We just gaped. I said, "That can't—*no*—what—what exactly did they say? What were the *exact words*?"

"They said, '*Scandal* is postponed indefinitely.' That's exactly what they said. My agent told me not to turn down any work."

The bottom dropped out of my life. The best analogy I can offer is being abandoned at the altar. With complete love and trust, I'd made a huge commitment, closed the door on other offers, and devoted myself to only this. A date was set, announcements made. I'd been fitted for the goddamn dress! Now here I stood, bereft and full of questions. This was before the days when anyone had cell phones. We were in this remote place; it was almost impossible to get a call through, and when you finally did, the operators all spoke French. The stage manager had left me the same cryptic message. No details. No reason. Just an unmistakable vibe of *don't call us, we'll call you.*

Thank God Margo was there with me. While I mourned, she held me and stroked my head. The next day, I sat in numb silence, and she set about the task of getting us home.

Michael called me after we got back. Put it all on Treva. Said she was making eleventh-hour demands, wanted casting and choreography approval. They were going back and forth through lawyers, barely communicating, so I begged him, "Let me talk to her. Please. We can still make this happen." I talked to Treva, and she was in a baffled panic, scrambling to appease Michael without completely screwing her own interests. Rumors had begun swirling that Michael had had a heart attack or heart trouble of some undefined nature, and then that became the story: Michael's heart trouble. Then it was, no, not that, something about the money. No, it was all that sexual overtone, what with this whole new awareness about high-risk behavior and everything. The only solid piece of information I got was that Michael had gone to London to direct *Chess* on the West End.

"You've given it all the time it deserves," Frankie advised. "Shake it off and move on. Keep chopping wood."

"Yes, why don't I just do that?" I said bitterly.

Easier said than done. I was heartbroken. And I was angry. I turned forty during those workshops. The only thing that really changed was that I no longer laughed at the old joke about how, in Hollywood, they euthanize you when you turned forty. Nonetheless, this show took a year from the middle of my performing prime, and my dear, those days are numbered for an actress just as surely as they are for a professional athlete. We must carefully choose where to invest our time, because every day of our professional lives, time and gravity are doing their merciless thing. (My tits have migrated three centimeters to the south since the beginning of this paragraph!) There was no getting back that lost year, but the brutal financial blow meant nothing to me compared to what I had emotionally invested in this show. "Can't forget what I did for love," as the song says. It also says "won't regret"—and it took me a while to get there. But Frankie was right. Bemoaning it served no purpose.

I took a nice part in the movie *Wildcats*, playing Goldie Hawn's sister. It was like rehab or like a sojourn at a sanitarium, the way ladies sojourned back in the day if grief or consumption got the better of them. Goldie is generous and outgoing and has a vivacity that energizes the people around her. I quite idolized her. She had everything worked out, the way one does if one is good at being a movie star: snacks at the right time, warm coats, lots of water, inner peace. We were up early and eating healthy. Goldie had us all happily doing aerobics during lunch. Everyone was cared for. No one was on a pedestal. A lot of my scenes ended up on the cutting room floor, but I was so grateful for this healthy work experience. It was the unbuttered wheat toast and Pedialyte cure for my Michael Bennett hangover.

While I was on the set, I got a call from the producer of *True Stories*, directed by David Byrne of Talking Heads.

"Here's the thing," she said. "We can only pay union scale. And it's a no-frills situation as far as—"

"I'll take it."

I got to marry John Goodman in bed. Who turns that down? (Turns out, Betty Buckley did, actually. I was their second choice and glad to have it.)

A while back, I saw Stockard Channing at some event or other, and when I asked her what she was working on, she said with a philosophical shrug, "The tide's out right now." Such a lovely way to put it. The work comes in waves. That's something I love about this life. One night, you're sitting there counting crickets, and the next morning, two opportunities are on the table, and you have to figure out how to fly back and forth between Hong Kong and exotic Alabama or make Sophie's Choice and let one go. (Chatting on set several years ago, I told Elisabeth Shue how much I loved *Leaving Las Vegas*, and she said she'd been up for *Waterworld* with Kevin Costner at the same time. Talk about a rising tide . . .)

The key to happiness is learning to enjoy the quiet moments, using them to gather the strength you'll need to enjoy your next ride on the rollercoaster. I'd love to say I finally have a handle on that, but I'd be lying. I go to a dark place sometimes when I'm between jobs. My family and friends have come to understand that I'm fully present in my work, so I suffer in its absence. Adrienne Rich wrote in her elegant poem about Madame Curie: "She died a famous woman . . . denying her wounds came from the same place as her power." I'd like to think it's a bit like that—to a lesser degree, of course—with tragedy and comedy instead of radium and polonium and a couple of Tonys instead of the Nobel.

∞

Omaha, 1941

The other reason I kept imagining Frank near Manila was the phone call that rang in our house at seven o'clock on the morning of December 19.

"Margo, quick—quick, get up—the phone. It's about Frank!"

And I stumble to the phone, asleep and awake in the same instant, almost, and the operator is reading me a message from Frank.

It's from Manila, but there is no date. But I hardly miss that yet—it is saying, "Am doing all right under the circumstances."

The second time I make her read it (I always do this, it's such pretty music)—I realize, this second time, she has started the cable, "Beloved flower."

Now you think these are rather soft words for a man who's been dealing in cold blood. They are soft, and Frank doesn't usually talk that way; but Frank said them over ten thousand miles for me to hear the softness. They told me a lot of other words.

These are quiet words, but I guess strong words are always quiet. And quiet words never seem to go away. It was Frank's own voice, speaking in the cable, not someone else making up a message for him. That was something so sure to hold to.

But then, when I had been staying a long time with the strong things this cable let me know, I began to realize how much it couldn't tell me, too. There was something very puzzling. After Frank told me he was "doing all right under the circumstances," he said: "Wire Eddie's brother."

Why hadn't he said anything about the rest of the boys?

Margo sits at the table, and I can feel her waiting for the other shoe to drop. The worst kind of curiosity. Not only is the answer out of reach, she's forgotten the question, which is a mercy, because of course, all the boys were dead, burned alive on the tarmac at Clark Field just a few days after Pearl Harbor. This is one of those times when Margo's bewilderment, as upsetting as that can be for her, is better than the memory that lies beyond the haze. The source of her uncertainty is nothing she can articulate, nothing I can guess at; quizzing her about it would only make it nag at her more deeply.

It's uncanny how much her present state of mind resembles Bananas's in *The House of Blue Leaves*. I gleaned bits and nuances from Margo's mannerisms when I created this character, but I never suspected I was peering through a keyhole, looking at Margo's future. Her poetic dementia.

John Guare's darkly quirky comedy was workshopped at the Eugene O'Neill Theater Center in 1966 while I was off learning the London tube system. In 1986, Jerry Zaks was directing a revival, and when he called me to audition—I have to be honest here—I read the thing and didn't understand it. I didn't get the jokes or even the gist of the story, which involves a zookeeper who wants to have his schizophrenic wife (Bananas) committed to a mental hospital so he can run off to Hollywood with his mistress (Bunny) to pursue his dream of writing music for the movies. And their son, who has gone AWOL from the army, is planning to blow up the pope, who happens to be in town that day. Really, it's the definition of "you had to be there."

I was asked to read for Bunny, which was great with me. Bunny had more lines, bigger laughs, cuter costumes, lots of lovability. Bananas, meanwhile, spends half the play in a bathrobe, haunting the upstage windowsill and saying strange, arcane things like, "I can't leave the house, my fingernails are all different lengths." Until you learn to love the poetry of her, she has the potential to be rather sad. Obviously, Bunny was much more up my alley, so I worked up a few terrific Bunny monologues (of which there are many) and trouped off to the audition, where they did a complete 180 and asked me to read for Bananas.

"We know what you can do with Bunny," said Jerry. "Would you mind reading Bananas? Take a few minutes—however long you need. Do the green latrine speech for us."

"The green . . ."

Apparently, this is a monologue that gets done all the time for auditions and competitions. I was completely oblivious.

"Could you talk me through it?" I asked.

He talked me through it. I still didn't get it.

The Green Latrine is a Buick that Bananas is driving in a dream, and she comes to an intersection where Jackie Kennedy, Cardinal Spellman, President Johnson and Bob Hope are all trying to hail a cab. Only two words in this monologue made sense to me: Bob and Hope. But I gave it my best shot.

My agent at the time, a very nice British woman, called and said, "Well, you've been offered *Ba-nah-nahs*."

"I wanted you for your wrists," Guare told me later.

The less poetic version: Stockard Channing was already on board, and given first choice of the two roles, she took Bunny, just as I would have done had I been in her shoes. Nonetheless, my friends kept telling me what a great play it was and what a great role Bananas is, and I knew the people involved would be great to work with, so I dove in.

At the first reading, my heart sank further. Stockard was terrific in this role and made the most of all those lavish monologues and big laughs. Our castmates, John Mahoney, Christopher Walken and Ben Stiller, were all familiar with the play. Ben (who was making his stage debut) had seen his mother, Anne Meara, playing Bunny in the original off-Broadway production. I alone was a *House of Blue Leaves* virgin and largely in the weeds.

"I'm so lost," I told Margo that night. "I don't know what I'm doing. I feel like I'm invisible. I can't even tell you what this play is about."

(Ironically, this is exactly what Bananas feels, so I was on the right track, I just didn't know it.)

Margo said the perfect thing: "Why don't you just quit?"

"*What?* No! I'm going to figure this out. Just because it doesn't jump up and kick you in the head the first time you read it doesn't mean . . . oh."

Even over the phone, I could tell she was smiling smugly.

I lay in bed at night, turning the lines over in my mind.

I don't like the shock treatments, Artie. At least the concentration camps—I was reading about them, Artie—they put the people in the ovens and never took them out—but the shock treatments— they put you in the oven and then they take you out and then they put you in and then they take you out . . .

Jerry Zaks's direction was a master class: "Swoose. Swoosie, dahling. You're the most normal housewife in Queens. Your husband works at the zoo, and you're the most normal couple in Queens. With your first line—'Is it morning?'—you just want to know if it's morning."

Throughout the entire run, Jerry continued to give all of us notes, which I lusted after and squirreled away for future reference. The breakthrough moment for me was when he said, "I need a sound from you every time she has a fit. Some ungodly, heart-wrenching sound. Then it needs to be a light switch change to a calm, serene 'Look at me, I'm a forest.' No transition."

That night, sitting on my living room floor, I thought about the epileptic fit I had to do in *Marigolds* and about the night sounds in a zookeeper's nightmares, and the sound reeled out of me. I have no idea where it came from, and I suspect my neighbors were equally baffled.

Ann Roth (who also designed my Eighth-Avenue-not-Park-

Al Hirschfeld's heart-wrenching rendition of
Bananas in The House of Blue Leaves

AL HIRSCHFELD

Avenue hooker garb for *The World According to Garp*) tried about six dozen bathrobes on me to find the one with exactly the right amount of weariness in the nap and buttoned it one buttonhole off kilter, which set the *you don't have to tell us who you are* tone.

I have to laugh now, because Margo's favorite robe is her staple wardrobe item. We have to go through all sorts of machinations to get her into something else long enough to launder the thing, and there are times when this is not worth the stress. Last year, we all gave her robes on her birthday in hopes of getting a rotation going.

At the time of *Blue Leaves*, Margo was a healthy, young-hearted seventy, still sharp and ready for anything, but starting to display some eccentricities. Her classic one-shoulder shrug was an easy bit to steal. The rest was more instinctive, subconscious even, particularly—though I don't want this to sound wrong—the scene where Bananas morphs into an eagerly affectionate little dog, guileless and cheerful, but with a vaguely dark undercurrent of insistent need. I certainly wouldn't have said so to Margo at the time, but I'd seen flashes of that in her devotion to Frankie. For the most part they were the dynamic duo, but their marriage—like any other marriage—went through passages of imbalance, and in those moments, it was debatable who had whom on a leash.

It wasn't until much later that I recognized how Bananas had inherited Margo's longing to fly, her wistful remembrance of past glory days, her willingness to please coupled with an unwillingness to keep quiet about something she knows is not right. There's her lonesome love for her distracted husband. She remains calm at his sudden outbursts, her flashes of anger and sadness firmly held at bay—until they're not, and she suddenly turns on him with rage, standing up for herself. Maybe as marriages go, all that is just another day at the office, because in a kinder, gentler way, it was all heartrendingly familiar.

It's uncanny how the lyric language of Bananas's craziness foreshadowed the frangible reality Margo lives in today, and having lived in Bananas's head for quite a while, I'm less frightened by Margo's dementia now. I'm able to let go of the urge to correct and reorient her, because I get that she is perfectly oriented on the only plane that makes sense to her.

I felt fairly confident by the final dress rehearsal, and the first night of previews, I knew I'd found it. This play knows no "fourth wall"—the actors speak directly to the audience at times, and it doesn't really work until the audience becomes part of it. Toward the end of the show, Walken's character even says, "The greatest talent in the world is to be an audience." The audience arrived, and I understood. This role was a turning point. Life-changing.

Tommy Schlamme and Christine Lahti came to a matinee, and it was so good to see them backstage. Tommy gripped my hand and said, "There's someone here to see you."

It was Michael Bennett.

I went cold and hot and weak and strong all at once, and the urge to get my arms around him won out. I suddenly realized I wasn't angry anymore. I couldn't remember when I'd let it go, but I knew it had been a while.

"How is your heart?" I asked him.

"It's okay. How's yours?"

"It's okay."

"You were spectacular. Did you see Frank Rich's review in the *Times*?"

"No!" I clapped my hands over my ears. "I never read reviews while the play is running, especially if it's a wonderful review. If the reviewer says, 'I loved the way she tilted her chin,' you'll never get that chin tilt right again."

"Honey," said Michael, "lock yourself in the bathroom and read this one."

He knew I wouldn't—and I didn't—but it was impossible to ignore the way the audience reacted; within a few days after we opened, we knew we'd be moved to Broadway in time for Tony nominations.

"I'm so glad this happened for you," Michael said before he left. "If it hadn't—honey, I would have slit my wrists. I felt like I owed you a year of your life."

It meant everything to hear him acknowledge that and to see that it caused him genuine sorrow. He didn't apologize or offer any further explanation. That's not how this business works. We parted with Hollywood half kisses and the standard promises to keep in touch, but there was more emotion in it than usual, both sadness and affection.

Before the Tonys, Brent Spiner sent me a telegram: "I think your Tony's going to have a twin sister." He was right. Stockard and I were both nominated, and I won. (If that bothered her at all, she avenged the decision by getting cast in *Six Degrees of Separation*, which I coveted mightily. So goes the tide.) John Mahoney and Jerry Zaks also won Tonys, and the following year, PBS filmed *The House of Blue Leaves* for the American Playhouse series with Christine Baranski coming in for Stockard.

The show had a luxurious long run. We were a tight-knit cast and went as a gang to a nearby coffee shop after most performances. One night after the show, several of us walked out the stage door and across the street to see *True Stories* playing in the

New York Film Festival, which was kind of a gratifying little Swoosie-palooza.

Things continued to ebb and flow. As the years went by, I was lucky enough to work with so many people that it was almost impossible to go to an audition or show up for a shoot where I didn't know anyone. Every time was a reminder that the industry had become my extended family—especially the New York theatre community.

As the 1980s unfolded, the AIDS epidemic took a terrible toll on Broadway, especially among the dancers. The first of my friends to die was Peter Coffield, my castmate in *Tartuffe* and in the A. R. Gurney play *The Middle Ages*. This was in the fall of 1983. Gurney had gone to see him in the hospital, and he told me, "They said he had pneumonia. They made me put on this mask." A few weeks later, we heard that Peter had died. We didn't understand yet, but it was dawning. At first, there was fear—no one knew what this thing was, how it was spreading, why nothing was being done to stop it—then the gravity of it settled over us. The funerals and missing pieces, the dwindling numbers at the dance auditions, the disappearing directors, playwrights, actors and producers. It felt as if we'd lost an entire generation.

Of course, it eventually came out that Michael Bennett's vaguely defined "heart problem" was in fact AIDS. He'd known it when the dancers and I went to Saint Bart's. That was the real reason he'd pulled the plug on *Scandal*. Even if he could have gone on working for a while, sooner or later, the truth would have come out, and the meaning of the play would have been forever changed, tinged with an irony that undermined its buoyant spirit.

During the summer of 1987, word traveled through the grapevine that Michael had bought a house in Arizona, and he was dying. He called me in June and said, "Honey, I just got a brand-new car. Rolls-Royce. Top of the line."

I heard his voice and started weeping. (I thought about this later during *And the Band Played On*; I play a character who's told she has AIDS, and her first task is to comfort her sobbing husband.) Michael sounded fragile but still strong and acerbically funny.

"You should come and visit," he said.

"I would love to see you, Michael. When can I come?"

"Soon. Don't come now, though. It's monsoon season."

"In Arizona?"

"Yeah. This is not a good time. But soon."

I was grateful to get the call from Michael's longtime assistant two weeks later before I saw on the news that Michael Bennett, the revolutionary choreographer and director, the innovator who'd given us *A Chorus Line*—which was, at that time, the longest-running musical in Broadway history—had died at age forty-four.

"You say every character you play gives you a gift," says Ethel the Oracle. "Did the fact that the show never opened take away Claudia's gift?"

I have to ponder a moment before I honestly answer, "Almost."

But with equal honesty, I can say that it would not be possible to be in a room with Michael Bennett for a year and not come away in some way blessed by his mercurial, unpredictable genius. I told myself that first day that it would be worth any amount of heartbreak. Famous last words. But from the here and now, I do see that I got more than I gave.

This character was so like me—same rhythms, same intellect,

same slanted, slightly sardonic view of the world, my voice with a stage spin on it—as though it had been written for me, but it wasn't. She refused to fall apart after her husband left her; she was proactive and chose to grow. I love the old saying, "If you fear the lion, walk up to the lion." Claudia showed me how to walk up to the lion, and I never forgot.

The article for the Genius series in the *New York Times* never happened, but after Michael's death, the writer, Barbara Gelb, wrote an important piece about Michael, "First, Last and Always a Dancer." In it, she mentioned his mysterious, last-minute abandonment of a fully staged musical called *Scandal*, which had evolved, like *A Chorus Line*, "through a prolonged and painstaking workshop process." She said, "I spent several months watching him ready *Scandal* for its Broadway opening, for an article that was aborted when the show was. Like the handful of others who saw it, I knew it would have been the best thing he'd ever done."

Last night I had a vivid dream that I was standing in the California sunshine, and Margo picked me up and tossed me and caught me, the way you'd toss a toddler in the air and catch her and kiss her and set her down safely.

I woke up waiting for the other shoe to drop.

Steaming things up with the Sisterhood in 1990:
Julianne Phillips, Sela Ward, Patricia Kalember and me.

WARNER BROS.

CHAPTER TEN

Degrees of Separation

———— ∞ ————

Omaha, 1943

The first time I saw war was in a man's eyes. It was a sergeant in the Air Corps, who stepped off a plane at the Municipal Airport in my city. I approached him as he came through the passenger gate. I said, "Sergeant Catarrius?"

His khaki uniform was dusty and spotted, and his leather jacket was worn thin and scratched raw. This sergeant had a thin face. Is Frank's this thin by now? His eyes look off into the distance, somewhere, and they look hunted. Could Frank's eyes look so hunted, tired, and frightened? Would I know them now?

I've heard lots of radio commentators talk about war, but

their voices never sounded like this man's. He doesn't tell me the big picture of war, the percentages and the logistics that the Congressmen and the newspapers give. They tell me "intelligent" war, all the black and white facts of this new business we are in.

"They found us again in Broome, Mrs. Kurtz, when we landed in Australia. We felt safe at last and then at daylight, they came in again, a skyful of them. I'm used to seeing soldiers and officers bombed, after Clark Field and after Java, but to watch them bomb women and children who didn't have a chance—to crouch there in a foxhole and watch their bodies cut to pieces. We are all very tired, Mrs. Kurtz."

Right now I'm glad he doesn't look at me—I'm not ready. And I know now, sitting next to this man who comes from war, the job at home is not only to get guns and equipment to the boys at the front, but we have to learn to be ready for these eyes. We need to be ready, to be ready for when they finally, someday, turn to us.

Will Frank and I ever look at each other again, or will he be looking off to the distance, somewhere?

"We are all very tired," the sergeant said.

And this is how war comes to someone at home.

On *Pushing Daisies*, Ellen Greene and I played two synchronized swimming sisters. I was Lily, whose exotic backstory includes the loss of one eye. This was deeply affecting to me in a completely unexpected way. Late in his life, you see, Frankie had lost the vision in one eye and went through hell, but I never really understood the enormity of it until I got inside Lily's skin. Sometimes a character's secrets manifest from the outside in: Bananas's bath-robe, the exoskeleton of corsets and lace in *Dangerous Liaisons*, the faux fur of the hooker in *The World According to Garp*, Honey's catalog-clipped ensemble in *Who's Afraid of Virginia Woolf?*

The costumer placed Lily's bedazzled silk patch over my eye, tilting the world just enough to make a difference in my balance, planting the seed of a vague but persistent headache. Having no depth perception is only one of the challenges, I realized. When I looked around the room, I could still see perfectly well, but somehow, wherever I looked, there was this palpable void look-ing back at me. Putting on the eye patch before every shot, I thought of Frankie, of the vulnerability to which he could never become accustomed and his anger at having part of himself so abruptly truncated. I remembered the ever-present sediment of bitter frustration that seemed to collect in him after that, and I put that into Lily.

Before this happened, Frankie was in tiptop health. A hale and hearty seventy-five, he was not thinking about retirement any more than I think about it now—meaning not at all. I went as often as I could to see him speaking, and he was a natural, which is not to say he didn't practice. He put the same assiduous effort into preparing for these performances that he put into the old aquacades. Just as she had back then, Margo sat in as his coach, giving him notes and keeping him impeccably styled. He'd get up there in his signature bow tie and have the room in the palm of his hand. People lapped it up and loved him. Great delivery and rhythm. I definitely inherited my comic timing from him. Can-didly, I cringed at some of his one-liners, but he always got huge laughs.

"So the psychiatrist says to his patient, 'Do you ever talk to your husband during sex?' And the lady says, 'I suppose I could. There's a phone right there by the bed.'"

You could almost hear the rim shots.

"They tell me Nixon is looking to buy a house in New Jersey. Hasn't this poor man suffered enough?"

Frankie and Margo continued to visit me frequently during those years, and overwhelmingly my memories are about what fun we had. They were always my best pals and favorite cohorts, game for anything from the time I was a teenager, all uptake and liftoff. If I said, "Let's go to Easter sunrise service at the Hollywood Bowl," alarms were set and coffee poured into thermoses. Someone was always coming up with a great idea—visit Pasadena, tour a museum, hunt up a book—I don't recall anyone ever saying, "Nah, not in the mood" or "maybe some other time." We went to baseball games, movies, shopping. There was Randy Newman at Avery Fisher Hall and Bobby Darin at the Copa. There was even an Orson Welles sighting at the unfortunately named Tail o' the Cock restaurant. We even went to Vegas a few times. (Frankie was a natural gambler who'd built his life on an addiction to calculated risk, and Margo, as you may recall, had grown up with poker players.)

In 1985, Frankie and Margo came to see me in yet another incarnation of *The Beach House*, and while they were in New York, Frankie suffered one of those little TIAs (a transient ischemic attack or "mini-stroke") while he was brushing his teeth. He felt basically fine, but Margo noticed his speech had become oddly slurry. I had to do a matinee, so a friend took them to see a doctor—a star doctor who was supposedly the guy for this sort of thing, which was supposedly a fairly routine operation to clear the carotid artery. *Why didn't we get a second opinion?* Margo and I grilled ourselves in retrospect. *Why didn't we insist he have it done at Mayo?*

The operation was botched, the optic nerve severed. Frankie, who'd zealously guarded his health all those years, felt maimed, robbed and benighted. He still had good vision in his remaining eye, so he was able to continue driving and do all the things he was accustomed to doing—not to mention all the things I was accustomed to having him do for me. There was much to be grateful for. He was, overall, in stellar shape for a man his age. But this was a major thing. It changed his life, changed him. Sadly, I wouldn't understand how deeply and why until thirty years later when Lily revealed it to me, quietly but without pity, long after Frankie was gone. In the same moment, I understood that I'm now capable of compassion I simply didn't have back then.

Back then, as Frankie found his new normal, I was focused on my own plate-spinning act, steadily working, constantly traveling. I wasn't ready to confront the fact that my father was getting old, that there might come a time when he would need me as much as I had always needed him. Frankie was happy to facilitate my denial. He liked being needed, being the hero, grounding me with wiry pragmatism, clotheslining me with an unsparing joke. He and Margo were both happily aware that their unconditional love was the steady fulcrum I needed as my life continued to seesaw between the ridiculous and the sublime.

In 1988, I was offered a part in the film of *Dangerous Liaisons*, which I kept turning down, until John Guare physically took me by the shoulders and said, "Swoose, you *are* doing this." Glenn

Sometimes a character's secrets manifest from the outside in. From Eighth Avenue to eighteenth century with Robin Williams and Glenn Close in The World According to Garp *(1981) (top) and Glenn Close and Uma Thurman in* Dangerous Liaisons *(1988).*

Close was on board, along with John Malkovich and Michelle Pfeiffer. I'd be playing Uma Thurman's mother. People kept telling me I'd have a great time, and I did.

We shot in Paris for ten weeks. My French steadily improved as I settled into the pleasant neighborhood surrounding my hotel where I could see the Eiffel Tower from the bathroom window. The costume designer, James Acheson, who'd just won an Oscar for *The Last Emperor* (and would win another for *Liaisons*), did not cheat on a thing. He piled it on, layer by authentic layer: crinolines, corsets, hoops. It was easier to lean against a tree and close your eyes than to try to lie down for five minutes. Glenn had her baby girl with her, an adventure in itself, but additionally challenging when bending over to adjust one's own shoe buckle was a three-man operation. Eyeing the narrow door of the Porta Potty in utter despair, she and Uma and I compared notes:

"We have an hour for lunch. Are you taking off your corset?"

"That's like taking off your boots on an airplane. Don't even go there."

"Three words: Eat. No. Bread."

"I won't even go into what it was like trying to change a Tampax," I told Margo when I got home. "On the upside, there was Courvoisier on the craft service table at lunch every day. You don't usually see that."

After that, I was flying back and forth between coasts, making *A Shock to the System* with Sir Michael Caine and *The Image* with Albert Finney. The two of them kept giving me messages to courier to each other:

"Albert, Michael says go fuck yourself."

"Michael, Albert says same to you with love."

(Joanne, the driven television news producer in *The Image*, was not an outside-in character; I did a research deep-dive with help from Don Hewitt and Mike Wallace at *60 Minutes* and Peter Jennings, who let me sit beside him, just off-camera, while he delivered the evening news.)

I moved on to *Love Letters* onstage in New York, and one night John Guare dropped by the theater to bring me a script—his new play, *Six Degrees of Separation*—which I immediately consumed and loved. This character, Ouisa, so resonated with me: her intelligence and urbane wit, her willingness to trust and to be open to connection even after her trust has been shattered.

"It's brilliant," I told him (though I'm not sure I'd absorbed yet just how brilliant it really was). "I want to play the young black guy."

I felt I had a good shot (at Ouisa) because the last John Guare play I was in was *The House of Blue Leaves*, and I'd won a Tony, so there was a happy history there. A love fest. Jerry Zaks was set to direct *Six Degrees* at Lincoln Center, and I had just done a staged reading of Stephen Sondheim's *Assassins* for Jerry Zaks where I played Squeaky Fromme alongside Nathan Lane and Christine Baranski, which was a blast. Jerry took me out to dinner, which was pleasant enough, but the purpose was a bit murky. I had the disquieting feeling that I was auditioning, but I didn't know what I was supposed to do.

Long story short, they cast Blythe Danner, and knowing I needed to vent, Frankie patiently listened to me unload about it at home in Toluca Lake.

"I appreciated that Jerry called to tell me himself, and if not me, yes, of course, I'm happy for Blythe, I love her, but . . ." I sighed. "Moving on. I'm just sad this play won't be part of my life. I really loved it."

"What else are you being offered?" Frankie asked.

"There's an interesting pilot at NBC. They're calling it 'the Sisters Project.'"

Frankie and Margo knew well by now that there were always pilots being pitched, and I was rarely interested in doing one. My upscale New York theatre niche suited me as comfortably as my Upper West Side apartment. Back then, the toniest theatre folk tended to think of TV as slumming (unlike now, the golden post–*Mad Men* reality), but this script was literate, grown-up, and funny from the very first scene, which had the Reed sisters in a steam room discussing the possibilities of multiple orgasms, to the emotional dénouement, which had them crossing paths with their younger selves in the empty rooms of their childhood home. The characters were warm and flawed, struggling with themselves and each other. It was created by Dan Lipman and Ron Cowen, a playwright who'd won a Drama Desk and been nominated for a Pulitzer. They were trying to get Sada Thompson to play my mother, and even if they couldn't get her, I thought, the fact that they wanted her was a good sign.

I was literally on my way out the door, when my agent called, telling me they wanted me for *Sisters*, and I should stay in L.A. and work it out.

"I'm on my way back to New York," I told him. "The car is out front waiting to take me to the airport."

He said, "Put your bags down. This is serious."

I sent the car on without me, and Frankie and I sat at the kitchen table. He poured himself a glass of milk, took a yellow legal pad and drew a line down the center.

"Okay. Pros and cons."

Right away, on the upside, I could see that if the show got

picked up, I could be living at Frankie and Margo's for the better part of five years. That was also a downside. Frankie had a my-way-or-the-highway approach to folding towels and parking the car, and I cringed to hear the way he barked at Margo for whatever little or big thing was out of place in his world.

An old joke he repeated over the years: "Sometimes I think you were born twins: Margo and an idiot. And Margo died."

Somehow it didn't sound so playful anymore, and at some point, Margo's laughter at the old joke started to sound a bit off key. He had a way of asking the hard questions and compelling self-honest answers, and generally, I appreciated that, but diplomacy had never been his strong suit. His idea of tact was to preface his unvarnished opinion with "Now, this isn't a criticism, but . . ." The starchier side of Frankie's character wasn't aging well. His impatience hardened to anger much more quickly than it did when he was younger. Frankie had the ability to inspire and enrage me like no one else.

"It's a huge commitment," I said, "but they're offering me a good deal. My agent says they think getting me will help them attract some other good people, so there's some leverage there."

Frankie listed all that, and we went back and forth, bouncing thoughts and questions. At the end of the day, I decided to sign on for the Sisters Project. I went to bed feeling blessed and loved and lucky to have Frankie in my corner.

I was the first sister cast (Alex), so I had the opportunity to sit in and read with the actresses auditioning to fill out the quartet. Patricia Kalember, cast as Georgie, was the next Reed sister to come onboard, then Julianne Phillips as Frankie, so the three of us were there the day Sela Ward came in to read for Teddy. It was evident in that moment that the four of us had that elusive chemistry you always hope for. With lovely Elizabeth Hoffman as our mother, we dove into shooting the pilot episode of *Sisters*. There's almost always a honeymoon period in the early days of a show, but I felt we had something beyond that. It was a mellowed, more mature version of an uncommon sorority I've experienced with only a few other ensembles over the years.

It's a high-diving horse trick for writing to be as gentle and humorous as this and still be groundbreaking. That steam room scene is, in microcosm, exactly how the show eventually found its audience. First we hear voices through the heavy clouds. Girl talk. We can barely make out the sisters sitting close together, wrapped in towels. The girl talk eventually leads to comparing notes on multiple orgasms.

"I had five once," says Alex. "New Year's Eve, 1981."

"What a memory!"

"What a New Year's . . ."

The scene was a perfect vehicle for all the exposition that needs to happen in a pilot. Immediately we see Alex's sterling pragmatism, Georgie's earthy honesty, Teddy's over-the-top bravado, and Frankie's longing to keep up. We also get a sense of the pecking order. But as the sisters go their separate ways, something extraordinary happens: an unseen woman somewhere in the room softly says, "Eleven." And another says, "Seven." Voices ripple through the steam, each one as sensual as a glimpse of wrist bone, saying exactly what so many women were about to say in response to this show: *You haven't seen us, but we're here. And we really do want to talk about all these things we're not supposed to talk about.*

The day before we finished shooting, Frankie called me at the studio. "Jerry Zaks is trying to get in touch with you."

Blythe had left *Six Degrees*. "Due to a family emergency" can be code for all kinds of things, so my first thought was, *I hope she's all right*. My second thought had a cynical edge I didn't like feeling. *Oh, so now I'm right for the part?*

"I guess you heard we've had a little crisis," Jerry said. "But I understand you're in the middle of a pilot."

"We finish shooting tomorrow. We won't know for a month if we're picked up, and if we are, we probably wouldn't be shooting again until the end of the year."

When we hung up, the tantalizing possibility of this play was hanging in the air again, but by the time the pilot wrapped, it was gone again. Long story short (I never heard the long version), they cast Stockard Channing. *Six Degrees of Separation* was hailed as the second coming, she earned the reviews we all envision in our sticky little dreams and was cast in the film, for which she would later earn an Oscar nomination. She really was magnificent in that role. I can't tell you how delighted I was for her.

Seriously. I can't.

It would be considered unbecoming to admit I ate my heart out. We're supposed to air-kiss these things good-bye and graciously walk off the stage like smiling pageant hopefuls, and we do that for the sake of propriety and so we can remain friends, but the truth is, almost every single one of us is harboring a ravenously covetous creative tapeworm. Without it, we wouldn't be in this business at all.

Moving on.

The *Sisters* pilot was shown to critics in January 1991, and the predictable howl went up about the opening scene—not in response to a lingering shot of a woman's backside in silk panties, but about "all that orgasm talk," which the producers had gotten past Standards and Practices and showed when I was a guest on *The Tonight Show* with Johnny Carson. Now they had to sell to advertisers and convince them that it would play in Peoria. As local affiliates started grumbling, Ron Cowen spoke up to defend what he felt was a "signature scene" similar to the roll call scene at the beginning of *Hill Street Blues* or the stand-up club at the beginning of *Seinfeld*. NBC's president, Warren Littlefield, issued a good-humored statement: "Corporately, we believe in orgasms." Disappointingly, when the dust settled, the shapely backside remained, but the intimate conversation between the sisters would be cut when the pilot aired in May. (It was later restored, and at this writing, you can see it in its entirety on YouTube.)

This was a different day and age in the television industry. We had no idea if we were going to get away with banter about orgasm or any of the other intimate subject matter being addressed or if audiences accustomed to a steady diet of *MacGyver, Magnum, P.I.* and *Baywatch* would embrace a thoughtful show about the kitchen cupboard wisdom, private triumphs and quiet disappointments of suburban women. On the upside, the show was different, which made it a creative joy. On the downside, the show was different, which made it a commercial long shot. When it was time for "upfronts"—a sort of flea circus in which the stars of all the network shows are marched before the media and potential advertisers in an effort to generate buzz—we Reed sisters gave it our leggy best. We would have preferred being heralded as one of the smartest shows on television, but if having the best gams got us picked up, we'd take what we could get for the moment.

Afterward, I had a break in my schedule, so Margo and I went to Hawaii to hike around the flowered trails and huddle like baby turtles under our beach umbrellas. The first day we were there, I was happily surprised when the *Sisters* line producer called to tell me we'd start shooting in October; the show had been picked up for six episodes.

When I called to tell Frankie, he predicted, "This show's going to go for five years."

"I don't know. They're not ordering a full season, but with all the tempest in the teapot, I'm grateful we had a chance to hit our stride."

"Five years," he said with certainty. "At least five, maybe six."

In my ear at that moment, five years sounded like a long time. But we could discuss that later, I figured, because it's human nature to think there's always a lot of *later* lying around—until there's not. A month or so after *Sisters* premiered, we celebrated my father's eightieth birthday. As he predicted, the final episode would air five years later, just a few months before he died. I don't know if I was imagining that he'd go on, invincible as ever, until I was eighty myself, or if I was simply incapable of imaging my life without him.

Or maybe it's just something about Hawaii. When you're there, you feel like you have all the time in the world.

"Frankie, Margo and I were thinking we might stay on here a little longer. Do you mind being a lone wolf for an extra week?"

"No, by all means, stay. You're there. Make the most of it. Have a good time."

The next day, Frankie called me at the hotel. "Jerry Zaks is trying to get in touch with you."

Stockard was leaving the play to shoot a movie to which she had a previous commitment. They wanted me to come in and replace her for three months. I felt a jolt of *No, thanks, I've just put one out*, but I kept that to myself and told Jerry I'd think it over.

"What's to think about?" Frankie said bluntly. "You said you wanted this play in your life. Then your pride got hurt. Which one means more to you?"

I could honestly answer, "The play."

"Besides," he harrumphed, "what'll you do all summer if you don't take it—sit on your ass?"

Part of my hesitancy was the fact that I'd never replaced before. It's like you're standing on the platform and they're asking you to jump on a ninety-mile-an-hour train. Back in New York, I sat in the audience and watched Stockard, stole everything I could and made it my own before she left and I stepped in.

You bring your unique heart to the character when you replace another actor, but you have to fit into the play as everyone else has already rehearsed and performed it. There's also an element of "if it ain't broke, don't fix it"; it's likely your predecessor—with the director's input—will have come up with bits and business that just plain work. You learn as much as you can as quickly as you can and dive in without the benefit of a long rehearsal process. (I've often said I could happily spend my life doing nothing but rehearsing, if only someone would hire me for that.)

But the play! This play—having John Guare's dialogue in my mouth again—it's like biting down on a tuning fork. Painfully resonant. It rings in the head. You feel it in your jaws. Speaking of the young con artist who's convinced her and her husband that he's the son of Sidney Poitier, Ouisa says, "We turn him into an anecdote . . . 'Oh, tell the one about that boy.' And we become these human jukeboxes spitting out these anecdotes to dine out on like we're doing right now. Well, I will not turn him into an anecdote, it was an experience."

Human jukeboxes, spitting out anecdotes. It seemed to me, when I was young and had reached critical mass on the repetition of wartime stories, that Margo and Frankie were caught in a loop, reliving and reciting those glory days over and over. Put another nickel in the nickelodeon, out comes the story of Ole 99, the story of the Swoose—all that Greatest Generation lore—over and over until the war stories became as mundanely rote as the fruitcakes and aquacades and Gigi's goiter. What did it even mean anymore? What had it meant in the first place?

"There I was in Okinawa with nothing between me and the cold, hard ground but one thin nurse."

I will not turn him into an anecdote. It was an experience.

∞

Luzon Island, 1941

Pearl Harbor was attacked before dawn, Philippine time, and Manila radio soon blared the news. That was what Frank awakened to, danger jerking him by the shoulder, shouting harshly in his ear, jerking him to the double quick.

Men at Clark Field who had been on the alert now for three weeks, tense, ready for whatever action, gulped breakfast and ran for duty, questions and orders crackling the air like static grown to explosions.

Is it rumor? A suicidal "incident?" The real thing—war?

Stop the camouflaging job on Ole 99—too late for that now. Load bombs. Keep the engines warmed up. Halt the bomb loading. Unload. Take on cameras for reconnaissance. Keep the engines warmed up. The news is true. It's war. The Japanese will try to strike here—don't know when, but it will come. Cameras ready? Go on with the camouflage. Engines ready. Wait for orders.

With Frank in the operations tent and the Ole 99's crew standing by her, ready to start the great engines—it hit.

Japanese bombers roared over, a black V and then another, and more zooming behind them. There was nothing to do but take it. Frank lay with two others in a foxhole for one, and took the ruin that seventy Japanese bombers could hurl on an easy target. In the sudden eternity of a few seconds—a roaring thunder, piercing screaming whistles downward, a grinding quaking shrilling roar. The ground he was lying in pitched and heaved and quivered.

The thunder roared away to nothing, and the earth shuddered to stillness except the crackling of our planes burning. Then a hum. More planes. Fighter planes—our own, the men thought, and straightened to watch. The fighters swooped in low, with orange suns on their wings.

This time Frank dived into a big ditch with about forty others—another man collapsed into it, streaming blood, and died. The attackers, strafing with machine guns and cannons, tore over the field, circled, returned, again and again. Gunshot spraying the edge of the ditch. Burning planes crackling. Gas tanks gone, with hissing and shattering explosion. One Fortress near the ditch being systematically shot to bits. Mission accomplished.

Frank walked past the ruined plane, across the bomb-dug field, past more burned planes, scorching with the heat of their burning. Then over the crest of a runway toward 99, hurrying to see—

The twisted, crumpled, blackened skeleton of our plane. Four men, burned, under the plane. The crew lying on the other side of her, eight of them, sprawled in a crooked line, one by one where each was struck as they ran toward shelter: boys Frank had worked with and lived with and depended on for his life; our boys whom he had kidded and cussed and bucked up—lying dead by their twisted ship.

And they were still so much themselves, and after the first moments, Frank walked to the farthest one, Tex, his co-pilot, and lifted him in his arms and talked to him. He talked to each one, somehow, slowly, puzzling with them how this terrible thing could have happened, talking it to them over and over, reaching to pillow them with something, some kind of sense in this utterly senseless horror, and telling them this couldn't be the end—whatever it took, we'd fight on and win, and Ole 99 somehow would be making the long flight, too, with all of us.

"Life," said Truman Capote, "is a moderately good play with a badly written third act."

This proved agonizingly true for Frankie. But if it hadn't, I might not have known how to go about rewriting Margo's third act. Or my own. That's how I'm able to live with mistakes that were made.

My father's last five years passed so swiftly. That time comes back to me now as an intense blur of work, play, accomplishment and airplane food. Through most of it, Frankie was going strong, still rocking that bow tie and motivating crowds for General Tel. Health conscious and fit throughout his life, he kept himself in condition as a point of honor. Now in his eighties, he could still dance, do handstands and drive like the wind. He refused to give in to the advance of gray in his receding hairline. The same colorist who kept me vibrantly red used to do his roots. Afterward, he'd stand and grin and declare, "I'm a new girl!"

It was harder to mask the cracks that began to appear in his mental and physical infrastructure. I see now that during those years, he must have been devoting a tremendous amount of energy to keeping up the heroic construct that had defined him all his life—and had, to a great extent, defined Margo, whose identity was so intricately woven with his. I saw my father as an immovable object; he saw me as an unstoppable force. For most of my life, that dynamic worked in my favor because Frankie and I shared common ground and goals, but Frankie and I could come to blows in a way I haven't with anyone else in my life—probably because I've never known anyone else who was so like me.

When I decamped to my parents' home in Toluca Lake where I would live while *Sisters* was being filmed at Warner Brothers, Frankie and I began to suffer something a friend of mine calls "proximity burn"—a series of small annoyances that are individually no big deal but collectively begin to chafe. This house was fairly small and seemed to be getting smaller by the day.

"Frankie." As I sat in my room, trying to learn lines with my hands cupped over my ears. "Do you have to have the TV at top volume all the time?"

"Frankie." As I walked in the door to find a porn video playing. "For God's sake. Must you?"

"Frankie." As I white-knuckled the passenger seat of his car. "It's not an airplane. You can't bank around the corners like that."

Because I was home so little, we managed to keep a lid on things (with Margo gently interceding as needed) for the first two years, but the driving issue slowly escalated from a simmer to a rapid boil. Frankie had always driven like a fighter pilot: skillful and dynamic with a serious need for speed. He did not respond well to criticism (to put it mildly), but I was certain my employers at Lorimar would not respond well to my face going through a windshield. How were we to tell this legendary flyer that he was losing his mojo?

Eventually, we would have to sit him down intervention style and take the keys away, but for the moment, Margo and I returned to the slow simmer when Frankie grudgingly agreed to trade in his eight-cylinder gunboat for a smaller car with less horsepower. Honestly, I don't think Margo was ready to give up on Frankie's reassuring presence in the driver's seat. We were used to being chauffeured and facilitated by our hero, and facilitating his self-denial was little enough for him to ask of us in return.

After the third season of *Sisters*, I did buy my own house (for those gentle readers who are thinking, *Why the hell doesn't she buy her own house already?*), but it was empty and needed work before I could move in, and at the end of every fifteen-hour day, I was grateful to go home to people who loved me, even if we did occasionally drive each other crazy. Frankie and Margo were still my greatest allies and trusted advisors—and never once did either of them say, "Swoose, wake up and smell the eviction notice." They liked having me there, and I liked being there. It wasn't exactly the quintessence of Hollywood glamour, but I was never about the trappings of success. The greatest luxury I could imagine was to spend every ounce of my energy working a fifteen-hour day, crash on the foldout bed in my old room and fall asleep over my homework, studying lines for the new day that was scheduled to begin in a few hours.

We had running jokes about "You know your call is too early when . . ."

". . . the moon is still up when you're driving to work."

". . . yesterday's hairspray has yet to wear off."

Frankie had the best one, a souvenir of his flying days: "The last thing I did before bed at night was get up in the morning."

Filming a television series (if not as life-threatening) can be equally life swallowing. The pesky problem of what to do on a Friday night is solved; you're usually shooting straight on through till dawn on Saturday.

I was the veteran of the *Sisters*hood, number one on the call sheet, and while that didn't endow me with any particular responsibility or privilege, I liked feeling like the Big Sister. I prefer a jerk-free environment when I work and wanted the tone on the set to be about kindness, collaboration and a strong work ethic. I hoped my younger sisters would look to me for that, the way we all looked to Goldie to set the tone of happy productivity on the set of *Wildcats*.

Patricia, Sela, Julianne and I fell into step right away and became very close. We were acutely appreciative every time the show was picked up, and while we always hoped we'd be picked up again, we never took it for granted. More important, we didn't take *each other* for granted.

Julianne introduced us to a favorite restaurant in Brentwood, and that became our Saturday night haunt—our version of the

Reed sisters' steam room, I suppose—where we talked girl talk, laughed until we cried (and sometimes cried until we laughed), and bonded over a single Death By Chocolate served with four forks and a round of vodka martinis. Julianne is generous, guileless and sweet, one of those people who's good to everyone around her and hard on herself, on the Stairmaster every morning before dawn, working hard at not being the baby of the family. Patricia is wicked smart with a sharp sense of humor and a New York sensibility—which in combination with her prowess as a mom would, in my humble opinion, make her a great director. Sela had started out as a successful model, so I used to tease her, "I thought I was gorgeous when I was in the makeup chair, but then I walked onto the set and remembered—*shit*, Sela works here."

People tend to project brotherhood when they see an ensemble of men, but they look at an ensemble of women and expect diva trips and cat fights. I won't pretend that never happens, but it's the exception, not the rule, and it didn't happen here. Toward the very end, there was some of the aforementioned proximity burn, but I can honestly say that the four of us started as friends and parted six years later as sisters. Here again, I wish I could accommodate the tabloids with some sexy mudslinging, but these disobligingly good women provided me with nothing salacious to report. It may fly in the face of conventional wisdom, but the truth is, beautiful women can be smart, and smart women can be kind, and a sisterhood can be as decent and compelling as a band of brothers.

A movable feast of supporting characters came and went over the years. Ashley Judd played my daughter and was a darling soul, mature and savvy beyond her years. (I wish I'd had that strong sense of self when I was starting out.) Paul Rudd came on as her husband, and (to my horror) I found myself playing a spectacularly menopausal grandmother, complete with hot-flash-simulating special effects. George Clooney was with us when he was still an undiscovered natural wonder—a dreamboat who knew he was funny enough to get away with just about anything. (Is there anything sexier than the dreamboat/funny/occasional smartass combination?) Robert Klein came in to play my husband (the tax evader, not the cross-dresser), and I developed a serious crush on him. If ever a straight man could make me forget Nathan Lane, it would be Robert Klein. I laugh harder and think more during dinner with him than I do during *The Colbert Report*.

Filming an hour-long show every week demands a tremendous time commitment from everyone involved, but with Frankie and Margo's tactical support, I was able to keep up the mad pace I thrive on, accepting theatre gigs and movie roles during every hiatus and sometimes even while we were shooting. During our first hiatus, I did Terrence McNally's *Lips Together, Teeth Apart* with Nathan Lane at the Manhattan Theatre Club, a wonderful way to be reunited with Christine Baranski. While we were filming our second season, I did *And the Band Played On* for HBO—a gratifying gift of a role that took only one day but meant so much to me. I also did *The Positively True Adventures of the Alleged Texas Cheerleader-Murdering Mom*, with Holly Hunter and Beau Bridges, a gloriously fun film with the smart edge I love. They accommodated my *Sisters* schedule by packing three weeks of work into a few seventeen-hour marathon days.

In 1993, Margo's sister Mici died, which was sad for all of us, but particularly hard on Margo. I tried to find time for her, but she understood that time was hard to come by. She went out of her way to make me feel free to leave, and I went out of my way to take her with me whenever I could. It made our lives immeasurably easier when Perry joined us. He'd been running a health food store in Laguna and bonded with Mici, who came to depend on him during the last years of her life. He was more than a trusted friend; he was her ally and aide-de-camp. It's hard to précis Perry's job description in ten thousand words or less: troubleshooter, office manager, domestic partner, travel cohort, colorist, archivist, accomplice, confidante, spin doctor, inertia disturber, dog wrangler.

There was a time when, if I needed someone to run interference for me on the phone, run errands for me while I worked late or run lines with me when I was cramming, I did what Frankie had always done: I depended on Margo. Perry stepped into her shoes somewhat, bringing a good soul and calming influence as friction between Frankie and me increased along with his need for Margo's attention.

In 1994, I had the opportunity to work with Katharine Hepburn on *One Christmas*, a TV movie adapted from a trio of short stories by Truman Capote. I initially turned it down, telling my agent, "It's impossible." But when I mentioned it to the makeup artist on the *Sisters* set that day, he rousted me bodily from the chair and said, "Call him back! Get out of this chair, call back right now, and say you'll do it. Are you insane?" I immediately came to my senses: this was overwhelmingly likely to be Katharine Hepburn's last film. Of course, *of course*, I had to do it. And conveniently, I knew someone who'd been making impossible things possible from the time he was a teenager.

"Frankie." It felt good to both of us when I turned to him for help. "Logistics issue. How can I commute between L.A. and North Carolina for a month or so?"

Truman Capote's One Christmas *(1994). I was incredibly honored to be with Katharine Hepburn in the last scene she performed on film.*

He called in the sort of favor only flyers can call in. Two or three times a week, I bounded off the *Sisters* set at ten o'clock. Frankie was waiting for me in the car, and we sped to the airport in Burbank where the pilot, Frankie's friend Clay Lacy, was pushing the time limit for takeoff. We flew away, leaving Frankie waving on the tarmac, the same way he used to fly away like a kite on Margo's string. We'd lift off under the stars and drop by Texas for fuel somewhere in the night. I'd wake up in North Carolina (nothing could be finer) in the morning. I'd sprint to the hotel for a quick shower and haul it to the set to get into my meticulously tailored 1930s suits, hair and makeup.

Every day was packed with activity, because they knew I'd have to leave again that night or early the next morning. Clay and his copilot were waiting to fly back to L.A. and deposit me as the sun rose in Burbank, where Frankie was waiting to take me to Warner Brothers so I could start another day on the *Sisters* set. Sela and I were both nominated for Emmys that year, and Sela won, but before I had a chance to stew about it, I was back on an airplane to go make a movie with Katharine Hepburn, which goes a long way toward consoling a girl.

People shook their heads with a mix of awe and apprehension, but I felt energized and exhilarated. Frankie felt heroic again. (I felt a bit heroic myself a few times.) Margo kept us all blissfully on the tight schedule. This was the three of us at our level best.

In the last scene Katharine Hepburn would do on film, she and I are perched on a bronze brocade settee. "I've had a life of no regrets," she says, "and that's what I wish for you, my dear. A life with no regrets."

With Kelly Preston and Laura Dern in Alexander Payne's Citizen Ruth *in 1995.*

MIRAMAX FILMS/KIMBERLY WRIGHT

A year later, during the hiatus before our last season on *Sisters*, I did an indie film called *Citizen Ruth*, written and directed by Alexander Payne (who later did *Sideways* and *The Descendants*) with Kelly Preston and me as militant lesbian partners, Laura Dern as a pregnant, confused, chemically dependent runaway, Mary Kay Place as our clinic-protesting adversary, and Tippi Hedren and Burt Reynolds as two Titans at the center of a pro-choice/pro-life controversy. One would not think it remotely sensible to attempt high camp comedy about abortion, but *Citizen Ruth* manages that while making a rather profound statement that caters to no political agenda and leaves neither side unscathed. The script was intelligently hilarious, and Alexander Payne is from Omaha, where we'd be shooting on location.

The shoot was grueling, especially for Laura, who was fearless and egoless and game every step of the way. The farmhouse where most of the action took place was freezing cold because all the electricity was devoted to sound cables, lights and consoles. Torrential rains created a sea of mud between the house and the no-frills trailers and craft service tent, where we ate grayish chicken thighs and broccoli stems almost every day. It could have been a misery, but it wasn't. It was fun, and the movie is unlike any other movie I've ever done—or seen for that matter. It's one of those unique creative projects, like *Pushing Daisies* and *Cheerleader-Murdering Mom*, where the script is the star. Roger Ebert praised its "reckless courage"; it ruffled some feathers, for obvious reasons, but I was proud to be in it.

While we were shooting, Frankie happened to be in Omaha for the annual meeting of Berkshire Hathaway shareholders, and we went to dinner at a local restaurant. When we first sat down, I was distracted, shifting gears after a long day on the waterlogged

set. One of the producers stopped by our table, and as I introduced Frankie and the two of them chatted for a moment, I was
stricken by the realization that something was wrong. Not rush-
to-the-emergency-room wrong or even go-back-to-your-hotel-
room-and-lie-down wrong. But distinctly off. It was like looking
at the vacant farmhouse, strangely at sea on a muddy swale,
drained of its electricity, fogged in and fragile.

During the labored conversation, it was impossible to ignore
the subtle shift in Frankie's personality or the more obvious gaps
in memory and articulation. That night, I lay in the dark feeling
sad and mystified. I tried to talk to Margo, but she did what she
always did where Frankie was concerned; she kept up the brave
face, assuring me everything was fine, changing the subject like a
magpie moving on to the next shiny object. By the time I got
home, my sadness had crystallized to a fear-based, childish anger.
How dare he be vulnerable like that? How dare he change, as if I
no longer needed him to be Frankie? This was not just some ordinary old man. This was the larger-than-life father under whose
broad steel wings I'd been born, *the majordomo that's known as
the honcho hippo.*

When I returned to work for the final season of *Sisters*, I could
feel the drift in my on-set family as well. We'd run our course,
and it was such a good run, but contracts were coming to an end,
and we were all getting restless, ready to move on. I'd been well
used, and this show had given me so much. I was certain my sisters felt the same way, and I hoped that we would forgive each
other for those moments when battle fatigue got the better of us.
We all have moments when we see our sand castles crumbling,
and we get a bit graspy, which can be as unbecoming as it is futile.

As the show drew to a close, articles were written about the groundbreaking subject matter we'd covered, the awards and nominations for acting, writing and editing, how the complexity of the characters had evolved and the significance of this show in the overarching genre of television drama. Patricia and I wondered wryly where all that laudation was when we really needed it—back in season two, when we were hanging by a thread and being dismissed as a Harlequin romance with tampon commercials.

Something I know because I grew up moving constantly: you learn, as a survival mechanism, to separate from the places you love best. The moment you know you're leaving, there's a devious little spin doctor on your shoulder, whispering, *"It's for the best. This place sucks."* And your need to feel okay about moving on begins to fill in the blanks, grasping every irritating detail, no matter how small, planting them like grains of sand in your shoe so that by the time you have to say good-bye, you've convinced yourself that what you feel is relief instead of grieving—until later on, when the grieving eventually demands its due. (Multiply that dynamic times ten thousand when applied to separating from people you love.)

At the end of the day, we were a family. We rose up for each other when someone was having a bad day. We pulled together—even through difficulties and the intrinsically competitive environment of the industry—to do the work that would only work if we did it together. It was a sob fest shooting the last scene. A major part of our lives was coming to a close.

The pace after the show wrapped was more relentless than ever, because now I was searching for a steady succession of smaller jobs to replace this one huge job, and Frankie, whom I'd always depended on for moral support and a strong sounding board, was the opposite of all that. During the last year or so of *Sisters*, the terrifying change in his personality progressed, circling tighter and darker until he was an absent, angry stranger who flew into a rage over everything and nothing. It was impossible to reason with him, impossible to ignore him, impossible to have a conversation with him, impossible for him to sit quietly.

He'd always been fastidious about personal grooming and hygiene, but now he entered a gray area where he was no longer handling it properly but angrily rejected the slightest insinuation that he might be slipping. If Margo or I gently inquired, "Frankie, do you need to visit the bathroom?" his embarrassment would instantly touch off a brush fire of indignant wrath. He was enraged that we would insult him so, that we would even suggest he was forgetting himself in some vital personal way. *What kind of idiots—*

Margo and I didn't know how to bring in help when Frankie was so vehemently opposed to it, and the two of us were not emotionally or physically equipped to handle him, because he was not about to *be* handled by us or anyone else. After a series of upsetting incidents, the situation breached one evening when I found feces smeared across the walls in the hallway. In less than a moment, Frankie and I were engaged in a horrific screaming match. *What the hell is wrong with you don't you even with me what the hell is why why why would you where do you get off accusing even know what don't you fucking talk to me like can't deal with your shit you know goddamn well I did not then who did it nothing to do with*—and more meaningless word storm. I wrenched a knife out of the block and cast it in the sink, not knowing if I wanted to stick it in his arm or my own.

"This is insane, this is insane." I covered my face with my

hands, wrecked and winded, clinging to the edge of a cliff. Margo stood between us, trying to keep things from escalating. I wheeled on her and said, "It's him or me, Margo. I don't want to leave you here alone with him, but I cannot do this anymore."

Not knowing how to respond, Margo pulled into herself like a little box turtle. Lacking any coherent input from me or the honcho hippo, she flailed for the best solution she could think of and made the decision to move Frankie to a nearby rental house they owned. By nightfall the following day, she'd installed him there with comfortable furnishings, his favorite chair, and a TV he could blast to his heart's content.

"So I've been exiled," he said bitterly.

Margo begged him not to think of it that way.

"Put out to pasture then."

"Frankie. You'll see. It'll be better this way," I said. "We can all take a deep breath and figure out what's best for everyone. We can talk about it later. When I get back. I have to go, but if you need—"

"I don't."

"Okay. Well. I need to get some sleep."

Margo and I closed the door and walked home in the dark and cried in the resounding quiet. This wasn't how anyone wanted this to be, but no one had ever brought up the subject of how we *did* want it to be. We were completely open with each other about so many things. I'd seen my parents naked as a child. I'd heard them fight and make up. They were well acquainted with all my personal and professional affairs. We had shared happiness and heartache of all the usual varieties. I could have asked Frankie and Margo anything, but it never even occurred to me to ask, *How does this story end?*

One morning he fell and struck the back of his head, and the injury was serious enough that the choice was made for us; he could never be left alone again. He was forced to allow full-time caregivers to come in. We found two male aids who were strong and dependable and willing to tag team in twelve-hour shifts. Frankie settled into an unhappy but functional stasis. Margo was deeply sad but remained tragically chipper, as if she was on a war-bond drive. Perry was Mr. Indispensable, my eyes and right hand at both houses while I was away on location. I felt rotten about the whole thing, but I did what I always had done, sunny skies or gray: I worked.

I went to Vancouver to do a remake of *Harvey*, which should have been better than it was. The script is classic. The director was a legendary *Playhouse 90* alumnus. My costars were funny, funny men. It didn't air and didn't air, and finally did air, buried in some under-the-cellar time slot. Which was a mercy. Frankie and I watched it together, and I told him, "I knew it was slow, but I didn't know it was *that* slow. Now I understand why they didn't want it to see the light of day."

Next box on the flow chart: playing the divorce attorney who goes up against the honesty-impaired Jim Carrey in *Liar, Liar*. This was a pretty beefy role in the original script, but while we were shooting in the courtroom, the director pulled me aside and told me that some of my scenes were being cut. I could make excuses, I suppose—the situation at home, the fact that I was exhausted because I was also shooting a TV show in front of a live audience that week. Bottom line, I was feeling a bit sullen and not "giving good set," as we say, which is very unlike me and impossible to maintain when you're on the set with someone like Jim.

So we were doing take after take of a heated little face-off:

HIM (TO MEG TILLY): *"Now, let's see. Weight . . . 105?*
    Yeah. In your bra."
ME: *"Your honor, I object!"*
HIM: *"You would."*
ME: *"Bastard!"*
HIM: *"Hag!"*

We experimented with a variety of invectives.

"Hog!"
"Cow!"
"Hack!"
"Jezebel!"

Makeup people stepped in to blot us down, and the director, Tom Shadyac, came over and whispered in my ear. We started the next take:

JIM: *"Weight . . . 105? Yeah. In your bra."*
ME: *"Your honor, I object!"*
JIM: *"You would."*
ME: *"Overactor!"*

And then we were all howling with laughter, including Jim, who threw his arms around me. They ended up including this moment in a montage of outtakes during the end credits, and to this day, it's what people remember most about my part in this movie. They shout out to me on the street: "Overactor!" Anyway, I'm certain there's a metaphor there. Something about the un-scripted moments in life and the efficacy of being able to laugh at oneself, or perhaps it's as simple as "What goes around comes around." I didn't have time to process it at the time; I had to sprint back to the TV series—a short-lived sitcom called *Party Girl* with Christine Taylor, who's terrific, but the show was one of those confections that seems to have the right ingredients until it falls flat in the oven.

I also had a recurring role on *Suddenly Susan*, playing Brooke Shields's mother, and I was happy to be called in for that because I so enjoy being around her. She has a philosophical survivor's-eye-view of life and the industry, so we laugh a lot, exchanging our war stories. Brooke told me she did an audition where she came in, set her purse down, read the scene. They said great and they'd be in touch, but as she got to the door, one of the producers said, "God bless you."

"I knew I'd never hear from them again," she said.

"I've learned over the years that I'm screwed if they say, 'You're a *brilliant* actress,'" I said. "It's like they're giving me a little something to take with me. Like a game show where they send the loser off with a lovely parting gift."

I told her about a movie with Jane Fonda and Robert De Niro—*Stanley & Iris*—which was quite a meaty role when it was offered to me. I played Jane's sister in the accidentally prophetic script about family members crammed into a small house, driving each other crazy. It was written by Harriet Frank Jr. and Irving Ravetch, who'd written *Norma Rae*, so expectations were high, even some dare to dream about the Oscars. We were rehearsing in Connecticut, and late one night, while I was out for a brisk walk around the chilly parking lot, I came upon Irving, who was also taking the evening air.

We greeted each other, and he said, "Great work today."

"Thanks," I said. "Great scenes."

And then he said, "Just remember, whatever happens . . . you're *great*."

I instantly knew I was hearing the hiss of the guillotine right before my head rolled across the cutting room floor.

"Ultimately," I said to Brooke, "there's no good way to be told something you don't want to hear."

Another accidental prophesy.

In October 1996, I was in L.A., shooting a Lifetime movie called *Little Girls in Pretty Boxes*. Coming home from the set at dusk on Halloween, I carefully wove through the neighborhood. The streets were busy with trick-or-treaters, the sidewalks bobbing with flashlights. *Suddenly Susan* was scheduled to be aired that night, and I was hoping I'd get home in time to see it.

As I pulled into the driveway, I saw my manager waiting for me, and because I am the daughter of Frankie and Margo Kurtz, I felt an optimistic surge of excitement. I thought, "He must have great news! He came all the way over to tell me in person." But then I drew close enough to see the expression on his face.

I ran toward him across the yard, saying, "Oh, God—not Margo! Not Margo!"

He shook his head. "Frankie."

"And when that happens, I know it," Truman Capote wrote at the end of his lovely Christmas story. "A message saying so merely confirms a piece of news some secret vein had already received, severing from me an irreplaceable part of myself, letting it loose like a kite on a broken string."

Frank Kurtz, September 9, 1911–October 31, 1996

COURTESY OF THE AUTHOR

CHAPTER ELEVEN

Heartbreak and Daisies

———— ∞ ————

California, 1939

Something that happened in the early days of our flying to-gether:

It was an early morning flight, and for some reason Frank was taking me quite high. I didn't know what he had in mind—maybe some stunting, because it always requires alti-tude. Then in case something goes wrong—a spin which won't unwind, for example—a pilot can bail out with safety because he has enough altitude left to get the chute open.

At 10,000 feet it was chilly in the open cockpit, with fog still camouflaging the sun. The beady dampness had crept inside my flying suit. Frank was giving me instructions over the interphone. He was going to fly blind. I was to be check pilot, and waggle the wings or take over the controls in case he was not flying level. Now I felt important. I had a title, and duties. Frank always gives me a title, and the job always is part of what he is doing.

I adjusted my goggles after cleaning them thoroughly. There must be no slips. Then, since Frank always manages to be as sweet as he is severe, he turned the controls over to me, "to see if you will be as hot a pilot as you are a check pilot," giving me the compass course, and instructions to "take 'er in" to Palm Springs.

While Frank rested, I flew until we were square in the middle of San Jacinto Pass, one of the roughest in the United States. The San Jack mountains jut up on each side, 12,000 to 14,000 feet high, and the down drafts have a pull that makes any aircraft seem puny.

Suddenly our plane drops, the endless drop of a nightmare; you hold to the stick because there is nothing else to hold to, and it seems to lift up out of its socket, lift with your stomach. Just as suddenly as it started, the down draft stops. My stomach goes down now, while everything else in the plane soars up.

Frank had told me of his encounter with those giants who reach up with strong claw-hands and pull aviators to their death. He did what saved his life; he dropped the nose and dived with the force which was pulling him down. Riding downward into that vacuum, he could gain control of the plane, and at the right moment pull it up and out into free air.

In my notebook I had written his exact words: "You see,

Margo, you never fight something which is stronger than you."

We had to go down with this thing, down until we could right our small strength, and pull up from ruin.

Margo wakes up in a downdraft. We see her in the grainy window of the baby monitor, struggling to sit up, clutching Randall to her breast.

"Oh, no!" she cries out. "Oh, God, he's not responding!"

Angela quickly rinses her hands under the kitchen faucet and says, "I got it." I take over lunch preparations while she helps Margo through the loo rituals and into a fresh bathrobe, which takes quite a while, so by the time we're together at the table, the home health nurse arrives at the front door. The vitals-taking ritual commences in congress with the med-taking ritual and the making of coffee.

"How are you feeling this afternoon, Margo?" asks the nurse.

"Like someone stuffed me in an envelope. Filled it out. Sent it off," Margo says.

"Well, you've got the blood pressure and oxygen levels of a high school football player." The nurse records the readings on a chart beside the celebratory notation: "XL beamer!" She checks my blood pressure and Angela's before announcing, "Margo, you're the winner again."

"Those Omaha women," I say.

Margo presses the back of my hand to her lips and tells me, "I am honored to know you. And so happy you're my wife."

"I'm happy about that too," I tell her, understanding exactly what *wife* means in the iconography of this moment.

Margo always crafted her own definitions, particularly when it came to defining herself and the role she played in the lives of the people she loved, and I've come to appreciate the reality that all those roles and modifiers are fluid. Frankie's final year was a terrible struggle with that dynamic. Despite all his certitude about who and what he was (or perhaps because of it), I believe he was more comfortable with the eventuality of dying than he was with the possibility of lingering in a life that no longer felt purposeful.

The day before the day he died, Frankie went for a walk, as he did every day, with one of the brawny young caregivers who were in place twenty-four/seven after he fell and hit his head.

"Do you think I should go on doing this?" Frankie asked.

I don't know how the aide answered or how I would have answered had Frankie put the question to me. I think I would have given the coward's answer: an upbeat *Don't even think about it!*— because that would have come off as good humored and casual and less childish than *Don't leave me.*

The next day, they returned from their walk, and Frankie settled in his recliner.

"I thought the colonel was just having a nap," the aide told us later.

Frankie had made his preferences very clear in properly documented advance directives: there were to be no extreme measures, but when the aide realized Frankie wasn't responding, he called paramedics, who were working on Frankie when Margo arrived, and because we weren't as organized then as we are now, she didn't know where the documents were, so they flailed away on him, trying to revive him, jarring his reluctant heart, shoving air (it could no longer be called breath) in and out of his lungs.

Ironically, Frankie was too tough for them. He resolutely remained dead.

The ambulance whisked him off to the hospital, and Perry tore back to Margo's house for the DNR papers. Perry told me that when he got to the house, the sloping lawn was covered with gray mourning doves. As he sprinted to the front door, they startled up, and the air was full of wings. We went to the morgue and stared at the paperwork. Came home and stared at food. *Suddenly Susan* came on, and we stared at me on TV in a poignant episode about Susan being tragi-comically tormented by guilt after neglecting her father.

The day someone dies can so easily become a litany of terrible details, small things that take on prescience and irony like a rowboat taking on water. Wisely, Margo buried what didn't honor Frankie; she kept the doves. And I too like that part of the story. *The Doves That Came When My Father Died*. We felt great significance in their presence, the way they mate for life, the sky full of wings.

I was twelve when Daddy Art died. Margo and I were out grocery shopping. I remember that when we pulled up in front of the house in Omaha, I checked the time because I wasn't going to school then, and I wanted to know if the kids would be coming home soon. It was ten minutes after three. Margo said to me, "I have the strangest feeling. Like something's been lifted from my shoulders. Out of nowhere—this lightness." As we carried our groceries into the house, the phone rang. Daddy Art had died at ten minutes after three.

Margo was given to this sort of metaphysical engagement; this kind of thing was rare enough to be special, but not especially rare. Frankie was always quick to diagnose vivid imagination or gas, and I'm no more prescient than he was, but I always wanted to believe in womanly intuition, spirits among us, unseen workings in the universe. When Frankie died, I waited for the lightness—longed for it—but my father's passing felt just the opposite to me. The weight of this loss piled like a millstone on top of all the frustration of the preceding year, and on top of that was my deep fear for Margo.

I kept thinking of Gigi in the wake of Daddy Art's death. The joy went out of her. She was exhausted by grief. The liquor was kept in a little room off the kitchen. (We called it the "butler's pantry," not that we ever had a butler.) Gigi visited that doorway with increasing frequency, as if she was visiting an old friend she could sit with and reminisce. No one else could truly know her secrets or keep her stories. Daddy Art was her history, and he was gone. Gigi had always enjoyed her bourbon, but it was different now—the needy shame with which she scuffed ice out of the tray and poured one more, one more, one more—while Margo tried to cajole the bottle away from her.

Margo didn't want to leave her. Gigi had never lived alone a day in her life. Her house had always been a hub, a spark plug, a parlor for cardsharps, a great long table for Thanksgiving dinner. But it was getting close to the time I'd have to start school. Frankie missed us, and Gigi readily told Margo that our life was with him. Gigi had always been a feisty, self-sufficient broad who rode bucking broncos and never fell behind on a hike or a hunt.

You go on now. I'll be fine.

She'd survived a number of harrowing maladies in her life—including the famous goiter, the colostomy, cancer, her own vices—but the loss of Daddy Art removed the invincible core that made her *Gigi* and kept her on her feet all those years. Her weaknesses ganged up on her. She died one year after Daddy Art, almost to the day, and that year was a physical and emotional trial.

Margo was quietly unbreakable in the wake of Frankie's passing. Art Sulzberger called from the *New York Times*. "Your husband was a remarkable man," he said, and that meant a lot to her. Robert McG. Thomas Jr. wrote a lengthy obituary for the *Times*. *People* magazine did a three-page story. Margo made sure everyone had all the correct information and photos. There was no military pomp and circumstance for Frankie. We're not funeral people. We sent out an austere memorial note with a photograph of Frankie soaring through the air in perfect dive form.

Margo and I shared many a good, hard cry, but we were honest with ourselves; we were grateful that it went down the way it did. The prospect of Frankie continuing his downward spiral had terrified us, and I suspect it terrified Frankie even more. Maybe because he was not lovingly mothered as a child, or maybe because he was Frankie, it was torturous for him to be recast as the diapered supplicant. The renegotiation of his dignity was intolerably stressful because pride—machismo even—was so key to his identity. Sustained fragility takes a different kind of strength. I didn't know then if Margo would have it in her.

"It was a lean life, and bright, and high. We'll never outlive it, never want to," she'd written in her book. But Frankie did outlive it, and now she would outlive it alone. Or she wouldn't.

Margo and I cocooned briefly after Frankie's death, then she picked herself up and forged on like Jackie Kennedy while I went back to work on *Pretty Boxes*. Busier is better. That's how we do in my family. During *Sisters*, I'd gotten one great offer after another. I could afford to be choosy, and I chose to work my tail off. Part of this life is the constant feeling that whatever show you're working on is probably the last time anyone will call you, notice you or take you to lunch. Beyond that scroll of end credits or that final curtain, there lies an abyss known as *between jobs*; the worst thing I could imagine would be falling into it.

"I feel like an acting machine," I told Margo after *Pretty Boxes* wrapped, and I should have known that would jinx me. The next year was fairly quiet. I might have been busier if I'd stayed in New York, but I decided to headquarter in L.A. While the tide was out, I finally had time to work on my house, which was also a nice creative endeavor for Margo, but I was always holding my breath, waiting for a play—make that *the* play—that would move me forward in a creative way I couldn't articulate but knew I was ready for. That perfect role. ("Is that so much to ask?" I keep asking, knowing that it is.) Of course, in my florid dreams, someone would lay this Heaven-sent script at my feet and invite me to step into it. That did not happen. Instead, my manager laid the script on my desk and told me I'd have to work for it. And it wasn't one perfect role, it was two.

In the production notes, *The Mineola Twins* is described thusly: "A comedy in six scenes, four dreams and seven wigs. There are two ways to produce this play: (1) with good wigs; or (2) with bad wigs. The second way is preferred. Myrna and Myra, identical twins, battle each other through the Eisenhower, Nixon and Reagan/Bush years over virginity, Vietnam and Family Values." On the front of the script were the words "DRAFT SIXTEEN"—which was extraordinary, I thought, first because the playwright had put it through such an arduous process and even more because she was willing to say so on the front of the script. In this remarkable play, Paula Vogel, who'd recently won a Pulitzer for *How I Learned to Drive*, blurred all boundaries, real

"There are two ways to produce this play: (1) with good wigs; or (2) with bad wigs. The second way is preferred." As Myra and Myrna (with Mo Gaffney as both my boyfriends) in The Mineola Twins *in 1999.*

JOAN MARCUS

or imagined, between time, gender, morality, plurality, sexuality and logistics. She cut political and cultural constructs into a string of paper dolls, paying no attention (as far as I could see) to conventional wisdom or the laws of physics.

As I turned the pages, knuckles as white as if I was on a rollercoaster, I stopped trying to count the lightning-fast costume changes. (There are seventeen.) Three actresses are cast as six characters: the twins, their lovers, and their sons. The actress playing Myrna and Myra is tasked with taking two polar opposite characters through ages fifteen to fifty-five in two hours, transitioning backstage in a matter of seconds from a busty Sandra Dee teenager to a Patty Hearst–prototypical bank robber, a right-wing Christian radio host, a lesbian radical, an abortion clinic bomber, a lunatic dancing in a straight jacket. With the exception of those inconceivably quick changes, either Myrna or Myra is onstage at all times throughout the entire play, making it as physically and mentally demanding as a one-woman show. For anyone ambitious enough to take it on, this play would be the artistic and dramaturgic equivalent of a ten-meter platform dive.

I called my manager. Breathless. "It's Everest! Like my own little *Hamlet*. We have to make it happen."

We knew *The Mineola Twins* was too peculiar for Broadway, but Roundabout Theater Company had an off-Broadway production in the works with Joe Mantello directing. The show wasn't being offered to me, but they wanted to do a reading, and I volunteered. I poured all my time and energy into preparation. I'd done some huge roles before, but this was beyond the beyond. Part of the thrill was genuinely not knowing if I could summon the physical and vocal stamina to pull it off and then discovering through months of coaching and rehearsal that I could. A role like this doesn't come down the pike very often, and when it does, it sure as hell doesn't get offered to a fifty-four-year-old woman, but even more than winning the opportunity to do it, I needed to prove to myself that I was still capable of the creative growth and physical conditioning required to run this marathon. (In retrospect, the dreaded ebb tide was probably a gift that allowed me to be still and gather my strength.)

Margo and I hadn't been apart much since Frankie died, but she was completely in my corner, as they'd both always been. She held down the fort in L.A. while I went to New York and did the reading, which was more upscale than your usual audition, but every bit as nerve scorching. Joe called me afterward and said, "You have to do this play." I was cast, with Mo Gaffney playing my lovers, male and female, and Mandy Siegfried playing the two rebellious sons.

We started rehearsals in the dead of winter in a huge, drafty space on the twelfth floor of a huge, drafty building near Times Square. This was an almost perfect marriage of script, director and actors. Joe Mantello was spectacularly imaginative with the staging. I couldn't have asked for better company, from his sure helm to the two wonderful girls who stripped, dressed and wigged me during the quick changes. (I still think of them fondly every time I hear the peppermill rasp of Velcro separating.)

The complex staging was very ambitious for the little Laura Pels Theatre, which had very little wing space and closed down shortly after our run. (I seem to have that effect, don't I? I do a show and hear a few months later, "Oh, that old firetrap, yes, they're tearing that place down.") It made for some iffy moments. There was a heavy twelve-foot plank that sailed down with a backdrop, functioning as a bank counter. When the lights came up, I'd be standing there with Mandy, and my opening line was, "I hate this bank." But one night during previews, the lights came up, and there was a suspended moment of *something* that made Mandy and me step back just as the bulky set piece crashed to the floor where our little feet had been. There was an audience-wide sphincter response, but then I inadvertently brought down the house by saying without a missed beat, "I hate this bank!" In another scene, Mo and I were supposed to cruise in on a big double bed, but for some reason, the thing lurched along as if we were driving an Edsel and didn't know when to clutch. We finally slipped out of bed and pushed it down center, scrambled back under the covers and commenced the scene as if nothing had happened.

The show is filled with parlor tricks and sleight of hand (including a moment when the audience gasped, thinking for a split second that they were seeing two of me onstage at once), but all that aside, I think the greatest gymnastic feat of *The Mineola Twins* is the way it skewers politics of all persuasions and manages to show us how these two women from one cell could grow to hate each other and how two women who hate each other could long for each other at the same time. This play is political satire at its best because it's so unsparingly funny, and it is feminism at its best because it genuinely loves and celebrates women but doesn't allow us to suffer any fools, including ourselves. It's a profound statement about the clashing ideals and supposed "wars" between women who've chosen different directions for their lives—which always baffled me, because Margo and I never judged each other that way; her love and acceptance came back to her because it taught me to be loving and accepting, and as I took that out into the world, it came back to me.

The moment was right for *The Mineola Twins.* Audiences loved the show and the critics loved me. I wish I could say I don't care (and if they'd panned me, I would probably convince myself that I didn't), but I'd been absent from the New York stage for almost a decade. This was a joyful, triumphant way to return. It would have been ungrateful not to wallow in sweetly fulsome satisfaction as the production was showered with awards and nominations, including another Obie for me, and the day the Obie was announced, I also got the call that *Love & Money,* a pilot I'd shot earlier, had been picked up for thirteen episodes.

Margo and I decided to celebrate with a trip to Hawaii before I started shooting again, and while we were there, we took in a Rolling Stones concert. The last concert I'd gone to before this, if memory serves, was Randy Newman at Avery Fisher Hall in 1983. So I had no idea that we were all standing up these days. Standing through the entire show, not just the high moments or big numbers. About forty minutes in, I was dying to sit down, thinking, "How can this be? The Stones are older than me, for God's sake! Surely, they'll be needing a nap or some heroin or *something* soon."

I tried to use my eighty-four-year-old mother as a human shield.

"Mommie, don't you want to sit down? Really. It's okay. I don't mind."

Margo would have none of that. She was grooving on the Stones, zeroing in particularly on Keith Richards, whom she found magnetic and sexy, and she was not the least bit interested in sitting down with her decrepit daughter. Time and again during the endless evening, I begged, I sat, I tried to pull her into the seat next to me, but she continued to dance in place, waving her arms erratically to the music, just like I had done as a teenager when Margo and Frankie searched out a motel where I could see Elvis on TV. Perhaps this was payback.

We had *fun*. The two of us. We were making new lives for ourselves, and it was fine, and it was fun, and we would be all right. Frankie had been gone for three years now, but we spoke of him often, keeping him close to the surface of our hearts and conversations. Margo was healthy and happy, eager to travel, showing no signs of slowing down. Her greatest fear had been with her since she was twenty: the very real possibility of Frankie's death. It had happened, and she'd survived it. A new century was about to begin, and Margo saw herself in it, vital, creative, needed and loved. She was grateful for every day, which made hanging out with her a pleasure. Everyone who met her came away with a sense of "*that* is how you do eighty-four." (In fact, that is how you do fifty-four. Or twenty-four or fourteen.)

Back in L.A., we finally moved into my house, bringing with us many of the old Japanese pieces Frankie and Margo had brought home from Japan in the 1950s, including the inscrutable fisherman on his little wooden scaffold and a heavy black chest of drawers that fit perfectly in the entryway across from the foot of the floating staircase. Margo settled in a downstairs bedroom, and I took the one upstairs, thinking it would be more comfortable for Margo and more private for me if I happened to have a gentleman caller.

The open air and practicality of the place was the polar opposite of my apartment in New York, which was beginning to feel cluttered and in need of updating. It wasn't sensible for me to be so homesick for the place. There's more money in film and television than you'll ever find between the catwalks and curtains of a New York playhouse. Broadway dressing rooms could be called "shabby chic," on a good day but are just plain shabby compared to the accommodations at Warner Brothers. Nonetheless, I felt myself keeping an eye out for another great script, knowing how hard it would be to top the last one.

We shot our thirteen episodes of *Love & Money*, a sitcom with a sweet premise: WASPish penthouse dwellers with a beautiful daughter, salt-of-the-earth building super with a handsome son, connect the dots. I was the Hervé Léger–clad, martini-swizzling WASP mother, David Ogden Stiers was my husband, and our beautiful daughter was played by Paget Brewster—a pro and someone I always click with. Paget and I were sent off to New York on a press junket to promote the show, and while we were there, we got a call from a PR person at Paramount.

"This is going to sound like *bad* news," she said, "but it's actually *good* news."

Has any good news ever followed that sort of preface? Ever—in the history of news? In the history of *good*? Certainly, in my experience, if it quacks like bad news . . . you get the picture.

The impending doom of our dear little show was spun to Paget and me as "finding a better time slot"—because they were expecting us to continue the junket with game faces firmly in place, which we did, but Paget and I had both done enough pilots to know for whom the bell tolls. We laughed about it, actually, and made the most of our trip to New York. I suppose shooting thirteen episodes and having only three air is as close as I'll get to my dream of simply rehearsing for a living. Next box on the flow chart, please.

Shortly thereafter, I was offered the role of Beaver Mother on a cartoon called *The Two Beavers*. Then Joe Mantello asked me to come back to New York and do *The Vagina Monologues*.

"Coincidence?" I said to Margo. "Or is the universe trying to tell me something?"

"Who can say?" she laughed.

Audra McDonald, Julie Kavner and I were to be the first rotating cast to perform Eve Ensler's infamously fabulous one-woman show. Having three actors performing the script brought another dimension to this play that was already a wall mover in the same way that *Uncommon Women* was in its day. It didn't seem so long ago that people were up in arms about the *Sisters* orgasm conversation; now I would be onstage—as myself, not hiding behind a character—in front of the New York theatre audience saying "twat," "come" and "clitoris" (does anyone actually say "clitoris" in real life?) and demonstrating seventeen different orgasmic moans in what came to be known as the "The Moanologue." (The climax of the evening—*ba-dum-bum-CHHH!*)

We were to have exactly one day of rehearsal in New York, so it was up to me to prepare for this in L.A. But how? Workmen were still in and out of the house all day. Our new address wasn't in an area you generally see featured on the Hollywood Star Maps, so the neighbors were very impressed to have the respected actress Swoosie Kurtz on their street. I was reluctant to destroy the illusion with my backyard interpretation of Marilyn Chambers in *Insatiable II*. My solution was to drive back and forth several times a day through Coldwater Canyon, car windows up, practicing my various forms of vocalized pleasure with as much abandon as I could while keeping an eye out lest a busload of tourists pull up alongside me.

The next few years kept us busy. While I traveled to New York and various film locations, Margo held down the fort in L.A. She was writing again, and though it was more for pleasure than publication, she was diligent about it, laboring over stories in longhand on yellow tablets and handing them over to Perry, who dutifully typed them up. They bore titles like "A Ring of Energy" and "The Purple Suit" and spoke mostly of small things she'd done and seen. She saw no need to endow these details of her life with any particular significance; the stories needed no excuse for being other than the exercise of her lyrical language, like a ballerina stretching her legs, and the simple postscript: "This is part of my journey."

I made *Bubble Boy*, playing Jake Gyllenhaal's mother as a Pat Nixon/Betty Crocker hybrid, and though the finished product went somewhat more to the scatological than the original script indicated, it was great fun and had a sweet spirit at heart. That original script prompted me to contemplate the bubble of my own childhood, how it had protected me as I bounced and floated through a sometimes-hostile world.

"But it also isolated you," Ethel the Oracle is quick to point out. "Perhaps, more than you like to acknowledge."

"We got hats!" I tell her. "The *Bubble Boy* cast and crew. We got hats, and I gave them to my plumber's kids. They were big, big *Bubble Boy* fans. So that was nice."

"Yes," she says. "Very nice."

While I was getting into makeup and a red carpet cocktail dress for the *Bubble Boy* premiere, I got a call from Konrad, who wanted to send over a script for *Rules of Attraction*, a horridly funny movie based on the novel by Bret Easton Ellis.

"They want to start shooting tomorrow," he said, and before I could tell him it was impossible, he added, "Trust me on this one. It's just a couple of scenes, but these are really good scenes—one great scene with Faye Dunaway."

Margo had been having trouble sleeping, and I knew she was planning to try Ambien that evening, so . . . okay, now I had two reasons to get home early, I decided. And I did try, but it was a late night. When I pulled into the driveway, the house alarm was at a full scream, and Margo was on her way down the sidewalk in her nightgown. I leaped out of the driver's seat and went after her as quickly as I could, mincing across the lawn in my hostile red carpet heels.

"Margo! Margo, what are you doing?"

Now, this could happen to anyone, really. Technology, right? And Ambien. Two dots that probably should not be connected. Whatever. All I could do at that moment was help Margo find her way back to bed and catch a few hours of sleep myself before heading over to the Ritz Carlton to act like I was getting smashed in a bar with Faye Dunaway. That was the reality of my life. And it was fine. We were still having fun. We would laugh about this later, I was certain, and we did laugh—and that drunk scene with Dunaway is the most tragically hilarious drunk scene I've ever participated in—but a seed of uncertainty started germinating in the back of my mind. I wasn't sure how much longer I'd be able to leave home with the peace of mind I'd been taking for granted.

I was still in L.A. two weeks later, on September 11. My heart was torn in two. It was agony not knowing what was happening at home in New York, who might be hurt or killed, but I was so grateful to be in L.A. with Margo. If she'd seen all that on television knowing I was there in the middle of it, that would have put her through Pearl Harbor all over again. We sat close together in front of the television, staring at the city we loved, cycling hourly through the seven stages of grief.

But after the holidays, as the dust settled, we agreed I should go home. The theatre community in New York faced a terrible struggle. I wanted to do what I could do to help, as a body in the audience and a name onstage. The Flea Theater had been doing a two-hander called *The Guys* since December. Based on playwright Anne Nelson's personal experience, it's a conversation between a fire captain who lost most of his men on 9/11 and a journalist who's helping him write their eulogies. The rotating cast began with Sigourney Weaver and Bill Murray, then Susan Sarandon and Anthony LaPaglia. I offered to come in and was paired with Tim Robbins. The show was a gift for me and for a lot of other people in New York and beyond, who needed to laugh so we could breathe again and needed to cry so we could move on.

Several of my friends were doing a Broadway revival of *Morning's at Seven*, and I left *The Guys* just in time to see them open. I bumped into director Jack O'Brien there, and that's how I happened to do Nora Ephron's *Imaginary Friends*. Jack told me later, "I saw you and said, 'She's our Lillian.'"

Truthfully, this made no sense to me. I don't resemble Lillian Hellman, physically or vocally, and I knew this for a fact, because I'd met her years before when she and Richard Avedon came to see *Virginia Woolf* at the Long Wharf Theatre. They met us in a dark cocktail lounge afterward, and she said to me, "Oh, darling, you were absolutely wonderful. Your facial expressions. Where's my vodka?" This is not a moment one forgets.

Thirty years later, I peered into the bathroom mirror, trying to recapture her farsighted squint and cigarette tenor.

"Wonderful facial expressions. Where's my vodka?"

"What did we do to deserve each other?" "Everything, apparently."
The magnificent Cherry Jones as Mary McCarthy and me as Lillian
Hellman in Nora Ephron's Imaginary Friends *on Broadway in 2002.*

JOAN MARCUS

No. I did not see it. I watched hours of interviews, observing her sounds and rhythms and facial expressions, thinking all the while, *Doesn't anyone else see that this is wildly miscast?* When I expressed these doubts to Jack O'Brien, he said, "We don't want you to be an impersonator." But I was playing *her*, not someone like her.

So get her essence, I decided. The play takes place in the afterlife. What goes with us there? Not our bodies. Not our voices. We take with us exactly what we leave behind: the singular spirit of who we are.

I read all of her stuff over and over again, trying to take her in by osmosis. I studied her testimony before the House Committee on Un-American Activities, one of the most terrifying episodes in American history. Knowing she'd be blacklisted from Hollywood, she refused to testify and wrote in a letter to the HUAC: "To hurt innocent people whom I knew many years ago in order to save myself is, to me, inhuman and indecent and dishonorable. I cannot and will not cut my conscience to fit this year's fashions."

Nora Ephron's script captures all that in a small but spiny vignette, and how Lillian handles herself in that chilling moment taught me so much about when you're terrified at the deepest level, your guts melting, your brain racing, making a case for why you're not going to cede your soul to the downdraft, doing it with authority and strength. Twenty-seven years later, almost blind and in failing health, she saw Mary McCarthy on television, telling Dick Cavett that Lillian Hellman was overrated and "every word she writes is a lie, including 'and' and 'the.'" According to legend, Lillian sat up and laughed in disbelief when she heard it, but then she stewed on it overnight. By the next morning, she was pissed as a newt and on the phone to her lawyer.

When we started rehearsals, I felt I had a grasp on it, and
Cherry Jones was magnificent, so the collaborative energy began
to hum. Nora was thrilled with the first reading. We opened in
San Diego to work out the kinks, then moved to Broadway. Before the first previews, Cherry and I were out on the sidewalk,
checking out the marquee, and she dryly observed, "Ninety bucks
a head. We'd better be good."

During one of the first performances, I was backstage on a
platform for a quick change. Three dressers manhandled me into
a wig and a little sailor dress for a musical number called "The
Fig Tree Rag," and I headed for a ladder to make my entrance,
but I missed the step and landed hard on my right knee. The impact knocked the wind out of me. I felt it from the back of my
neck to the tips of my tingling toes. A drawstring of agony drew
me into a tight ball on the floor.

"No, no, please! It can't be!"

Stagehands and dressers were immediately dragging me to
my feet, fixing my wig and dabbing tears away from my makeup,
whispering concern and encouragement as they hoisted me up to
make my entrance. That's how it works. An unvoiced alarm rip-
ples through the dark silence backstage—*Man down! Man
down!*—a shared adrenaline rush grips every midsection, because
we've all seen it happen and constantly pray it won't happen to us.
The pain has to be postponed. There's no lack of compassion, but
the show quite literally must go on. My only battle injury previous
to this was during *A History of the American Film*; I pulled the
trigger on a gun-shaped cigarette lighter, and searing flash pow-
der sprayed my face. That time and this time, whatever god is in
charge of such things moved me like a marionette through a

stunted choreography of the musical number and back off the stage where ice and painkillers were waiting. This business is not for sissies. I think Lillian Hellman would agree.

The theater kindly provided me with a car during the run so I wouldn't have to hobble after a taxi every night. When Margo came up to see the show, she made quite an impression on the driver.

"I gotta tell you. I'll never forget your mom," he said after she went back to L.A.

"I hear that a lot," I said, and I did. (I still do.)

"No, I mean it," he said with great seriousness. "She did something for me. I had one of the worst days of my life and was feeling pretty devastated. The way she said what she said—it changed my whole day, my whole outlook."

I've come to understand that Margo has always moved through the world with an extraordinary kind of creativity—a kind of 960-degree vision—beyond the full circle. She was able to intuit the story that went deeper than that. She never cast a person as a prop or extra in the Margo Show. She recognized that *she* was a moment in *his* life, and she cared enough to make that moment sing. I can strive to practice that emotional art form, but Margo had an innate talent for it. A bit of her singular spirit remains with so many people she met in her long journey. When I took her to the annual Berkshire Hathaway stockholder's meeting in Omaha a few years ago, Warren Buffett took the two of us to lunch at his country club, then drove us around on a merry tour of their old stomping grounds. The family connection was no longer there (Susie had died, and they had separated long before that), but he treated Margo with such deference and affection.

What goes around comes around, as they say, and in Margo's world, what goes around is unequivocating respect and friendship whether she's riding around with Warren Buffet or a New York cabbie.

After *Imaginary Friends*, I shuttled back and forth a bit between coasts, keeping one eye on Margo, who was still insistently on her own. Her cadre of acquaintances from the military days had dwindled over the years, but Perry was there working, and our new neighbors were lovely people, so I felt comfortable signing on to do another Broadway play. I'd been approached to do *Paper Doll* (about the life of Jacqueline Susann) with Judd Hirsch, which seemed like a fine idea, but my heart was with a play called *Frozen* by British playwright Bryony Lavery. I'd read it a month earlier when I heard they were doing it at a small theater downtown, and I told Margo, "Holy mother of God—this play. I have to do it."

Frozen deals with the most disturbing subject matter possible, the horrific abuse and murder of a child, and unfolds from the perspectives of the little girl's bereaved mother, the murderer, and a psychologist. The script takes you to the darkest places without mercy, but there are moments of laughter—little pockets of oxygen here and there—and at the end, there is light, redemption, a return to the surface of the deep. (It's up to audience members to visit a nearby bar, singly or in groups, for decompression afterward.)

Unfortunately, it seemed that *Frozen* wasn't going to happen, so I committed to *Paper Doll*, but just a few days before we started rehearsals, I heard that *Frozen* was moving forward, and they wanted me. It felt like walking down the aisle with the wrong man. My manager rode in like Barbarossa and got me out of the

The audience deserves to see someone who truly, madly, deeply wants to be on that stage, with that show, in that moment—and that is how we all felt about this play. (Laila Robins, Brian F. O'Byrne and Swoosie Kurtz in Frozen, *New York, March 15, 2004.) © The Richard Avedon Foundation*

PHOTOGRAPH BY RICHARD AVEDON

contract. I hated to do it, but you can't "stay in it for the children" on Broadway. The audience can feel that missing piece, and they deserve to see someone who truly, madly, deeply wants to be on that stage, with that show, in that moment—and that is how I felt about *Frozen*.

We opened in the spring of 2004 at Manhattan Class Company Theater with me playing the mother, Bryan O'Byrne as the murderer, and Laila Robins as the psychologist. Reviews were stellar, and we quickly moved to Broadway in time for Tony nominations and ran for another 128 performances, which is all I had in me; this play is so viscerally draining. One night a group of families of missing and murdered children came to see the play, and the weight of their heartbreak was overwhelming. Standing there in front of them, attempting to do some justice, give some voice to their experience—it was humbling, a privilege I will never forget.

Toward the end of the run, I was asked to play Paget Brewster's mother on *Huff*, a Showtime series with beautiful, whip-smart writing and a terrific cast. My character had been written with cancer, so the gig wasn't going to last (television drama is as unsentimental as the state of Texas when it comes to doling out death sentences), but the potential in those emotional scenes was irresistible.

I found myself doing another stint of bicoastal commuting, flying in the dead of night like a drug smuggler, arriving on set in L.A. as the sun rose, catching a nap over Kansas and sprinting to the stage in New York for an eight o'clock curtain. Exhausting and exhilarating. By the time *Frozen* closed, my *Huff* character had gotten a stay of execution, and I had Tony and Emmy nominations in my hip pocket. Not a bad year.

Margo and me warming up for the red carpet at the 2004 Tonys.
(Hard to believe she was about to turn 90!)

In 2005, Margo turned ninety. After the additional *Huff* episodes and *Lost*, which was an extraordinary thing to be a part of, there were several other projects that weren't quite as extraordinary, but for which I was grateful. I was glad to be in L.A. with Margo most of that year. There's something about that zero candle on a birthday cake. Another decade down. You feel the need to take a breath, take stock, think about what comes next. But Margo wasn't ready for that, and neither was I.

I didn't understand it then, but looking back now I get it: what I felt when I was offered a Broadway revival of *Heartbreak House* was the separation anxiety of a new mother who's never left her child in daycare.

"Why would you turn it down?" Margo was nonplussed, hands on her hips. "Not because of *me*."

"No! Of course not. It's because . . ." I searched for another reason. Something that meant more than Shaw and another chance to work with Laila Robins and Philip Bosco. And *Shaw*. "I just—I don't know if I love this play that much. And you know how it is with Shaw, all that coming and going, you end up sitting backstage a lot. And look at the greats who've played Hesione Hushabye before. Remember Rosemary Harris with Rex Harrison?"

"Swoose, why worry about who's done what or who's onstage or off? You're who you are. Tell them yes."

"I'll sleep on it," I said.

"Go call them now," said Margo. "Just say yes."

I spent the summer thrashing over having committed to it. Too much time to think. I went from worrying about Margo to questioning if it was even possible for Shaw to be relevant in a hundred-forty-character culture. "How do we even keep audiences in their seats?" I asked the director, Robin Lefèvre. His unsentimental answer: "Cut, cut, cut." I was in love.

It was very hard to leave. I didn't want Margo cooking or cleaning while I was gone, so I arranged for meals to be delivered and hired a housekeeper to come in every day.

"Not because you can't do it," I told Margo. "Just as a treat. Enjoy being a lady of leisure."

I flew to New York in August to start rehearsals. Not the kind of rehearsal I'd do for a lifetime. This was more like Viking rowing galley practice. It was hard. I struggled with the complex language and the core strength it took to deliver the baroque lines in a single breath. But George Bernard Shaw, gentleman that he was, stepped in to help me. Reading about his life and poring over the long preface he provided for *Heartbreak House*, I came upon a passage he'd titled "War Delirium":

> *Only those who have lived through a first-rate war, not in the field, but at home, and kept their heads, can possibly understand the bitterness of Shakespeare and Swift . . . I do not know whether anyone really kept his head completely except those who had to keep it because they had to conduct the war at first hand. I should not have kept my own (as far as I did keep it) if I had not at once understood that as a scribe and speaker, I too was under the most serious public obligation to keep my grip on realities.*

He was talking about Margo—the scribe, the speaker—telling stories about love because the war stories have been told to death. And because it is in the love stories, with all their small but terrible stakes, that we understand what human beings are. Margo's take on all this is, of course, remarkably less cynical than Shaw's. She'd kept her heart as well as her head, but they spoke the same language, and it was a language I loved.

As I absorbed all this, Robin offered another unsentimental but universally helpful bit of direction: "It's Shaw. Just keep talking."

The show went well, to say the least. Reviews were boffo, and I heard through the grapevine (because I really don't read the reviews) that in the *Times*, Charles Isherwood called me "the most seductive woman on a New York stage right now," which is not something you usually see written about a sexagenarian (a word that does not mean what I wish it did). Our extraordinary costumer, Jane Greenwood, and I were nominated for Tonys, and the play was extended until mid-December, a lovely time in New York when everything is as Christmassy as—well, as Christmas in New York.

Things in L.A. were not going as swimmingly. The first week of November, just after the show opened, I came off stage, and the stage manager whispered, "Your phone's been ringing." I ran to my dressing room and grabbed my cell. The calls were from Perry. I hit the speed dial to call him back as I stumbled down the backstage passage, trying to hitch up my Victorian dressing gown and clutch the cell phone with my shoulder.

"I have ninety seconds," I said when Perry picked up. "Is Margo all right?"

"Everything's fine, but we're at the ER. She fell and hit her head. She needs five or six stitches, but she'll be fine."

"Oh, no! What happened?"

"She was visiting next door. Their dogs got excited. She must have lost her balance. They said it's not serious enough to keep her overnight or anything."

"Oh, damn it. *Damn* it. Okay, um—I have to . . . *damn it*!"

"Everything's fine," he repeated evenly. "You can talk to her after the show."

"She can't be alone anymore."

"I know. We'll talk later. Go do what you have to do."

"Tell her I love her."

"Margo, Swoosie loves you," he said aside, and I heard her wan reply in the background. "She loves you, Swoose."

"Perry . . . thank you. Thank God for you."

"Go," he said, and I went, dropping my cell phone into the stage manager's outstretched hand as I swept back onstage. Keeping my head. My head would be kept.

Margo resisted the idea of help, just as Frankie had, but we found an agency who sent caregivers on rotating eight-hour shifts. A few weeks later, Perry told me a neighbor had called him because Margo was wandering down the street in her nightie. When Perry arrived at my house, the caregiver was outside yelling at Margo to come in, and a distraught Margo was giving as good as she got, equally insistent that it was time for this stranger to go home.

By mid-December, Margo had recovered from her tumble. I asked Perry to bring her to New York so she could see *Heartbreak House* and come with me to the closing night party. Margo was excited about coming—as she always was—but when they arrived at my apartment, she absently told me she had a headache and went to lie down. When Perry and I were alone, I warily asked him, "How was the flight?"

"Harrowing," he said bluntly.

On the trip over, Margo kept demanding vodka and became obstreperous when the flight attendant tried to quietly tell her she'd already had two. Perry was visibly shaken.

"She was making a scene," he said. "She became someone I didn't know."

The following evening, they came to the performance. Seeing Margo backstage afterward, there was something missing in her eyes. A connection. A vital light I couldn't define.

"It's a long play," I said, squeezing her hand. "You must be jetlagged. I can't imagine—because you know, I get so terribly jetlagged. We'll sleep in tomorrow."

Perry flew back to L.A. on Sunday morning, but I kept Margo with me in New York.

"After the party tonight, I'll be done," I told her. "We can do whatever we want for the next two weeks. We'll just walk around and go shopping. We'll sit in the audience and watch other people work their tails off onstage, all right?"

Margo responded with some tepid affirmation. I got ready to go to the matinee, donning the glamorous red dress I intended to wear to the after party, but just as I was leaving, I discovered that Margo had had a bowel movement on the floor in the bathroom. I stood there for a moment with my heart pounding, sinking, echoing with that screaming scene in the hallway at Frankie and Margo's house.

I stepped into the hallway and said, "Margo? Are you all right?"

Hesione Hushabye in Heartbreak House, *2006*

JOAN MARCUS

"I'm fine," she said without any particular emotion.

"Did you . . . do you need help with anything?"

"No."

A few minutes later, on my knees in my red carpet dress, I glanced up and saw her standing there.

"What are you doing?" she asked.

"Cleaning this up." I tried to keep the edge out of my voice.

"Oh. That's . . . how strange."

She watched me vacantly while I scrubbed the floor. Far more disturbing than the physical aspect of it was the emotionless void in her face.

"Are you sure you're all right?" I asked as I washed my hands.

"I'm fine."

Right. Great. I forced myself to swallow the childish annoyance and raw fear spiking inside me. I had a matinee I had to get to. I had a person I had to be, and that person had to perform Shaw in this show and then go to a party and smile in this dress.

Before I left, I said, "Margo, a friend of mine is coming to bring you to the restaurant after the show, all right? If you still want to come. You don't have to."

"Of course, I'll come," she said. "I always want to be there for you."

"I know." I gathered her in my arms and kissed her soft temple. "I know you do, sweetheart."

I loved doing this play, but I was ready for it to be over. This is why a person can't do plays all the time. Everything is sacrificed on the altar of performance. In 1921, in a letter to the producer of *Heartbreak House*, George Bernard Shaw said this about the actress playing Hesione: "You must pamper her for all you are worth. Those three hours onstage must be paid for by a worth-

Playing Lily in Pushing Daisies, *2008. Putting on the eye patch before every shot, I thought of Frankie, of the vulnerability to which he could never become accustomed.*

WARNER BROS.

less, luxurious, lie-a-bed, lazy spoiled life during the other twenty-one." When I first read this, I smartly tucked it in my metaphorical hip pocket as a great excuse to sleep late. But now, waiting in the wings to make my entrance, leaning against the wall in the dark, I realized how mentally and physically exhausted I was, and I was stung by the true extent of what Margo and Frankie's support had meant to me throughout my career.

All my life, I'd had the luxury of this singular focus on my work—just like Frankie did. I have to give my parents credit; they had the greatest respect for that focus, whatever had to be sacrificed. What a wonderful space of concentration. Everything was about the work at hand. They never bothered me at work, would not dream of calling me when I was getting ready to go to the theater. I never had to worry about anyone but myself. This was the dawning of a new era.

Sadness descended on me when I thought of Margo and realized that what I witnessed with Frankie must have been the tip of the iceberg, a sliver of what Margo must have gone through with him. I'd never given this much thought because Margo was always so *Margo* with her penny-bright smile and her unstoppable upbeat charm. I was capable of being that sort of trouper too, but it was like wearing a bulletproof vest; nothing gets through, but oh, the weight of it, the heavy cost of that impenetrable armor.

Margo and her escort were late arriving at the restaurant. I kept checking my cell phone, pacing to the front door, peering out into the frozen night street. They finally arrived, and I pulled Margo into a booth beside me, warming her hands between mine. She was always the life of these parties, and the group in our booth was a rotating cast of artists and writers and theatre folk, the kind of people Margo loved being around. She sat smiling a remote smile, saying small-talk things one would expect a person to say at a party, which is not at all what I would expect from Margo.

The next day, depressed and exhausted, I tried to rally for a little shopping and lunch, but it was too much for both of us. We curled up in my bed together and slept most of the afternoon away, then got up and picked at a sparse dinner. It wasn't unusual for Margo to have a nip of vodka in the evening, but the way she scuffed the ice into her glass made me nervous now.

But the next morning, Margo was bright and talkative over coffee. We went to see a revival of *A Chorus Line* and out to a late dinner after that, reminiscing about other Christmases in New York and making plans for the coming week. It was as if a shade had been drawn down over her personality and now, suddenly, it had been raised again, perhaps not quite all the way, but enough for me to breathe with profound relief.

There's a wonderful moment during the first season of *Pushing Daisies* when the two synchronized swimming sisters, Lily (me) and Vivian (Ellen Greene), have been dredging up the past and tearing each other up about it.

"I think it's brave to try to be happy," Vivian says. "You've gotten so comfortable being unhappy. Wouldn't it be wonderful to wake up in the morning and choose to be happy?"

They walk out of their rambling gingerbread house into a steady rain that gives way to a sun shower and then to resilient sun as Ellen sings "Morning Has Broken" and they dive into a pool and swim with pagodas on their heads, because that's the kind of thing that could happen at any moment on *Pushing Daisies*.

It was that sort of morning in L.A, the first week of January 2007, when Margo and I sat out on the patio, home from the last holiday we would spend in New York. With a resilient sun above and blue sky beaming on the calm surface of the swimming pool, Margo took my hand and told me she wanted to die.

*"There would be no easy routes into these new horizons.
But here was my realm, and here my way." (Margo and Frankie
on the wing of Yankee Boy in the late 1930s.)*

CHAPTER TWELVE

More Later

Pacific Theater, 1943

"On our homeward trip," Frankie said, "we cracked the trans-Pacific record wide open. The old Swoose, with her war-worn motors, made it from Brisbane to San Francisco in thirty-six hours ten minutes flying time, the only one of the original 35 on Clark Field to see home again.

"Then there was our last night flight in. Clear, so the stars were out, even down to the horizon. And calm, so I could put the Swoose on automatic pilot and sit there half-dozing, thinking about Ole 99 and my other crew. And the way old Tex used to sit beside me, slumped in his seat. You'd think that happy-go-lucky kid was asleep, and yet somehow he always kept an eye cocked on the instrument panel and the horizon, so if anything started to go even a little funny, Tex would snap up, quick as a fox terrier pup, bless him.

"And then I thought of that sprawling line of my crew on Clark Field. And of Ole 99, crumpled, sagging on the ground.

"But at times like these, half-dozing, it seemed like I was back with the old gang again, who had brought me safe out East and now were bringing me home again. Everything easy and comfortable; all I had to do was sit here and follow those two wing lights, so steady ahead in the dark, those unwavering wing lights which would lead me safely back. On calm nights like this, in formation, there's little flying to do; those wing lights ahead seem to pull you home.

"I guess I must have been dozing, because a little motor undulation roused me, and I realized, of course, there was no plane ahead—never had been one. It had only been two blue stars which are close together in the eastern sky. The Swoose was alone, over the Pacific."

Margo stroked my hand while I broke down and sobbed. She was clear and serene, remarkably lucid, as articulate as she had been at forty-one.

"Darling, I want to go now," she said. "I've had a good life, and I'm not afraid of death. I'm done here. I want to move on to my next assignment. You've taken such good care of me over the years, but I don't want to keep this going. I want to go while everything is good. Why keep driving the car until everything falls off and breaks?"

It hit me in the heart. A blunt, hard blow. I felt the same bleak helplessness I'd felt the last time I heard from Michael Bennett. *Don't come,* he said. *Monsoon season.* Unlike Michael, Margo didn't keep me at arm's length. She wanted my help, and I tried hard to listen, to not let the conversation be about me or my feelings, to get the best information I could find for her. A few years earlier there was a lot of publicity about a book, *Final Exit: The Practicalities of Self-Deliverance and Assisted Suicide for the Dying.* I procured a copy and forced myself through it, but even the table of contents gave me a knot in my chest. Along with chapters on "Shopping for the Right Doctor" and "Letters to Be Written" were unbearably bald candor slaps like "Self-Deliverance Using a Plastic Bag" and "Death in the Family Car." The physical, legal and emotional logistics of Margo's request were inconceivable.

That winter, in January of 2007, at age ninety-two, Margo was still here with her faculties largely intact. She was not afraid of death. She never was. She proved that in the fearless way she lived. "But Mommie," I said, "being ready to die and wanting to die—these are two very different things. And *needing* to die is something way beyond either of those."

It does appear that some people decide their life is over and just die. Frankie sat down in his chair and simply left off living. Gigi folded her life like a tent after Daddy Art died. We watched her do it. These days Margo seems to dwell in two worlds. Sometimes it seems she is surrounded by the spirits of Gigi and Daddy Art and Frank and Mici. But something keeps her here. I experience waves of guilt, knowing that in large part, it's me. I worry that every time she sees me, she feels compelled to come up to the Margo that I know, obligated to play that exhausting role rather than "let go and let God," as they say. My devotion to Margo was undeniably selfish. Nothing altruistic about it. I wasn't ready to let her go.

We talked about it at length and in depth, and if nothing else, these conversations, and the reading of that terrifying book, were catalysts for a much-needed reality check. The paradigm by which I valued my time—especially time away from L.A.—shifted dramatically, which changed the way I evaluated projects coming across the transom. What a gift that the next big thing to come my way was *Pushing Daisies*, a whimsical series about a pie maker who is able to restore the dead to life and sets to solving mysteries with his formerly deceased childhood sweetheart.

When I read the script (appropriately titled "Pie-lette"), I told Konrad, "It'll never go. It's too brilliant." But the creator and writer, Bryan Fuller, was a rising star, having done three other acutely quirky but critically successful shows—*Dead Like Me*, *Wonderfalls*, and *Heroes*—so I dared to hope. I was asked to come in and meet with Bryan, the director Barry Sonnenfeld, and the two producers, Bruce Cohen and Dan Jinks, which felt like an audition to me, though I was assured it was not. It was completely out of character for me to jump the turnstile and do my own thing at an audition, but I brought along some photos of Frankie and me from the old aquacade days, just to show them that I had this connection to Lily's world, and by the time I got home, Konrad was calling to tell me they wanted me.

I was over the moon—and this was before I realized *Pushing Daisies* would be a unique and vibrant bit of television history. The extraordinary cast was drawn from all over the theatrical map: Kristin Chenoweth and Ellen Greene were Broadway divas of the highest order, but like me, Kristin had jumped the turnstile;

she'd proven herself in film and television and a series of wall-moving symphony concerts as well. Anna Friel was a Brit (sporting a flawless American accent) who'd been on TV since she was a kid. Chi McBride started out in a blues band. Lee Pace grew up in Texas and went to Julliard. New technology and a definitive design concept gave the show a highly stylized look; walking on set in these weirdly beautiful costumes was like living in a richly illustrated storybook. The writing was gentle genius—poetry and music, magical realism, and unabashed romanticism. Lily's lines were tersely eloquent à la "Vermouth reminds me of mother" and "Esther Williams would piss her cotton panel at the sight of those rocket splits."

When the show debuted, critics raved, but our first season was truncated by a writer's strike. The second season, ratings faltered, and there was a bit of follow-the-bouncing-time-slot, but the show was showered with critical praise and awards, including seven Emmys after we were canceled. Thanks to a solid core of diehard fans, the last three episodes eventually aired.

Candidly, it's a small miracle it lasted as long as it did. I was grateful every day to have this meaningful work just a few minutes away from Margo. The shooting schedule was erratic, and there were many long days, but there were also days off, and Margo and I began the shift toward a home life that revolved around her needs instead of mine. I tried hard to respect her privacy and preferences, but that evening vodka was beginning to be an issue. I found myself keeping an ear out for the slide of the freezer drawer followed by ice clinking in a tumbler, but I always hoped to avoid the wrestling match over the bottle.

"You know," I'd wheedle and nudge, "we should be drinking more water. To be hydrated, right? I read recently that hydration is very important. How about some sparkling water instead? I'll have some too."

She didn't want caregivers around all the time, but I knew I couldn't do it all, so we compromised and found a wonderful lady who came for four hours every afternoon. My thought was to expand that as needed. I didn't understand yet that by the time you know you need it, it's too late.

One evening after Perry and the caregiver had gone home, I was headed upstairs to my room and didn't realize that Margo was following me until I heard her behind me, thrashing for balance. I turned and saw her fall backward from the steps below—too far for me to reach out and grab her—plummeting back and back in sickening slow motion. She landed in a heap against the old Japanese chest, gashing her head on one of its ornate iron handles. Blood rivered down her neck and pooled on the floor as I fell to my knees beside her.

"Margo! Oh, no! Oh, Mommie . . ."

She mumbled up at me, dazed and trembling, and yes, I know how lame this sounds, but I ran for a bag of ice. I told you, we are big ice people in my family. That is our panacea of choice. Wrenching open the freezer drawer, I seized the giant plastic bag Margo had been tapping for her evening vodka, then ran back to her side and piled the bag on her head. The weight of it toppled her over sideways like a rag doll.

"Oh, God! Damn it! I'm sorry . . . sorry, Mommie. It's okay. We're okay."

Our neighbor had been a medic in the army, so my next flailing thought was to call him. Looking back on the slapstick lunacy of the ice bag, me calling the neighbor—*"Medic!"*—the whole scene might have been comical if it had been a Nora Ephron movie and not our life. Margo was alert and not enthusiastic about another trip to the ER, where the cheerful doctor pointed to the previous head gash and said, "Oh, I remember you. These are my stitches."

It's hard to condense the downward spiral that followed, to recall some sense of it without imposing a litany of medical records. Doctors and issues and tests and scans. Bone density, blood viscosity, brain function, meds, meds, meds. The soft comings and goings of nurses. The chirping of monitors. The sinking of my heart.

We made the decision to take Margo to intensive care, and I followed along numbly as they walked her bed down the hall. Suddenly, the orderlies bolted forward at a sprint, and I ran to catch up, not knowing what was happening, terrified that her vitals were crashing or spiking or doing something urgently horrific.

"What is it? What's wrong?" I cried as I caught up.

"Oh, there's a long ramp there," said one of the nurses. "We always speed up there to get some momentum going."

I stood there panting, feeling like I'd aged five years. Margo was wracked with pneumonia and lay delirious with fever, barely able to breathe. The treating physician drew me to the corner for a hushed conversation. To make it through the night, Margo would have to be intubated. I told him about the advance directives both of us kept in our purses now. She had specified that no extreme measure were to be taken.

"I understand," he said, "but she could come back from this. Pneumonia is treatable, but we have to get her through the night."

For the first time in my life, I wished I had a sibling. I'd always cherished being an only child, but in this moment, I'd have given anything to turn to a big brother—"Bruce, what do you think?"

I told the doctor to proceed with the intubation and spent the rest of the night agonizing over it. In the morning, as Margo emerged from a drugged haze, her eyes fluttered open, widening with pain and fear when she realized where she was and what was happening. I stroked her arm, cooing and coaxing, trying to reassure her that it was only for a little while, that she would be all right, everything would be all right. She made a weak motion with her hands, as if she was writing something down, and Perry quickly produced a pen and notepad.

In shaky blue letters, Margo spelled out a single word.

kill

Monsoon season was upon us.

∞

Omaha, 1942

I had seen Frank beaten before, but I had never seen him look like this. So this was what the Japanese had done to our men in the beginning. It was a defeated look, and I had never seen this before, not in Frank's eyes.

I knew the room would get a little dark when I mentioned the letter, but somehow I wanted the darkness.

"Frank, honey, before you go away again, tell me about

that letter. The one from the Philippines that you made me promise not to read. The one I never received."

"I wrote the letter, Margo, at Clark Field. I wrote it because I knew I could never get out of the Philippines alive. I wrote it in a foxhole. And I cried while I wrote.

"I told you to—to marry again. I told you to have the baby we have hoped for. And I said—it would be our baby."

"Frank—why didn't you want me to read it? You told me not to in every other letter and in the last phone call from Java. Why?"

"Well, in Java there seemed a little chance I'd get away all right, but I might be listed as 'missing' for a long time. If the Fortress hadn't come for us, we were going to try to escape in a small boat. If that failed, we were going to take to the hills. So you might not have heard from me for a long time. And while I was just 'missing' I didn't want you to get that letter."

Frank was almost cross now. I could see I had gone too far.

There is only one thing about my life that Margo never knew: I had an abortion in 1963, when abortion was illegal—and terrifying. Because my boyfriend was wealthy and my doctor was kind, I was able to have it done in a relatively safe environment where my health and privacy were protected. (If I were to make any political statement about that, it would be to say that I dread a return to the days when the healthiest circumstances are reserved for the wealthiest people and "relatively safe" is considered a luxury.) I never experienced a moment of doubt about the decision; the question that lingers for me is why I never told my mother, in whom I confided everything. I haven't spent a great deal of time pondering it, but honestly, I never even considered telling her at the time, because that would have been telling her I was having sex, and such things were simply not discussed. It also occurred to me that, because she had tried so hard and waited so long to get pregnant with me, it would be agony for her to know that I got pregnant so easily and then chose not to be a mother. It was my decision. A decision that was as intimate as it was important.

Standing there in the hospital, looking at the word Margo scrawled on Perry's notepad, I felt stricken to the core. Had I taken from her the right to make the most intimately important decision of her life? When the question was put to me—to implement the extreme measures or let her go—it was like standing on a platform ten meters above an empty pool. Watching Margo suffer, I cried, guilt and gratitude warring in my ruined stomach.

This is where Ethel the Oracle and I nearly come to blows.

"All's well that ends well," she says, "but it seems to me that Margo's advance directives should have been honored by the hospital staff."

"I had power of attorney," I tell her. "It was my decision."

"But the whole point of having advance directives is to spare your loved ones those difficult decisions."

I get that. I really do. And I am horribly aware of the alternate storyline that could have played out from that point. It almost did. But I can't regret my decision—because it's futile to regret decisions made while one is in the crucible with only the information at hand and because I'm so intensely grateful for every day

Margo has lived since that morning. The advance directives specify that no extreme measure should be taken "when there is no hope of recovery," and hope is something from which I will never recover. I am my mother's daughter, and for better or worse, the two of us are chronically hopeful. All that said, what I hope for now is that Margo's life will end as peacefully and painlessly as possible, and should the same situation arise again, I hope I'll be there holding her hand.

These issues go so quickly to the political, don't they? John Guare wrote in *Six Degrees of Separation*, "This world has been so heavy with all the right-to-lifers—'protect the lives of the unborn'; constitutional amendments—'when does life begin?'; or the converse, the end of life: the right to die. Why is life at this point in the twentieth century so focused upon the very beginning of life and the very end of life? What about the eighty years we have to live between those two inexorable bookends?"

Every decision Margo made on my behalf early in my life and all the decisions I make on Margo's behalf now—it's all shadow-boxing a future we have no way of divining. You do your best with the information at hand, and how you make peace with the outcome—whatever that may be—pretty much sets the tone for everything else that happens between the bookends.

Margo slept most of that day and the next. By the time she came around again, the tubes had been removed, her lungs had cleared somewhat, and her fever was under control. Ellen Greene came by to visit us. She'd fallen in love with Margo, like everyone always has. We were due to start shooting again soon, and I was worried about finding people to help me with Margo's care, because now I was determined to expand the schedule for round-the-clock coverage.

"There's a very nice young man in my building—Antonio—he's a nurse," Ellen said. "I'll ask him if he's available."

He was, and he's still with us. I'll always be grateful to Ellen for bringing this wonderful person into our lives. Margo cherished her independence, and I cherished my private space and time; bringing caregivers into our home didn't come naturally for either of us. I've never been one to lay down the law, and I'll go many extra miles to avoid conflict, but I located the enforcer within myself, realistically vetted applicants, being kind but clear about boundaries and expectations.

Margo came through the crisis, but as she recovered, vague headaches she'd been experiencing escalated and plagued her. I took her to a neurologist at Cedars for scans and a series of injections, to an acupuncture guy at UCLA, to chiropractors and nutritionists—nothing helped. We went through a hellish period during which she was combative and depressed, and there was a nightly battle for the bottle just as there had been between her and Gigi. There's heavy irony in some of the *Pushing Daisies* dialogue I delivered during that year.

"Look carefully, ladies. This is your future," says Olive Snook, and Lily says darkly, "Is it vodka?"

In *The House of Blue Leaves*, Bananas has a line about whiskey and ginger ale at dusk. That seems to be the cocktail hour ingrained in the women of Gigi's generation and passed down to their daughters. Margo also believed strongly in the medicinal value of gargling vodka. (Frankly, she's got me convinced; during *Fifth of July*, as my castmates dropped like flies from a vicious flu bug, Margo and I stayed hale and hearty with our afternoon Grey Goose gargle.) So, as the Headache descended on Margo every afternoon like clockwork, we'd hear the freezer drawer and the clink of the ice. We tried simply not having vodka in the house, but Margo circumvented that standoff by slamming out the front door and setting off down the sidewalk. She was still mentally and physically active enough that getting between her and any given goal could be harrowing.

The wonderful qualities that had always made Margo so *Margo* turned against her now, especially when mixed with alcohol. Her tenacity became a hard stubborn streak. Her clever wits turned cunning. Her spunk and self-determination became intractable mulishness. As her short-term memory became more and more checkered, her rich imagination filled in the blanks with harsh conclusions and dark fears. Her boundless energy became a frenetic compulsion. For years we couldn't get her to take a nap or even put her feet up, and now as she fought her own fatigue, the fallout rained down on whoever was trying to convince her to rest.

To avoid the conflict, she'd retreat to her room and range back and forth, taking things out of drawers and putting them away again, rearranging the items on her dresser. The more exhausted she was, the more determined she became to push herself through another hour. Disconcertingly, my presence seemed to make it all worse, because a caregiver's presence cast her in the role of someone being cared for while my presence cast her in the more familiar role: my partner in crime.

After *Pushing Daisies*, I did a few episodes of *Heroes* and several other recurring and guest roles, but I longed to be in New York. When I was asked to fly east to play Blythe Danner's lesbian spouse on *Nurse Jackie*, I dashed like a bandit, leaving Perry in charge. Oh, the cool crisp evenings in Central Park, the silent austerity of my apartment, my table for one, brisk walks at my own pace—I reveled in it. It felt so good to work without the weight of worry on the back of my neck. We were in the studio all night, watching snow fall outside the dressing room window. In the morning, I went home and breathed in the solitude of my own space.

I hadn't allowed myself to acknowledge it—and I knew she certainly didn't mean to—but it seemed these days that Margo took up all the oxygen in the house in L.A. She was intrusive and needy, and sometimes I needed to be in a space by myself to look at a script uninterrupted and not feel fragmented and not have someone walking in and out of my office literally every seven minutes, asking me the same four hundred questions over and over and over.

Nora Ephron asked me to participate in the first workshop of *Love, Loss, and What I Wore.* Afterward we sat together at one of our usual haunts, and I poured my heart out on the table.

"We seem to have gotten past the drinking thing, but it was bad. We've tried different drugs, and I'm always researching anything that comes up. I see stuff advertised on TV, and they make all these promises and then reel off all these side effects. This last one we tried—it's like she became a different person. Meanwhile," I sighed, "all my friends here keep asking, 'Where have you been hiding? Why haven't we seen you lately?' As if I'm off at a spa or something."

"Your friends want you to have your own life," said Nora, because Nora was wise and kind. "We're looking out for you. And *you* have to look out for you."

I confided in her that I'd been thinking about the possibility of residential care for Margo, and she said, "I think that's an excellent idea." I didn't know then that Nora had leukemia. She'd been diagnosed three years earlier, but she chose to share that information with very few people. In retrospect, it makes sense that she was keen on the idea that no one should put off the living of her own life.

"I've been doing all these guest shots—and thank God, because it's just one or two days here and there—but there's no way I can take care of her by myself, and she's not happy with caregivers coming in. I'm basically damned no matter what I do."

"Then you may as well do as you damn please," she said.

I talked it over with Konrad and Perry. Konrad arranged visits to a number of places and went with me to check them out. Nice places, every one of them. But there was always . . . something. Not the right setup, too far away, window treatments that stifled the sun, fluorescent lights, a strange smell in the hallway, a single lady eating at a table in the vast dining hall. At the last place I looked, a nurse with severely squared shoulders and arms like lug wrenches told me, "I know how to handle this situation. Your mother needs structure. We get everyone up at the same time, we have classes they go to, lunch, reading—"

I said, "My mom doesn't respond well to being told what to do . . ."

"Give us time," Nurse Ratched replied. "We'll get her used to it. Trust me. This is the best thing for her."

"This won't work," I told Konrad as we hurried out to the parking lot. "Not for Margo. I'm glad we did this. It was important to get the information, and if things become intolerable, I'll reassess, but for now . . . I just want to keep on keeping on."

With all the assiduous preparation Frankie would have put into a perilous trans-Atlantic flight, I began to research and study nutrition, homeopathics, comfort care equipment and palliative care pharmacology. I didn't want her to be zoned out on a lot of drugs, but with her peace and safety at stake, it was clear we'd have to incorporate some ongoing medication. I kept thinking of how Bananas opens her mouth for her daily dose in *The House of Blue Leaves*, that achingly real moment when she says, "You see, they give me these pills so I won't feel anything. Now I don't mind not feeling anything so long as I can remember feeling. You see? And this apartment, you see, here, right here, I stand in this corner and I remember laughing so hard . . ." We experimented and juggled the chemistry until we found a delicate balance, which Margo did her best to maintain with the imperiled grace of a wing walker.

We still had difficult moments. At times she would rail at me, and one day I lost myself and started railing back at her, "Stop it! Just stop! Why are you being this way? Can't you see, Margo, you're making this a thousand times harder on everyone including yourself?"

Cielito, who'd arrived for the evening shift, placed his hands on my shoulders and looked into my eyes.

"Swoose," he said, low and calm. I can't explain why, but it's meaningful to me that he always calls me Swoose. "It's going to be all right."

And eventually it was. It was all right.

This is, of course, an appalling oversimplification of a long process, but I devote a lot of time to chronicling Margo's ups and downs these days—the specifics of her pains, the particulars of her ingestion and digestion—those details aren't what's important here. Right now, I just want to say to you—whatever monsoon season you're weathering—it's going to be all right.

No, listen to me: *it is going to be all right.*

Long ago, doing my duty for some best-forgotten movie, I was sent on a press junket with a young starlet who was not a happy participant.

"Don't they know I have a life?" she groused.

"Honey," I said, "right now, this *is* your life."

When days get gritty around here, I have to rap my own knuckles with that same ruler. This is my life right now. Caring for Margo. I'm finally fully present in that life, and I've been far better off since I admitted I couldn't do it alone.

People marvel at the quality and longevity of the support network that surrounds Margo and me, and while I certainly won't minimize the fact that I'm blessed with the resources to swing all this, I believe the key to keeping these excellent people in our lives is that we care about their lives. We're a family. Which isn't to say that nothing ever goes awry, but when it does, we're better equipped to cope with it because that foundation of mutual respect and compassion is in place.

In his book *Family Meals: Bringing Her Home*, Michael Tucker writes about the tectonic shift he and Jill—and their whole family—made as Jill's elderly mother Lora made the same inexorable journey into dementia that Margo is making now. Michael beautifully states a painfully resonant reality with the profound observation that a devoted professional caregiver was able to give Lora something Jill could not: "She was able to love Lora—Lolo to her—as Lora was now. She had no expectation of seeing the former Lora, the intellectual, the elegant hostess, the mother . . . She had none of Jill's disappointment and frustration, none of Jill's sadness for the Lora who used to be. She knew only Lolo. And she loved her."

Michael also observes, always with his wry sense of humor,

that there's a broad spectrum of people working as caregivers—
as in any profession—some wonderful, "a few stinkers" but the
majority somewhere in between. Our quest for a few precious
wonderful ones was rocky and prolonged, but so well worth the
effort.

Oddly, things became easier over the next three years as Margo's short-term memory became more and more spotty. She began to think that these people who kept showing up at the door
were just bothersome houseguests. When either Antonio or
Cielito arrived, she'd greet him with genuine warmth, ask about
his family, and invite him to sit with her at the table and chat.
After an hour or so, with her best hostess face firmly in place,
she'd guide him back to the front door.

"Now, I know you have things to do, darling, so I don't want
to keep you, but it's been so *wonderful* having you! Really. So
wonderful."

If I tried to step in and steer things back on track, she'd drag
me into a corner of the kitchen for a conspiratorial word.

"Swoose. You have got to get rid of this guy. Some people just
don't get the hint."

Finally one afternoon, I took Antonio to the front door with a
breezy, "Bye now! Thanks so much for stopping by. Hope to *see
you again soon*," I added, ticking my thumb toward the patio out
back. Ten minutes later, there came a knock on the glass door in
the kitchen.

"Now who could that be?" I said casually. "Why, Antonio!
Margo, look who it is."

"Hello, darling!" Margo said in delighted surprise. "We're so
happy to see you."

We became an ensemble of dedicated method actors. When

Margo didn't want to go to the doctor, I suddenly developed terrible pain in my abdomen and needed her to take me to the doctor, which she was immediately eager to do. If she insisted that she wanted to go home and see her mother, we'd go through the elaborate machinations of checking a foul weather forecast and include her in the process of deciding to wait an hour before embarking on a long drive. One day she was insistent that we were late for some event we needed to be at.

"I'll call and let them know we're running late," I said, taking up the kitchen phone. "Hello, this is Swoosie Kurtz calling regarding the event this afternoon? Oh, it's been rescheduled? Next Thursday. Yes, of course. Thank you so much."

The overall effect of Theatre Domestica was a general step down in conflict-fueled stress. There was no help in arguing with her and no harm in agreeing. These performances took on a playful attitude that further eased tensions. I play many roles. In addition to recurring roles as Gigi and Mici, I play Swoosie (cast as type), a handsome gentleman caller (nontraditional casting), a complete stranger (improv), and a variety of spear-carriers and redshirts.

As time went on, Margo began laughing again, and we laugh too—with not one scintilla of disrespect—as she goes out for a walk with her beautiful Brazilian caregiver, accessorizing her bathrobe with a pair of panties looped over her arm like a purse. At times it seems that she's swept us all with her into a world of magical thinking and serendipitous comings and goings.

Edie was the most serendipitous of all. Getting a dog was always on my list in theory, but the practical reality of having a dog never seemed to fit in. I'd facetiously say, "The right dog will show up on my front lawn." Of course, I meant this as a metaphor, and I envisioned the right theoretical dog as some huggable Hollywood purse-denizen like Kristin Chenoweth's storied Maltese, Madeline Kahn. One evening, just after Perry had left for the day, he reappeared in my office doorway and said, "Swoose, I have to go, but you need to know—there's a dog in the yard. I think someone dropped it over the fence."

"*What?* No. That can't happen today. No way."

Way. I went out and found a smallish gray dog of indeterminate breed and not the sweetest disposition—definitely not the portable, Maddie-flavored dog I'd ordered from the Universe. We did our due diligence—took her to the vet to see if she had a chip, put up flyers, asked around the neighborhood—then accepted that Edith, as we'd been calling her, was here to stay, so we might as well love her. And the more we loved her, the sweeter she seemed.

One evening not long ago, Margo sat on the sofa in my office petting Edie while I studied my lines for *Mike & Molly*. After a while, I set my work aside and came to sit next to them, laying my head on Margo's breast.

"Oh," said Margo, "the soft land."

The past few years, I've been doing my best to vaccinate myself, make myself immune to the impact of the Final Good-bye. There is no real way to inoculate against heartbreak, but I kept telling myself that maybe small doses of it would result in a less severe case and shorten the duration.

It has been a kindness of the universe that I've been given this time to get used to less and less of Margo—the genuine and complete Margo who was my mother, my world—losing a little of her each day, each week, each month. Her spirit and her true self emerge every now and then, suddenly and unexpectedly out of the fog, and I am once again seduced into this soft land—my home, my original comfort zone—and the illusion that it will be there forever.

David Mamet (paraphrasing E. M. Forster) says, "The job of the dramatist is to make the audience wonder what happens next." Jerry Zaks would tactfully request that actors "give the emotion on the line." Because a so-called dramatic pause is usually just masturbation for the actor, and it gives the audience too much time to think. It doesn't move the story along, and I feel that impatient tug under my skin as I pace the stripped floors and spackled walls of my apartment in New York.

The summer of 2013 has offered up one of the hottest, rainiest Junes on record. Central Park is as green and swampy as an Amazon jungle. In the three weeks since my arrival, I've seen many good friends and several good plays. I've gone to yoga, dined at my favorite restaurants and accomplished a tremendous amount of work, but at a certain point, no matter how lovely a hotel is, you get crazy. You don't see the sun in New York like you do in L.A., and I need to see the sun. I need to see Margo and get my arms around her. Being away from her for a few weeks makes me freshly aware that our days together are numbered. Suddenly, I get verklempt and think, *Please, God, let her hold on till I get back.*

The story arc, I realize, has become clear at last. My parents loomed large in the early years of my life; I was small, but my great need for them was immediate, and they were always there. As is natural and healthy, I let my own work and life and loves take center stage until my parents loomed large again, but now they were the ones who needed me. The full circle feels right; it brings me back to Margo and Margo back to me. When I take in the full arc of her story, an enormous new understanding of who she is—and who Frankie was—humbles and delights me. I forgive the small childhood scars, and I know I had their forgiveness long before I needed it. I'm grateful, gobsmacked at my own good fortune. On top of everything else, Margo has given me that part of myself I'd never believed in: the caregiver, the nurturer. I have become, in essence, a mother.

Lucky me.

There are always a thousand reasons to stay in New York. With only one reason to leave, I return to L.A., and the evening I arrive happens to feature clear skies and a spectacular perigee moon riding just above the trees on a thin eddy of rose and lavender smog. Margo has always had a special affinity for the moon, which is so feminine. She always liked thinking of someone far away looking up at the same moon that was shining down on her. In that same spirit, she always lit a special lamp on nights I was performing under the bright lights onstage.

"Mommie, I have a surprise for you." I lead her out to the patio, and she gasps, clasps her hands in front of her chin and laughs out loud.

"*Oh!* There's a full moon for you. There's a *honey*moon."

I report what I've read online: "It's the super-super-moon. The moon's closest encounter with Earth for the whole year."

"We'll be back." She waves to the enormous amber moon. "Don't you worry. We'll meet again."

Gathering Margo in my arms, I am overtaken by unexpected weeping, overwhelmed with a liquid light show of emotion. I have known this feeling before: those moments onstage when I find myself felicitously cast in a rare, perfect-for-me role. I feel the best of my aptitudes shining beyond what I'd imagined I was capable of. Something is brought out of me I would not have believed was there. Startled and profoundly grateful, I soar.

This is not a state of grace in which one is allowed to live. It is a zephyr at best, and I have finally learned to cherish it instead of questioning my worthiness or pre-grieving the inevitable. If we're lucky, and I have been, it presents itself many times in a life and career, but always in a different guise, so we must be wise enough to wait for it, brave enough to take on the difficult day in which it comes, and strong enough to let it go.

The name of this particular zephyr is love. I have felt it before, and I know it will pass by me again.

∞

California, 1944

Goodbyes have become standard, I think. I watch people and I hear their stories, and it seems they all say goodbye just about the same.

This goodbye has all the trimmings. There's the bottle of champagne. Two tall-stemmed glasses standing together tell a story, a dramatic one.

The little item of the book I'm to write is all settled. It's been put on the shelf until Frank leaves. Then I'll go to work.

"Margo. I've been wondering. About the other little item. What are you going to name it?"

"Why, 'Little Swoose' of course," the pilot's wife said.

We toast with our champagne. But mostly silent toasts. You don't need to talk a love story. Everything has been said.

Tonight there are just a few sentences, but they are important. We want them to stick. I want them to go all the way

On top of everything else, Margo has given me that part of myself I'd never believed in: the caregiver, the nurturer.

to Italy and to stay there as long as they need to. Frank wants them to follow me wherever I am.

And now it's so quiet here on a dark airport, quiet and so calm. I get out of the car, and stand up. I like to take things standing up. Lights lead the way to our Swoose. The men are all at attention, and now they follow Frank inside. And with her four motors growling, our Swoose starts the turn which will take her down the runway.

I flick our car lights on and off three times. I smile and wave, good and strong.

Until, at last, a ship big enough to be a Fortress is lifting into the sky, and for this panicky moment I want to reach up and pull my Frank back to me.

I won't get back into the car being afraid. I cannot take panic home with me. So I stand here on the running board. I guess you just naturally look up when you don't know what to do, and I do.

I look up.

There is some noise, now. Loud noise. Four engines of a plane just above my head. A Fortress is flying over me with its nose pointed into the east, and there are two little lights on this plane and they are blinking on and off, and on and off, and on. And they are brighter than all the stars in the sky.

And a pilot's wife is waving and she is shouting. You can see now how she's smiling and laughing all at once.

"Hello, Frank!"

Over and over again.

"Hello, Frank!"

Even in the dark you can see she is happy.

ACKNOWLEDGMENTS

Henry James wrote in *The Tragic Muse*:

The insufferable side of her life will be just the side she'll thrive on. You can't eat your cake and have it, and you can't make omelets without breaking eggs. You can't at once sit by the fire and parade about the world, and you can't take all chances without having some adventures. You can't be a great actress without the luxury of nerves. Your nerves and your adventures, your eggs and your cake, are part of the cost of the most expensive of professions. You play with human passions, with exaltations and ecstasies and terrors, and if you trade on the fury of the elements, you must know how to ride the storm.

As an artist and a woman, I've done my best to tell my story here with decency, candor, love and discretion. While it's not possible to recount every detail or recall every conversation verbatim,

I've tried to remain true to the spirit of events and dialogue as I remember them. Getting the housekeeping out of the way: views expressed are my own and may not reflect the views of Warner Bros. or any other organization with whom I've worked in the past, present or future. No part of this manuscript should be misconstrued as medical or legal advice. Some characters and events have been composited for the sake of economy. Some names have been changed to protect privacy.

There's not room in all the pages of a book—or a bookshelf or a library full of books—to express my love and gratitude to my parents, Margo and Frank Kurtz. Their zest for life and spirit of adventure defined and freed me while their love and wisdom kept me grounded.

Enormous thanks to Perry Patton for your light heart and solid shoulder. You bring out the best in me and forgive the worst. The color red and the greater part of any given day would be impossible without you. Roger Bean, thank you for being Perry's rock while he's busy moving mountains for me. Konrad Leh, thank you for being my lionhearted advocate and steadfast friend. Without you, I'd be working half as much and having only a fraction of the fun. Jonathan Howard, my special agent man, you play an important role in my heart and career. Josh White . . . use your imagination. Brent Spiner, you opened my eyes, inspired me and made me laugh through it all. Michael Prochelo, thanks for taking care of business, as the song says. John Breglio, your help bringing *MRTS* out of the vault was greatly appreciated. Karl Austen, thanks for keeping the wolf pack at bay. Jeff Bernstein and William Briggs, your advocacy is greatly appreciated.

Special thanks to Margo's amazing team of caregivers: An-

gela, Antonio, Cielito and Lillian. I'm so humbled by, grateful for
and in awe of what you do. And to our special friend David Gris-
wold, who brings so much to Margo's life—and to mine. I need to
do a shout-out to my New York City pals, who supported and
encouraged me and got excited for me, long before I had a book
contract, or a book: Jim (Jimbo) Baldassare, Charlotte Moore,
Melvin Bernhardt, Jeff Woodman, Mary Pat Walsh, Meryl Gor-
don, Walter Shapiro, Maureen Anderman, Tommy Kail, Jill
Eikenberry and Michael Tucker, Bi-ko, Trish and Lou Mustillo,
and Carol Muske Dukes. To all my coworkers and castmates: you
are my family, and I treasure you. Special warm embraces to
Chuck Lorre, Melissa McCarthy and Billy Gardell.

I'm grateful to the characters I've played and from whom I've
learned so much—and to the writers who invited me to journey
beyond myself. Thanks for getting me out of the house. Lasting
love to Nora Ephron and Wendy Wasserstein.

This book was made possible by the laser-sharp expertise,
dogged faith and tireless efforts of an exceptional team: my literary agent Ian Kleinert, who believed in the idea of this book several years before I was ready to write it; my editor John Duff, a
warm and intelligent shepherd who fell in love with Margo and
Frankie's story and made it possible for me to tell my story in my
own way; all the people at Perigee who worked hard to make our
vision a reality; and Jerusha Rodgers, our cheerfully tenacious
permissions whip.

Joni Rodgers, if I could write like you, I would have the words
to tell you that your genius vision turned black and white into
Technicolor, amusement into hilarity, touching into heartbreaking and a very interesting life into a literary page-turner. That is

what I believe they call *art*. You promised to be my Sherpa on this mountain climb; you have also been my friend. I am touched by your heart and soul and so very glad serendipity and Kristin Chenoweth brought us together.

—Swoosie Kurtz
April 2014

CREDITS AND PERMISSIONS

Every effort was made to secure permissions and credits for the photographs and excerpts used in this work; however, in certain cases the rights holder was unresponsive or could not be found. Excerpts from *My Rival, the Sky* (Putnam, 1944) by Margo Kurtz have been edited for length and appear with the permission of the author. Quotations from *Queens Die Proudly* (Harcourt Brace, 1943) by W. L. White, *Six Degrees of Separation* by John Guare, *The Effect of Gamma Rays on Man-in-the-Moon Marigolds* by Paul Zindel, *Sundays in the Park with George* by Stephen Sondheim, and "A Plea for the Uncommon Woman" by Richard Glenn Gettell are used in accordance with U.S. copyright laws pertaining to fair use. *The Tragic Muse* by Henry James, originally serialized in the *Atlantic Monthly*, 1889–1890, is excerpted in accordance with U.S. copyright laws pertaining to public domain. *Heartbreak House* and the letters of George Bernard Shaw are excerpted with special thanks to the Society of Authors, on behalf of the George Bernard Shaw Estate. *Family Meals: Bringing Her Home* (Grove Press, 2010) by Michael Tucker is excerpted in accordance with U.S. copyright laws pertaining to fair use with heartfelt thanks to the author for his kind permission.

Photos

Pages ii, 146, 197: © The Al Hirschfeld Foundation. AlHirschfeldFoundation.org. Al Hirschfeld is also represented by the Margo Feiden Galleries Ltd., New York.

Page 3: © The Associated Press

Page 15: Photo by the U.S. Air Force

Page 152: © CBS

WORK AND AWARDS

1962: The Donna Reed Show
To Tell the Truth

1968: The Firebugs

1970: The Effect of Gamma Rays on Man-in-the-Moon Marigolds

1971: As the World Turns

1975: Ah, Wilderness!

1976: Great Performances: Ah, Wilderness!
Children
Kojak

1977: Slap Shot
First Love
Uncommon Women and Others (Drama Desk Award
    nomination, Obie Award)
Tartuffe (Tony nomination)

1978: A History of the American Film (Drama Desk award)
Mary
Oliver's Story

1979: Great Performances: Uncommon Women and Others
Walking Through the Fire
Wine Untouched

1980: Fifth of July (Tony Award, Drama Desk Award, Outer
    Critics Circle Award)
Marriage Is Alive and Well
The Mating Season

1981–83: Love, Sidney (Primetime Emmy nomination 1982, 1983)

1982: The World According to Garp
       American Playhouse: Fifth of July

1983: A Caribbean Mystery

1984: Against All Odds

1985: Guilty Conscience
       A Time to Live
       The Beach House

1986: The House of Blue Leaves (Tony Award, Drama Desk
           Award nomination, Obie Award)
       Wildcats
       True Stories

1987: American Playhouse: The House of Blue Leaves
       Trying Times

1988: Baja Oklahoma (Golden Globe nomination, ACE
           nomination)
       Vice Versa
       Bright Lights, Big City
       Dangerous Liaisons

1989: Love Letters

1990: Carol & Company (Primetime Emmy Award)
       The Image (Primetime Emmy nomination)
       Six Degrees of Separation
       Stanley & Iris
       A Shock to the System

1991: Walking the Dog

1991–96: Sisters (Screen Actors Guild Award nomination 1995,
              Primetime Emmy nomination 1993, 1994)
          Lips Together, Teeth Apart

1992: Terror on Track 9

1993: The Positively True Adventures of the Alleged Texas
           Cheerleader-Murdering Mom

And the Band Played On (Cable ACE Award, Primetime
    Emmy nomination)

1994: Reality Bites
     One Christmas

1995: The Magic School Bus
     Hope & Gloria
     Betrayed: A Story of Three Women

1996–97: Suddenly Susan
     Citizen Ruth
     A Promise to Carolyn
     Harvey
     Storybook
     Party Girl

1997: Touched by an Angel
     Little Girls in Pretty Boxes
     Liar Liar

1998: ER (Primetime Emmy nomination)
     Armistead Maupin's More Tales of the City
     My Own Country
     Outside Ozona

1999–2000: Love & Money
     The Vagina Monologues
     The Mineola Twins (Drama Desk Award nomination,
        Drama League Award nomination, Outer Critics Circle
        Award nomination, Obie Award)
     Cruel Intentions
     The White River Kid

2000: The Outer Limits

2001–02: That's Life
     The Fighting Fitzgeralds
     Get Over It
     Bubble Boy
     The Wilde Girls

2002: Street Time
The Rules of Attraction
The Guys
Imaginary Friends

2003: Intrigue with Faye
The Wild Thornberrys
Duplex
The Guys (audio book) (Audie Award, Best Audio Drama)

2004–06: Huff (Primetime Emmy nomination 2005, 2006)
Frozen (Tony Award nomination, Outer Critics Circle
Award nomination)
Sleep Easy, Hutch Rimes

2005: Lost
Still Standing
True
Category 7: The End of the World
Nadine in Date Land

2006: Heartbreak House (Tony Award nomination)

2006–present: American Dad!

2007–09: Pushing Daisies
Superman: Doomsday

2008: Living Proof

2009–11: Nurse Jackie
Desperate Housewives
Hank
Heroes
Law & Order: Special Victims Unit
Rita Rocks
An Englishman in New York
Chuck

2010–present: Mike & Molly

INDEX

Page numbers in *italics* indicate photographs or sketches.

abortion, 291–92
Acheson, James, 211
actors, 1, 8, 9, 46, 54, 80, 82, 92, 106, 131,
    164, 172, 191–92, 201, 213, 249–50, 264
    See also Kurtz, Swoosie
advance directives, 247, 289, 292–93
agents, 118–20
Ah, Wilderness, 130
AIDS, 201, 202
Air Force HQ, Margo, 135–37, 142
Albee, Edward, 160, 163–64
Aldredge, Theoni, 188
"Alexander the Swoose" (Kyser), 29
Alfonse's Diner in California, 75
all-seeing eyeball, 102, *105*, 107
Amadeus, 168
American Dad, 132
American Daughter, 143
American Playhouse series (PBS), 200
Anderson Yiddish Theater, 102
And the Band Played On, 202, 227
Angela (caregiver), 20, 21, 128, 245
"Angel Tits," 164, 170
Antonio (caregiver), 13, 41, 42, 43, 294, 300
aquacades, *viii*, 16, *19*, 22, 23, 59, 94, 159, 207,
    220, 286
Arizona, 201, 202
Arnaz, Lucie, 169
Artist, The, 23
Ashcroft, Peggy, 96
Assassins, 212
As the World Turns, 119
Avedon, Richard, 261, *267*
Avery Fisher Hall, 208, 255

B-17D Flying Fortress. *See* "Swoose, the"
backstage drama, 187
Baez, Joan, 61
ballet and Swoosie, 57–59, *58*, 70, 88
Bancroft, Anne, 112
Baranski, Christine, 200, 212, 227

Bardot, Brigitte, 74, 104
Barrymore, Diana, 110, 124, 148, 168, 172,
    179
Barrymore, Ethel, 82
Bataan Death March, 55
battle injuries, acting, 264–65
Baywatch, 217
Beach House, The, 159–60, 208
Bennett, Michael, 8, 180–81, 182, 183–85,
    184, 186–87, 188, 189–90, 191, 199–200,
    201–2, 203, 285
Berkshire Hathaway, 68, 232, 265
Berlin, Germany, 158–59
Bernhardt, Melvin, 114, 118
Blondell, Joan, 117–18
Booth, Shirley, 69
Bosco, Philip, 270
Brady, Diamond Jim, 114–15
Breaking Bad, 85
Brewster, Paget, 257, 268
Bridges, Beau, 227
British dialects and understatement, 99–100
Brooks, Albert, 76
Brooks, Mel, 111
Brown, Arvin, 160
Bubble Boy, 259
Buckley, Betty, 191
Buffett, Warren, 68, 265–66
Burnett, Carol, 81
Burton, Richard, 163
Byrne, David, 76, 191
By the Beautiful Sea, 69

Caesar, Sid, 70
Cage, Nicolas, 76
Caine, Sir Michael, 98, 211
California, 16–17, 32–33, 45–46, 49–50,
    65–66, 127–28, 243–45, 305, 307
Capote, Truman, 129, 222, 228, 229, 239, 240
Carnegie Tech (Carnegie Mellon), 92, 94
Carol Burnett Show, The, 151

Carol & Company, 81
Carrey, Jim, 237–38
Carson, Johnny, 217
Carver, Mary, 166
Catarrius (Sergeant), 205–6
Cavett, Dick, 263
CBS, 71, 153
Chambers, Marilyn, 258
Channing, Stockard, 191, 195, 200, 216, 218, 219
Cheerleader-Murdering Mom, 232
Chekhov, Anton, 98
Chenoweth, Kristin, 182, 286, 302
Cherry Orchard (Chekhov), 98
Chess, 190
Chicago, Illinois, 72, 79, 121
chicken breast before show, 130, 140, 164
Chicken Inspector No. 23 (Perelman), 80, 82
childhood homes, 50, 52, *53*, 70, 73–74, 76, 234
Chorus Line, A, 181, 183, 202, 203, 279
Cielito (caregiver), 13, 298, 300
Circle Rep, 166
Citizen Ruth, *231*, 232
Clark Field, Philippines, 20, 31, 32, 193, 206, 220, 283, 284, 291
Clooney, George, 227
Close, Glenn, 142, 145, 155, 156, 209–10, *210*
Coca, Imogene, 70
Coffield, Peter, 201
Cohen, Bruce, 286
Colbert Report, The, 227
Collier, Constance, 82
Colony Inn in New Haven, 164
committing to a given moment, 98–99
communication, words, and language, 42
Conant, Homer (Gigi's brother), 57
Cosby Show, The, 9
Costner, Kevin, 191
costumers, 206–7, *210*, 211, 272
Cowen, Ron, 213, 217
creativity encouraged by Gigi, 57–59, *58*
Cronyn, Hume, 144
Crucible, The, 31
cucumbers and Margo, 75–76
Cuervo, Alma, *126*
Curie, Madame, 192

Dangerous Liaisons, 207, 209–10, *210*
Danner, Blythe, 187, 188, 212, 216, 295
Darin, Bobby, 208
Dark Victory, 78
Davis, Bette, 26, 134
Dead Like Me, 286
Death of a Salesman, 134
Dee, Sandra, 75, 76, 79, 88, 104, 252

dementia, Margo's, 10–12, 14, 18, 20, 41–42, 99, 128, 193–94, 199, 273–74, 276, 278–79, 295, 296, 302–3
De Niro, Robert, 239
Dern, Laura, *231*, 232
Derricks, Cleavant, 186
Descendants, The, 232
diving and Frank, 2, 12, *19*, 21–22, 36, 37, 38, 66, 69, 73, 79, 158–59, *242*, 249
Donahue, Troy, 75
Donna Reed Show, The, 79, 80, 97
doves when Frank died, 247
down drafts, 243–45
Downy fabric softener commercial, 114
Dr. Strangelove, 134
Drama Desk Awards, 149, 168, 213
Dreamgirls, 181
Dreyfuss, Richard, 76
Dunaway, Faye, 260
Dunnock, Mildred, 134
Durang, Christopher, 134, 143
Duse, Eleanora, 82
Dylan, Bob, 121

Earhart, Amelia, 4
East 61st Street apartment, 102, 110–11, 124, 148, 168, 172, 179
Ebert, Roger, 232
Edie (dog), 301–2
Ed Sullivan Show, 71, 80
Edwards, Tommy, 71, 72
Effect of Gamma Rays on Man-in-the-Moon Marigolds, The, 106, 111, 113, 114–18, *115*, 180, 196
Eikenberry, Jill, *126*, 141, 142
Eleven O'Clock Number, 186–87
Elliott, Patricia, 155, 156
Ellis, Bret Easton, 259
Emmy Awards, 30, *81*, 180, 230, 268, 287
English Guy, 122–25
Ensler, Eve, 258
Entertainment Tonight, 180
entrances, 163
Ephron, Nora, 61–62, 140, 172, 261, 263, 288–89, 296–97
Equity Deputy, 115
Ethel Barrymore Theatre, 70
"Ethel the Oracle" (therapist), 61, 128, 182, 202, 259, 292
Eugene O'Neill Theater Center, *139*, 194
Eugene O'Neill National Playwrights Conference (1977), 138–40, *139*
Eureka! moment, 78–79, 113–14, 160

Fabares, Shelley, 80
Family Meals: Bringing Her Home (Tucker), 299

Farrell, Suzanne, 171
feminism, 137–38, 141
Fifth of July, 144, 145, *146*, *165*, 166–68, *167*, 169, 172, 179, 294
50 Shades of Intellectual Sadomasochism, 163
"Fig Tree Rag, The," 264
Fillmore East, 102, 149
film actors, 131
Final Exit: The Practicalities of Self-Deliverance and Assisted Suicide for the Dying (Humphry), 285, 286
Finney, Albert, 211
flashlight, classmate's birthday gift, 52, 82
Flea Theater, 261
flying and Margo, *15*, 32–33, 41, 45–46, 49–50, 198, 243–45, *282*
Fonda, Henry, 134
Fonda, Jane, 239
"For Esmé-with Love and Squalor" (Salinger), 111, 112
Forster, E. M., 303
fourth grade, doing her own thing, 60
"fourth wall," 199
Foy, Eddie, III, 79
Frank, Harriet, Jr., 239
Franny and Zooey, 112
Friel, Anna, 287
friendliness of Margo, 48, 70, 118, 154, 265–66
Fromme, Squeaky, 212
Frozen, 266–68, *267*
fruitcake story, Frank, 36
full circle, parents and children, 303–4, *306*
Fuller, Bryan, 286

Gaffney, Mo, *251*, 253
Ganz, Bill, 147
Garber, Victor, 134
Gardell, Billy, 5–6, *7*, 8, 9, 10
Garland, Jack and Helen, 73, 112, 159
Garland, William May, 73
Gelb, Barbara, 203
General Hospital, 76
Germany, 4, 158–59
Gernreich, Rudi, 92
Gettell, Richard Glenn, 138
Gielgud, Sir John, 96
Gleason, Joanna, 76
goodbyes, 305, 307
Goodman, John, 191
gratitude of Margo, 21, 26, 57, 256
Graziano, Rocky, 80
Great Performances (PBS), 140, 142, *176*
Greene, Ellen, 206, 279, 286, 293, 294
green latrine speech, 194–95
Greenwood, Jane, 272
Grenoble, Russia, 159

Grimes, Tammy, 134
Guare, John, 194, 195, 209, 212, 219, 293
Guilty Conscience, 187–88
Gurney, A. R., 201
Guys, The, 261
Gyllenhaal, Jake, 259

Hagen, Uta, 160
Hair, 121
"half-assed" after colostomy (Gigi), 26
Hamlisch, Marvin, 61
Hampton, Jim, *152*
Harris, Harwell Hamilton, 13
Harris, Rosemary, 270
Harrison, Rex, 182, 270
Harvey, 237
Hawaii vacations, 217–18, 255–56
Hawn, Goldie, 149, 190–91, 225
Hayes, Helen, 171
Hayes Registry, 120, 131
HBO, 227
Hearst, Patty, 252
Heartbreak House, 270–72, 273–74, *275*, 276, 278
Hedren, Tippi, 232
Hellman, Lillian, 61, 261, 263, 265
Helsinki, Finland, 159
Hendrix, Jimi, 103, *105*, 107
Hepburn, Katharine, 228, *229*, 230
Herman, Cynthia, *126*
Heroes, 286, 295
Hershey, Barbara, 76
Hewitt, Don, 212
Hill, Arthur, 160
Hill Street Blues, 217
Hirsch, Judd, 266
Hirschfeld, Al, *146*, 149, *197*
History of the American Film, A, 134, 149, 151, 264
Hitler, Adolf, 28, 158
Hoffman, Dustin, 114
Hoffman, Elizabeth, 215
hogs and love, 147, 148
Holiday, Billy, 79
Hollywood High, *64*, 74–80, 88, 114
home of Swoosie, 12–13, 256–57
"Home on the Range," 57
Hoover, J. Edgar, 52
hope, 2, *3*, 4
Hope, Bob, 73, 76, 195
Hopkins, Anthony, 187, 188
Horovitz, Israel, 112
House Committee on Un-American Activities (HUAC), 263
House of Blue Leaves, The, 82, *176*, 193–201, *197*, 207, 210, 212, 294, 298
Howard Johnson's, 162

"How I Came to Be Named Swoosie," 29–30
How I Learned to Drive (Vogel), 250
Huff, 268, 270
humility, 1, 2
Humphry, Derek, 285, 286
Hunter, Holly, 227
Hurt, William, 166

Ikeda, Atsuko, 56
Image, The, 211–12
Imaginary Friends, 61–62, 70, 124, 261–65,
     262, 266
Ingle, John, 76, 78–80, 98, 114, 160
Insatiable II, 258
Iraq War, 18
Irish Repertory Theatre, 149
Isherwood, Charles, 272
"It Ain't Me, Babe" (Dylan), 121
"It's All in the Game" (Edwards), 71

Jack Be Nimble (O'Brien, J.), 124
Japan, 20, 54, 55, 56–57, 256
Java, 206, 291
Javitz (toy), 47–48, 49, 102, 157–58
Jennings, Peter, 212
Jews slaughtered in WWII, 28
Jinks, Dan, 286
Joe Allen's Restaurant, 82
Johnson, Lyndon, 50, 52, 195
Johnstown, Pennsylvania, 132
Jones, Cherry, 61, 124, *262*, 264
Joshua Light Show (White, J.), 102–3, *105*
Judd, Ashley, 226
Justice for All, And, 149

Kahan, Judy, 151, *152*
Kalember, Patricia, *204*, 214, 225, 226, 234
karma, 5
Kavner, Julie, 76, 258
Keaton, Michael, 151, *152*
Kennedy, Jackie, 88, 89, 130, 195, 249
Kennedy, John F. (President), 102
Kill a Mockingbird, A (Lee), 129
Klein, Robert, 227
Klosters, Switzerland, 100
Kojak, 121
Korean War, 54–55
Kurtz, Dora Fenton (Frank's mother), 38, 40
Kurtz, Frank (Dr.) (Frank's father), 38, 40
Kurtz, Frank "Frankie" (Swoosie's father)
     aquacades, 16, *19*, 22, 23, 59, 94, 159, 207,
        220, 286
     birth of Swoosie, 27, *27*, 28–29
     Brent Spiner and, 148, 174
     childhood of, 35–36, 36–38, 40, 56
     Daddy Art and Grace "Gigi" (Margo's
        parents) and, 40–41, 46, 56, 67

death of, 10, 13, 218, 240, 246–47, 248, 249,
     253, 256, 285
decline of, 232–33, 235–37, 246, 249
diving career, 2, 12, *19*, 21–22, 36, 37, 38,
     66, 69, 73, 79, 158–59, *242*, 249
driving cars, 224
feminist (accidental), 137–38
first flight with Margo, 32–33, 41
fruitcake story, 36
gambling, 208
Japan and, 54, 55, 56, 256
Josh White and, 92–93, 148
letter to Margo, never received, 290–91
marriage, imbalance, 198–99
motivational speaking, 112–13, 114, 207–8,
     223
Ole 99, 220–22, 283, 284
Olympics and, 73, 158–59
personality of, 47, 59, 60, 131, 214
post-traumatic stress disorder, 112
postwar, 60, 72–73
real estate, 73, 112, 178, 179–80
Republican, 75, 137
Kurtz, Frank "Frankie" (*cont.*)
     road trips with Margo and Swoosie, 46–47,
        49, 50, *51*, 71–72
     Sisters and, 5, 213–14, 218
     sleep and voice of Javitz, 49, 156–58
     support of Swoosie, 22, 76, 96, 97, 132, 151,
        169, 185–86, 190, 212–13, 218–19, 227,
        228, 230, 278
     "Swoose, the" (B-17D Flying Fortress), 4,
        15, 17, *24*, 29, 30, 31–32, 38, 283–84, 305,
        307
     transient ischemic attack (TIA), 208–9
     Vietnam War view, 55, 75, 137
     vision, loss of, 206, 207, 209, 277
     visiting Swoosie, 111–12, 112–13, 180, 208
     war-bond tours, 2, 4, 16
     wedding night and locked suitcase, 93–94
     World War II pilot, 4, *15*, 16–17, 18, 20, 22,
        23, *24*, *27*, 28, 29, 30, 31–32, 38, 48,
        55–56, 67, 70, 71, 89–90, 127–28, 136,
        192–93, 220–22, 283–84, 305, 307
     Yankee Boy, 33, 41, 45, 46, 48, *282*
Kurtz, Margo Rogers (Swoosie's mother)
     aging well, 125
     air cadets and, 136–37
     Air Force HQ, 135–37, 142
     alcohol and, 287–88, 294–95
     Ambien and, 260
     bathrobe, staple wardrobe item, 198
     birth of, 34–35, 169
     birth of Swoosie, *3*, 27, *27*, 28–29, 138
     Bob (Margo's brother), 33, 57
     Brent Spiner and, 148, 174
     care of, 9, 13–14, 21, 22, 25, 26–27, 41,

42–43, 85–86, 132, 144, 228, 245, 256, 259, 270, 271, 272–73, 287, 288, 293–94, 296–305, *306*
Christmas (1941), 177–78
cucumbers and, 75–76
dating Frank, 65–66, 67, 78, 89–91, 94, 96
death of Frank, 246–47, 249, 256
decline of Frank, 235–37
dementia, 10–12, 14, 18, 20, 41–42, 99, 128, 193–94, 199, 273–74, 276, 278–79, 295, 296, 302–3
down drafts, 243–45
dying, wanting to, 280, 284–86, 290, 292
ER visits, 272–73, 288–89, 293
"ever-fixed mark," 2
fertility problems, 26, 28
flying and, *15*, 32–33, 41, 45–46, 49–50, 198, 243–45, *282*
friendliness of, 48, 70, 118, 154, 265–66
gambling, 34, 208
gratitude of, 21, 26, 57, 256
"Here I be," 79
Homer (Margo's brother), 23, 35, 57, 68
Japan Air Lines and visit to Japan, 56–57
Josh White and, 92
marriage, imbalance, 198–99
Mary Alice "Mici" (Margo's sister), 11, 67, 227, 228, 283
money and, 68, 69, 97
motivational speaking by Frank and, 207, 208
My Rival, The Sky, 4, 16, 17–18, 34, 37, 55, 67, 131, 149
Nippu Ji Ji (roadster), 48, 110, 127–28
passing gas fear, 94
phone calls intercepted by, 150–51
quiet, strong words, 192–93
road trips with Frank and Swoosie, 46–47, 49, 50, *51*, 71–72
sexuality, 75–76
support of Swoosie, 30, 118, 151, 182–83, 186, 189, 195–96, 227, 230, 253, 254, *269*, 278
vacations with Swoosie, 188–89, 201, 217–18, 255–56
visiting Swoosie, 111–12, 112–13, 180, 208
war, in a man's eyes, 205–6
war-bond tours, 2, 4, 16, 34, 41
wardrobe of Swoosie's and, 74–75, *77*
wedding night and locked suitcase, 93–94
writing (second book) and stories, 36–37, 40, 259
See also Rogers, Daddy Art and Grace "Gigi" (Margo's parents)
Kurtz, Swoosie
beach house at Winter Olympics, 147–75
birth of, 27, *27*, 28–29, 138

degrees of separation, 205–40
descendants of Art and Grace, 25–43, *44*
enter breathing, 1–24
heartbreak and daisies, 243–80
imaginary friends, 45–62
love and squalor, 109–25
more later, 283–306
my last first day, 65–82
name and, 29–31, 120
singing, dancing, schizophrenia, 177–203
uncommon women, 127–45
why I wasn't at Woodstock, 85–107
works and awards, 315–18
See also Kurtz, Frank "Frankie" (Swoosie's father); Kurtz, Margo Rogers (Swoosie's mother); Rogers, Daddy Art and Grace "Gigi" (Margo's parents); *specific works and awards*
Kyser, Kay, 29

Lacy, Clay, 230
Lahti, Christine, 148, 149, 199
Lake Placid, 159, 160
Lane, Nathan, 122, 148, 212, 227
LaPaglia, Anthony, 261
Last Emperor, The, 211
Las Vegas, 208
Laura Pels Theatre, 253–54
Lavery, Bryony, 266
"lead with the breastbone," 8
Leaving Las Vegas, 191
Lee, Harper, 129
Lefèvre, Robin, 271, 373
Leh, Konrad, 13, 14, 118–19, 121, 150, 259–60, 286, 297
Lennon, John, 102, 168–69
Leonard, Hugh, 166
lesbian, 87, 88
Letterman, David, 151, *152*, 153
Levine, Anna, *126*
Liar, Liar, 237–38
Lido Excelsior Hotel in Switzerland, 100
life fright, 52, 54
Lifetime, 240
Light, Judith, 142
Lindbergh, Anne Morrow, 67
Lipman, Dan, 213
Lipman, Maureen, 100
Lips Together, Teeth Apart, 227
Littlefield, Warren, 217
Little Girls in Pretty Boxes, 240
London Academy of Music and Dramatic Arts (LAMDA), 96–100, 102, 112, 114
Long Wharf Theatre in New Haven, 159, 160, *161*, 163, 261
Look Homeward, Angel, 70
Lost, 270

Love, Loss, and What I Wore, 296
Love, Sidney, 48, 169–72, *173*, 179, 180
Love and Squalor, 112, 114
Love Letters, 212
Love & Money, 255, 257
Loy, Myrna, 171
Luckenbill, Lawrence, 169
Lupone, Patti, 182
Luzon Island, 20, 220–22

Macbeth, 96
MacGyver, 217
Macowan, Michael, 98
Madame Romaine de Lyon, 111
Mad Men, 13, 74, 79, 213
Magnum, P. I., 217
Mahoney, John, 195, 200
Malkovich, John, 211
Mamet, David, 303
Manhattan Class Company Theater, 268
Manhattan Theatre Club, 227
Mantello, Joe, 252, 253, 258
March Air Force Base, 109–10
marriage and children, 86–88, 104
Martinique at the Edison Hotel, 122
Mary, 151–54, *152*, 155, 172
Mary Tyler Moore Show, The, 151, *152*, 181
Mascoutah, Illinois, 50, 74, *77*, 147
Mating Season, The, 169
May, Elaine, 160, *161*, 163, 164
Mayo, Charlie, 34, 35
McBride, Chi, 287
McCarthy, Mary, 61, 263
McCarthy, Melissa, 5–6, *7*, 133, 134
McCartney, Paul, 153
McDonald, Audra, 258
McDonough, Ann, *126*
McFarlane, Seth, 132
McKechnie, Donna, 155
McNally, Terrence, 227
Meara, Anne, 195
Mercer-O'Casey Theatre, 114–15
Meredith, Burgess, 70
Mexico City, 159
Middle Ages, The, 201
Mike & Molly, 5–10, 6, *7*, 8, 86, 132, *133*, 134,
    141, 302
Miller, Glenn, 67, 72
Mineola Twins, The, 250–55, *251*
Mixon, Katy, *7*
modesty, 1, 2
monokini, 92, 94, 95, *95*
Monroe, Marilyn, 88, 89
Montreal, Canada, 159
Moore, Charlotte, 149–50
Moore, Mary Tyler, 151–54, *152*, 155
Morning's at Seven, 261

"Most Important Thing, The," 187
motivational speaking, Frank, 112–13, 114,
    207–8, 223
Mount Holyoke College, 138
Munich, Germany, 159
Murray, Bill, 261
Murray, Brian, 121
Mussolini, Benito, 28
My Fair Lady, 181
My Rival, The Sky (Kurtz, M.), 4, 16, 17–18,
    34, 37, 55, 67, 131, 149

Napier, Alan, 96
National Theatre in Washington DC, 121
Naughton, James, *161*, 162, 164
NBC, 5, 169, 213, 217
Nelson, Anne, 261
New Apollo Theater, 166
new carpet for your dressing room, 122
Newman, Paul, 132–34, *133*, 143–44
Newman, Randy, 208, 255
New York Athletic Club, 179, 186
New Yorker, 69, 112, *267*
New York Film Festival, 201
New York Times, 82, 102–3, 149, 154, 163,
    166, 188, 199–200, 203, 249, 272
New York trips as child, 69–70
Nichols, Mike, 160, *161*, 162, 163, 164, 170
19th Bombardment Group, 31
Nippu Ji Ji (Margo's roadster), 48, 110, 127–28
Nixon, Richard, 75, 137, 208
Norfolk, Virginia, 50
Norma Rae, 239
Norwegian play, 155, 156, 157
nothing yet, what's next, 180
nude picture taken by Josh White, 107, *108*
Nurse Jackie, 295–96
Nyambi, Nyambi, *7*

Obie Awards, 144, 149, 255
O'Brien, Edna, 129
O'Brien, Jack, 124, 261, 263
O'Byrne, Bryan, 268
OCD/hermetic tendencies, 59, 88, 170
Old 99, 220–22, 283, 284
Olivier, Laurence, 130, 131, 166
Olympics and Frank, 73, 158–59
Omaha, Nebraska, 20, 33–34, 41, 46, 54, 56,
    57, 60, 68, 70, 72, 89–91, 135–37, 177–78,
    192–93, 205–6, 232, 245, 247, 265,
    290–91
One Christmas, 228, *229*, 230
One Life to Live, 142
orgasms, 71, 213, 215, 216, 217, 258
origins of life, 113
Oscars, 145, 149, 211, 216
Oslo, Norway, 156

Other Voices, Other Rooms, 129–30
Outer Critics Circle Awards, 168
Oxford Players, 96

Pace, Lee, 287
Pacific Theater, World War II, 4, 20, 31, 32, 136, 177, 192, 220–22, 283–84, 291
Pacino, Al, 149
Pagan Place (O'Brien, E.), 129
Palmer, Betsy, 103
Palmer Chiropractic School, 38
Paper Doll, 266
Papp, Joseph, 149
Paramount, 257
Paris, France, 211
Parker, Ellen, *126*
Parker, Dorothy, 178
Party Girl, 239
Pavlova, Anna, 57
Payne, Alexander, 231, 232
Payton-Wright, Pamela, 114, 117
PBS, 140, 142, 144, *176*, 200
peanut allergy, 111, 123–24
Pearl Harbor, 20, 31, 32, 220
People, 188, 249
Perelman, S. J., 80, 82
Perfect Day for Bananafish, A, 112, 114
Perkins, Anthony, 70
Perlman, Itzhak, 171
Philanthropist, The, 79, 121
Philippines, 4, 20, 31, 136, 177, 192, 220–22, 291
Phillips, Julianne, *204*, 214, 225–26
phone booth request, Earl's Court, 100
Pie-lette, 286–87
Place, Mary Kay, 232
Playhouse 90, 237
"play practice," 76, 78
"Plea for the Uncommon Woman, A" (Gettell), 138
Poitier, Sidney, 219
Positively True Adventures of the Alleged Texas Cheerleader-Murdering Mom, The, 227
post-traumatic stress disorder, 112
pot, smoking, 148–49, 157, 172
Powers, Stefanie, 76
Presley, Elvis, 71, 72, 256
Preston, Kelly, *231*, 232
Pretty Boxes, 249, 250
Prime of Miss Jean Brodie, 103–4, 114
"proximity burn," 223–25

Pulitzers, 115, 117, 180, 213, 250
Pushing Daisies, 171, 206–7, 209, 232, *277*, 279–80, 286, 287, 294, 295
Putnam, G. P., 4

Queens Die Proudly (White), 4, 32, 55
quiet, strong words, 192–93

Rainbow Room, 122–23
Rand, Ayn, 13
Randall, Tony, 169, 170–71, *173*
Randall and Big Red (toy), 48, 125, 245
"Rat Musical, The," 153
Ravetch, Irving, 239–40
Reader's Digest, 75
real estate, Frank, 73, 112, 178, 179–80
redhead, Swoosie, 129–30
"Red Sails in the Sunset," 57
Reeve, Christopher, *165*, 166, 168
retirement, 207
Reynolds, Burt, 232
Rich, Adrienne, 192
Rich, Frank, 163, 168, 199–200
Richards, Keith, 255
Rimbaud, Arthur, 129
road trips with parents, 46–47, 49, 50, *51*, 71–72
Robbins, Tim, 261
Robins, Laila, 268, 270
Rogers, Daddy Art and Grace "Gigi" (Margo's parents)
    alcohol and Gigi, 34, 72, 248–49, 294
    birth of Margo, 34–35, 169
    boyfriends, beating, 174–75
    childhood of Swoosie, 33–34, *39*, 54, 60, 79
    creativity encouraged by Gigi, 57–59, *58*
    cucumbers and Gigi, 75–76
    death of, 72, 247, 285
    Frank Kurtz and, 40–41, 46, 56, 67
    "half-assessed," Gigi's colostomy, 26
    money from Gigi, 68
    See also Kurtz, Margo Rogers (Swoosie's mother)
Rolling Stones concert, 255–56
Rome, Italy, 159
Rose, 144
Roth, Ann, 196
Roundabout Theater Company, 252
Rudd, Paul, 226–27
Rules of Attraction, 259–60

SAG card, 80
Saint Bart's, 188–89, 201
Salinger, J. D., 110–11, 112
San Antonio, Texas, 50
Sarandon, Susan, 261
Sardi's, 17, 70, 155, *156*, 168

Sassoon, Vidal, 92
Savalas, Telly, 121
Scandal, 181–82, 183–85, *184*, 186–87, 188, 189–90, 201, 202–3
Schlamme, Tommy, 148, 149, 163, 199
Seinfeld, 217
self, only consistency in life, 54
Sellers, Peter, 134
September 11 terrorist attacks, 260–61
"serial enema," 26
Sex and the City, 131
sexuality, 75–76
Shakespeare, William, 2, 98
Shalit, Gene, 169
Shaw, George Bernard, 270, 271–72, 276, 278
Shawn, Dick, 151, *152*, 153, 154
Shields, Brooke, 239, 240
Shimazu, Takako, 56
"shitting on the table," 121
Shock to the System, A, 98, 211
Showtime, 268
Shue, Elisabeth, 191
shyness, 52, 113, 118, 154
Sideways, 232
Siegfried, Mandy, 253
Silverman, Treva, 181, 185, 187, 189–90
Simon, Paul, 112
Sisters, 5, 12, 78, 171, *204*, 213–15, 216–17, 218, 223, 224, 225, 226–27, 228, 230, 232, 233–34, 235, 249, 258
Six Degrees of Separation, 200, 212, 216, 218–19, 293
60 Minutes, 212
Skin of Our Teeth (Wilder), 79
Slap Shot, 132–34, *133*
Slavin, Susan, 155
sleep as ongoing struggle, 49, 156–58
Smith, Liz, 188
Smithsonian Institute, *24*, 30, 38
Sondheim, Stephen, 212
Sonnenfeld, Barry, 286
Spellman, Cardinal, 195
Spiner, Brent, 134–35, 140, 148–49, 151, 156, 160, 162, 163, 168, 172, 174, 179, 200
Springsteen, Bruce, 148, 175
stage actors, 131, 213
Standards and Practices, 171, 173, 217
Stanley & Iris, 239–40
Star Trek: The Next Generation, 174
Stiers, David Ogden, 257
Stiller, Ben, 195
Streep, Meryl, *126*, 141, 142, 143
Suddenly Susan, 239, 240, 247
Sugar Plum Fairy, 57, 59, 74
Sulzberger, Art, 249
Summer, 166
Sunday in the Park with George, 174

Sunflower, The, 100
Superman, 166
Sure Antiperspirant commercial, 120–21
Susann, Jacqueline, 266
swimming pools, 21, 22, 66, 280
Swing Shift, 149
"Swoose, the" (B-17D Flying Fortress), 4, *15*, 17, *24*, 29, 30, 31–32, 38, 283–84, 305, 307
  See also Kurtz, Swoosie

table reads, 98, 106, 169
Tail o' the Cock restaurant, 208
Talking to Myself (Terkel), 79
Tampa, Florida, 50, 147, 174
Tandy, Jessica, 144, 145
taping TV show with live audience, 171
Tartuffe, 134, 149, 201
Taylor, Christine, 163, 239
Teahouse of the August Moon, 70
television actors, 131, 213
Terkel, Studs, 79, 121
That Girl, 131
Thomas, Richard, 168
Thomas, Robert McG, Jr., 249
Thompson, Sada, 114, 115, 117, 213
Thompson, Susie, 68
Thurman, Uma, 211
Time magazine, *84*, 88–89
Tinker, Grant, 151, 154
Today show, 168–69
Toluca Lake, California, 12–13, 73, 75, 94, 137, 150, 166, 212, 223
Tonight Show, The, 217
Tony Awards, 82, 144, 149, *167*, 168, 172, 180, 187, 192, 200, 212, 268, *269*, 272
tossing/catching child, Swoosie dream, 203
True Stories, 76, 200–201
Tucker, Michael, 142, 299–300
TV Guide, 180
Two Beavers, The, 258
typing class, 111

Uncommon Women and Others, *126*, 134, 138, 140–42, 144, 149, 258
"upfronts," 217
Upper West Side apartment, 172, 178, 179–80, 213
USC, 66, 78, *84*, 88, 92, 94, 96, 97

Vagina Monologues, The, 258
Vancouver, 237
Variety, 154
Venice Film Festival, 100
Vietnam War view of Frank, 55, 75, 137
virginity, 88, 93
vision, loss of (Frank), 206, 207, 209, 277

visiting with parents, 111–12, 112–13, 166, 180, 208
Vogel, Paula, 250, 252
voiceovers, 132

Waldorf Astoria, 69, 93, 94
Walken, Christopher, 195, 199
Wallace, Mike, 212
Ward, Sela, 204, 214, 225, 226, 230
"War Delirium" (Shaw), 271
Wardman Park Hotel, Washington DC, 122
Warner Brothers, 257
warring of countries and differences between people, 57
Wasserstein, Wendy, 134, 138, 140, 141, 142–43
Waterworld, 191
Weaver, Sigourney, 261
Webb, Jimmy, 186
wedding night and locked suitcase, 93–94
Weissmuller, Johnny, 37
Welles, Orson, 96, 208
West Side Story, 69, 93
White, Betty, 170
White, Josh, 89, 91–93, 94–95, 95, 100–103, 101, 104, 105, 106–7, 108, 111, 141, 143, 148
White, W. L., 4, 32, 55
Who's Afraid of Virginia Woolf?, 134, 160–64, 161, 166, 207, 210, 210, 261
Whose Life Is It Anyway?, 155
Wichita, Kansas, 70–71
Wildcats, 190–91, 225

Wilder, Thornton, 79
Williams, Esther, 23, 287
Williams, Treat, 188
Wilson, Lanford, 166
Wilson, Reno, 7, 9, 10, 14
Wine Untouched, 155–57
"With a Little Luck" (McCartney), 153
Wolf, Donna, 74
woman alone, uncomfortable with a, 178
Wonderfalls, 286
Woodstock, 104, 107
works and awards, Swoosie, 315–18
    See also specific works and awards
World According to Garp, The, 144–45, 155, 198, 207, 210
World War II
    Pacific Theater, 4, 20, 31, 32, 136, 177, 192, 220–22, 283–84, 291
    pilot, Frank, 4, 15, 16–17, 18, 20, 22, 23, 24, 27, 28, 29, 30, 31–32, 38, 48, 55–56, 67, 70, 71, 89–90, 127–28, 136, 192–93, 220–22, 283–84, 305, 307
    war, in a man's eyes, 205–6
    war-bond tours, 2, 4, 16, 34, 41

Yale, 133, 134
Yankee Boy, 33, 41, 45, 46, 48, 282
YouTube, 10, 151, 152, 217

Zaks, Jerry, 70, 194–95, 196, 200, 212, 215, 216, 218, 303
Ziegfeld Follies, 57
Zindel, Paul, 114

About the Author

A graduate of the London Academy of Music and Dramatic Art, **Swoosie Kurtz** is a Broadway icon whose work onstage and screen has been recognized with Tony, Emmy, Obie, Drama Desk and other awards. She's played an astonishing range of characters—synchronized swimmer, identical twins, spy, schizophrenic, criminal, cancer patient, televangelist, hooker, Lillian Hellman, a variety of lesbians—who have been murdered, mugged, seduced and stricken by a variety of diseases and untoward circumstances. She's played the mother of Melissa McCarthy, Ben Stiller, Seth MacFarlane, Ashley Judd, Uma Thurman, Winona Ryder, Brooke Shields, Jake Gyllenhaal and Janeane Garofalo; the sister of Jane Fonda, Goldie Hawn and Sela Ward; the wife and/or lover of Sir Anthony Hopkins, Sir Michael Caine, Blythe Danner, Nathan Lane, John Malkovich, Judith Light, Robin Williams, Beau Bridges and Carol Burnett.

Swoosie divides her time between New York City and Los Angeles. This is her first book.

About the Coauthor

New York Times bestselling author Joni Rodgers has written several critically acclaimed novels and memoirs on her own and collaborated on fiction and nonfiction with Kristin Chenoweth, Rue McClanahan, Ambassador Nancy Brinker and other extraordinary people. Her work in *Part Swan, Part Goose* is dedicated to the memory of her mother, author/historian Lois Lonnquist.